AMERICAN & TEXAS
Government Essentials

JOHN OSTERMAN

Kendall Hunt
publishing company

Cover image © 2012 Shutterstock, Inc.

Kendall Hunt
publishing company

www.kendallhunt.com
Send all inquiries to:
4050 Westmark Drive
Dubuque, IA 52004-1840

Printed in the United States of America
10 9 8 7 6 5 4 3 2 1

CONTENTS

Chapter

THE FOUNDING AND THE CONSTITUTION

THE FOUNDING: BACK IN GREAT BRITAIN

The founding of the United States began with the American Colonies of Great Britain. The British experienced political turmoil as tensions mounted between Charles I and Parliament during the 1630s. Civil War occurred between Charles I and Parliament from 1642 to 1646 ending with the surrender of Charles I to the army of Oliver Cromwell and Sir Thomas Fairfax. Charles I was beheaded January 30, 1649. Cromwell then established a Protectorate, which ran from December 1653 to May 24, 1659. Later, Charles II returned to England and was restored to the monarchy on May 25, 1660. James II, a Catholic, became King of England on February 6, 1685. A power struggle between the King and House of Commons ensued with religious tensions between Catholics and Protestants. The Glorious Revolution bloodlessly overthrew James II in 1688. Finally, William III, a Protestant, ascended to the throne in 1689.

THE FOUNDING: THE ESTABLISHMENT OF THE AMERICAN COLONIES

Virginia (1607)

The first permanent colony was established in Virginia under a royal charter to the Virginia Company who ruled through an appointed governor and a council of advisors. In 1618, a representative assembly was established called the House of Burgesses. This was the first legislative assembly in the colonies. Laws had to be approved by the Virginia Company.

Massachusetts (1620)

The Plymouth colony was established by Puritan Separatists, and they drafted the Mayflower Compact, which established consensual government. It was eventually absorbed into the Massachusetts Bay colony, which was established by Massachusetts Bay Company. A colonial legislature was created with representatives. Voting was limited to church members.

New Hampshire (1629)

New Hampshire was established after a land grant from the Council of New England, and Puritan colonization began. In 1639, the Exeter Compact was signed, which was similar to the Mayflower Compact.

Maryland (1634)

Maryland was established as a proprietary colony under Lord Baltimore as a refuge for English Catholics although still dominated by Protestants. Lord Baltimore's right to govern autocratically was challenged by the legislative assembly of delegates.

Rhode Island (1636)

Rhode Island was established by Roger Williams as a refuge for religious dissenters, religious tolerance, and government by consent. It was established as a confederation in 1640, and elected a governor and representative assembly. It would remain self-governing until the American Revolution.

Connecticut (1636)

Connecticut was settled by Dutch traders around 1633. Thomas Hooker and his congregation moved into the area after being driven from Massachusetts over the issue of participatory rights. The Fundamental Orders of 1639 established a popularly elected governor and a representative assembly. Connecticut would also remain self-governing until the American Revolution.

North Carolina (1653)

North Carolina was a proprietary colony that was never developed and was eventually ceded to eight aristocratic families who split territory into two colonies. It was officially recognized as a colony in 1691.

Delaware (1664)

Established by Sweden in 1638, it was taken by the Dutch in 1655, and then by England in 1664. In 1682, the Duke of York granted Penn the area of Delaware, which had been part of the Dutch territory. In 1701, Delaware was granted the right to choose their own assembly but had the same governor as Pennsylvania.

New York (1664)

New York was originally a Dutch colony, and a trading post was established on Manhattan Island in 1614 as a fur trading center. It came under British control in 1664, and New Amsterdam became New York. King James appointed a governor but did not allow a representative assembly in New York.

New Jersey (1664)

New Jersey was originally part of New Netherlands and split from New York after the British defeat of the Dutch in 1664. King James II issued land grants to supporters of the monarchy and established a proprietary governor and elected assembly.

South Carolina (1670)

The Colony of Carolina was created by King Charles II in 1663, which included North Carolina, South Carolina, and Georgia. It was settled and relied on the Fundamental Constitutions of Carolina, which was drafted with the assistance of John Locke.

Pennsylvania (1682)

Pennsylvania was settled by William Penn, who converted to Quakerism in 1667. Penn received a proprietary land grant from King Charles II in 1681, and recruited Quakers, Mennonites, Amish, Moravians, and Baptists. Pennsylvania was founded on the principles of toleration and religious freedom. A written constitution was drafted known as a Frame of Government. It guaranteed political and religious freedom, prohibited official church and religious taxes, and prohibited religious tests for voting or holding office.

Georgia (1732)

Georgia was the last of the British colonies to be established. King George II issued a land grant to twenty-one trustees. Georgia was promoted as a debtors' prison and a military buffer.

COLONIAL POLITICAL AND ECONOMIC DEVELOPMENT

Commercial enterprise ✱

England's internal problems along with the economic policy of mercantilism allowed the colonies to develop a degree of independence. Mercantilism was the dominant economic policy of England. Colonial policy emphasized trade over governing. The colonies were a source of raw materials and market for finished goods. There were attempts under Stuart rule to control the colonies, but following the Glorious Revolution and under the rule of the Hanoverian Monarchs colonial reigns were loosened ever more. Edmund Burke referred to the policy as salutary neglect. British

✱ *Wholesome Healthy*

colonists developed colonial governments along very similar lines to the British Parliament. There was a governor appointed by the king or proprietor with the power to call the assembly into session, prorogue (adjourn or recess) sessions, dissolve the assembly for new elections, postpone elections indefinitely, create courts, as well as hire/fire judges. He may or may not have worked closely with the assembly but was generally on a tight leash because the assembly controlled the purse strings on salaries.

There was a council appointed by the king or proprietor that served as an upper house of the legislature and the highest court of appeal within the colony. The assembly represented the people and was elected by them with the power to legislate and control the purse. The governor had the power to veto. The Crown could set aside the law within a specified period of time but rarely did so.

During the course of the 1700s, the legislative assemblies assumed more power as a result of the salutary neglect by the British Government, which established a precedent for self-government. The power of the purse was controlled by voting on taxes and expenditures that must be proposed and approved by legislation.

The colonists began to acquire wealth and economic sectors developed with a distinct middle class accustomed to self-government. These colonial economic sectors included the royalists, New England merchants, southern planters, shopkeepers, small farmers, artisans, and laborers.

New England merchants, southern planters and royalists maintained a loose alliance in governing the new colonies that also served to hold the more radical elements in check. The Royalists served as governors and bureaucrats, and New England merchants and Southern planters served in the legislative assemblies. This alliance was threatened after 1760 by British trade and tax policies that endangered the economic interests of the New England merchants and Southern planters.

The period from 1765 to 1781 was marked by taxes, revolution, and independence. The French and Indian War led to changes in colonial policy. The French and Indian War was sparked by tensions between the French and British colonists regarding the Ohio Valley territory, known as the Seven Years War in Europe, which lasted from 1754 to 1763. The war culminated with the Peace of Paris in 1763. England granted control of the French possessions in North America east of the Mississippi River. New Orleans was not included in the peace agreement. Conflicts between British colonists and the Indians of the Ohio Valley continued to occur increasing the cost of controlling the frontier. King George III issued the Royal Proclamation of 1763, which prohibited colonial migration beyond the Appalachian Mountains. This was an attempt to secure peace with the Indians and only angered the colonists. The costs of the war and the continuing costs of defending the frontier led to rising debts for the British government. England turned to the colonies as a source of new tax revenue. Until this time, the colonies had paid only a small share of the tax burden.

The Sugar Act of 1764 taxed sugar, molasses, and other commodities such as foreign textiles, wines, coffee, and indigo. This clearly angered New England merchants and southern planters.

The Currency Act of 1764 prohibited the colonies from printing their own currency and devalued the currency being issued by the states.

The Stamp Act of 1765 created revenue stamps to be affixed to all printed and legal documents including newspapers, pamphlets, advertisements, notes and bonds, leases, deeds, and licenses. This angered attorneys and newspapermen.

The fact that the Quartering Act of 1765 required the colonies to supply British troops with provisions and barracks and maintained a standing army amongst the people was considered a symbol of a tyrannical government. This became the basis for the Third Amendment to the U.S. Constitution.

These actions led to colonial resistance and the battle cry, "No Taxation Without Representation." The colonists argued that the British government lacked the authority to impose taxes on the colonies without their consent. The British government argued that there was virtual representation. Demonstrations against the Stamp Act were organized, which included the hanging and burning in effigy of stamp agents and sacking the home of the lieutenant governor. In addition, Royalists were tarred and feathered. Think about this when you read the Eighth Amendment to the U.S. Constitution regarding cruel and unusual punishment. The Virginia House of Burgesses passed the Virginia Resolves, which declared that the colonists were entitled to all the rights of Englishmen. The Stamp Act was repealed by Parliament in 1766, but Parliament passed the Declaratory Act to acknowledge its powers to enact legislation affecting the colonies. Colonists recognized Parliament's authority over trade policy. The Sugar Act and the Stamp Act severed the loose alliance with the Royalists and realigned with the other two social and economic groups: the New England merchants and southern planters.

The conflict between the colonies and England intensified. Charles Townshend, Chancellor of the Exchequer, attempted to reinstate control over the colonies. The Townshend Act of 1767 was passed and suspended all of the acts of the New York Assembly because New York failed to comply with the Quartering Act. The Revenue Act of 1767 levied taxes on colonial imports of glass, lead, paints, paper, and tea. A Board of Customs Commissioners was established in Boston. The Vice-Admiralty courts were established in Boston, Halifax, Philadelphia, and Charleston. Colonial resistance intensified in response to Townshend's policies. Then a boycott of British goods was called, which led to the development of colonial manufacturing to replace British goods. Essays critical of British policy were published by colonial papers by essayists such as the Pennsylvania Farmer. Samuel Adams of Harvard and the Sons of Liberty produced essays and organized protests. One such protest turned into the Boston Massacre in 1770. British troops fired on unarmed Bostonians. The British troops were represented by John Adams of Harvard to ensure they received a fair trial. All but two were acquitted, and the guilty were branded on the thumbs for the offense of manslaughter. Again, think of cruel and unusual punishment. Another protest was the Boston Tea Party. In 1773, the East India Company was granted essentially a monopoly on tea eliminating colonial merchants pursuant to the Tea Act of 1773. New England merchants feared that this was the beginning of future monopolies on all types of goods. The Boston Tea Party was led by Samuel Adams and John Hancock, also of Harvard, and the Sons of Liberty. England responded with the Coercive Acts of 1774, also known as the Intolerable Acts. The Boston Port Act closed the Port of Boston, and the trial of British officials would be transferred to England. A new Quartering Act required colonists to provide housing to troops even if it meant private homes. All Boston officials would be appointed rather than elected. These acts alienated the colonists even more as a strengthening radical element led by the likes of Samuel Adams asserted that British power supported an unjust political and social structure within the colonies and began to advocate an end to British Rule.

On September 5, 1774, the First Continental Congress met in Philadelphia, which included representation of twelve states. Georgia was absent. It called for a boycott of British goods, which led to King George III declaring the colonies in rebellion. On April 18, 1775, The Battles of Lexington and Concord began, and orders were received to suppress the rebellion. British troops went after radicals John Hancock and Sam Adams. They attempted to seize the militia's supply depot, and shots were fired in Lexington as militia were routed. The Concord Militia regrouped and chased the British back to Boston.

The Second Continental Congress met on May 10, 1775. Ethan Allen of Vermont and the Green Mountain Boys along with Massachusetts volunteers under Benedict Arnold of Connecticut captured Fort Ticonderoga in New York on May 10, 1775. George Washington of Virginia was named General and Commander-in-Chief of the Continental Army. The Battle of Bunker Hill in Boston occurred on June 17, 1775. The Olive Branch Petition of July 5, 1775, attempted reconciliation with the king but was rejected when King George III declared the colonists as enemies of the crown.

Thomas Paine's published *Common Sense* in January 1776 was responsible for moving public opinion towards independence.

DECLARING INDEPENDENCE: CLASSICAL LIBERALISM AND A NEW NATION

The Second Continental Congress met at Independence Hall in Philadelphia from May 1775 to March 1781, and served as government during the Revolutionary War. Richard Henry Lee introduced a resolution calling for independence, and a committee was formed that included John Adams, Ben Franklin, Thomas Jefferson, Robert Livingston, and Roger Sherman. Jefferson, from William & Mary, was chosen to draft the document. A Virginian was the principal author thus bringing Virginia into the group of principle states. Jefferson would avoid the political scrutiny and bias that would have been directed towards a document written by Adams. Jefferson was respected for his writing style, although not his oratory skills.

The principles of the Declaration were rooted in the writings of John Locke. It declared that people have God-given or natural rights that cannot be taken away by government. Government exists to preserve those rights and has authority based on consent of the governed. The governed retain the right to resist or remove rulers who persist in acting against these principles. Jefferson may have also drawn from state and local declarations that had been drafted during the period. Other influences include the colonists' understanding of the British Constitution and the English Bill of Rights.

THE DECLARATION OF INDEPENDENCE

The Declaration says, "We hold these truths to be self-evident; that all men are created equal." Of course this did not mean "all" men. Jefferson is basically saying that the king is not above any other man based on his birth alone. It further says, "That they are endowed by their creator with certain inalienable rights." In other words, your rights do not come from man. If they did, man could simply take them away. Man, by his birth, is not entitled to grant or remove rights. The Declaration also says, "That among these [rights] are life, liberty, and the pursuit of happiness." Locke said life, liberty, and property. Slaves were considered property, and it would not have been wise for Jefferson to include property here. Of course, the definition of these terms is a matter of much debate. Next, it says, "That to secure these rights, governments are instituted among men, deriving their just powers from the consent of the governed." Therefore, the true purpose of government is to provide order and protection. Moreover, the public is responsible for holding the government accountable.

Next, the Declaration says, "That whenever any form of government becomes destructive of these ends, it is the right of the people to alter or to abolish it and institute new government." This is a powerful statement indicating that the originally established government is not perpetual and that the government is to serve the people. The Declaration observes that "Prudence, indeed, will dictate that governments long established should not be changed for light and transient causes . . . but when a long train of abuses and usurpations . . . evinces a design to reduce them under absolute despotism (tyranny), it is their right, it is their duty, to throw off such government, and to provide new guards for their future security." This declarative statement makes it clear that the colonists have suffered long enough and it is time to take action.

The second part of the Declaration of Independence outlined complaints against King George III. Although Jefferson's original draft condemned the people of England for their support of the crown. It says, "He has refused his assent to laws, the most wholesome and necessary for the public good," and that "He has dissolved representative houses repeatedly." It is well understood the laws are a product of man for man. If one man thinks he is above the law, the system will not work.

Article III of the Constitution addresses the issue of the judiciary, and evidence for its formation can be found in this passage of the Declaration where it says, "He has made judges dependent on his will alone for the tenure of their offices, and the amount of payment for their offices."

It further says, "He has kept among us, in times of peace, standing armies, without the consent of the legislatures." As mentioned earlier, this is the basis of the Third Amendment.

Article I, Section 8 of the Constitution deals with commerce. This is driven, in part, by the clause, "For cutting off our trade with all parts of the world." Clearly, trade and commerce were the life blood of the colonies.

Of course much of the battle cry for the Revolution came from the clause, "For imposing taxes on us without our consent." No taxation without representation.

The next clause is the foundation for the Sixth Amendment. It says, "For transporting us beyond Seas to be tried for pretended offenses."

Both the Sixth and Seventh Amendments concern this next clause where it says, "For depriving us in many cases, of the benefits of trial by jury."

The Declaration says the king "has abducated government here, by declaring us out of his protection and waging war against us." This certainly justifies the need to take up arms.

The king has also "constrained our fellow citizens, taken captive on the high seas to bear arms against their Country." This is called impressments.

The original draft also blamed King George for slavery in the colonies. The draft says, "He has waged cruel war against human nature itself, violating its most sacred rights of life & liberty in the persons of distant people who never offended him. Captivating and carrying them into slavery in another hemisphere, or to incur miserable death in their transportation. He is now exciting those very people to rise in arms among us, and to purchase that liberty of which he has deprived them, by murdering the people whom he also obtruded."

This provision was omitted, but can be seen as a clever mechanism to blame slavery on the King of England thus expediting its end. In conclusion, we are free and independent states.

This next clause sounds familiar to the First Amendment. It says, "That we have at every stage petitioned for redress in the most humble terms, but our petitions have been answered by repeated injury."

Finally, the nail in the coffin says, "A prince, whose character is thus marked by every act which may define a tyrant, is unfit to be the ruler of a free people."

The result of all this leads the Declaration to say, "We, therefore, the representatives of the United States of America, in general congress, assembled, appealing to the supreme judge of the world for the rectitude of our intentions, do, in the name, and by authority of the good people of these colonies, solemnly publish and declare that these united colonies are, and of right, ought to be free and independent states; that they are absolved from all allegiance to the British Crown, and that all political connection between them and the State of Great Britain, is and ought to be totally dissolved."

On July 2, 1776, Second Continental Congress voted 12-0 for independence. There was disagreement between the states and within the states regarding a declaration of independence from England. South Carolina and Pennsylvania voted against independence on the first vote, and Delaware was split. New York only had instructions to vote for reconciliation and abstained on the vote for independence. New delegates, absent delegates, and additional debate shifted the vote with only New York abstaining. On July 2, 1776, the vote was 12-0 with 1 abstention. Editorial changes were made on July 3 and July 4. The Declaration of Independence was finally approved July 4, 1776. On July 9, the New York Convention formally agreed to the declaration and signed off on the document. The Declaration was not signed until August 1776.

The Revolutionary War continued until October 19, 1781, with the surrender of the British at Yorktown. England recognized American independence in 1782, and final peace treaties were signed in September 1783.

THE SECOND FOUNDING: FROM COMPROMISE TO CONSTITUTION

The Articles of Confederation

Colonists were in no mood for a strong central government having declared their independence from England and opted for a confederation. A confederation is a loose alliance of states who agree to cooperate with one another. In a confederation, states retain their sovereignty with supreme power over their population and territory. The central government is weak and serves primarily to coordinate rather than control the actions of the sovereign states. The Articles of Confederation were approved on November 15, 1777, but did not go into effect until March 1781.

It created a Congress of the Confederation with a <u>unicameral</u> assembly. Each state had one vote regardless of population or taxes. Each state sent between two and seven members or representatives who were maintained by the state. Delegates were chosen by state legislatures and paid by the states. They were subject to recall by the state authorities. Passage of legislation required nine out of thirteen votes. Amendments to the Articles required thirteen out of thirteen votes. An executive committee governed during congressional recess. There was no chief executive and no judicial branch. States maintained sovereignty. Congress was given very few powers and lacked many of the very essential powers of a national government. Congress could not compel states to respect treaties, meet military quotas, draft soldiers, regulate interstate and foreign commerce, collect taxes directly from the people, share the costs of government, or maintain a sound monetary system.

Lack of powers resulted in almost immediate problems. The Congressional lack of taxing powers resulted in the inability to pay the war debt and devaluation of bonds (defaulted on loans from France, Spain, and was on the verge of defaulting on Dutch loans). Congress could not maintain an army and was thus unable to secure the western lands (learning the hard way that securing a frontier is costly). Trade wars erupted between states with each state imposing tariffs that benefitted themselves at the expense of their neighbors. England closed its ports to American products and flooded colonies with British goods. Government would now retaliate by closing off American ports and forcing negotiations for free trade. States issued their own currency causing rising inflation and unstable finances.

The Annapolis Convention took place in September of 1786. There was a discussion with regard to revising the Articles, which began as early as 1785. Delegations from five states (Virginia, Delaware, Pennsylvania, New York, New Jersey) met in Annapolis in September 1786 to strengthen government by revising the Articles. There was poor attendance, which meant nothing could be accomplished. Alexander Hamilton, a thirty-four-year-old lawyer from New York educated at Kings College, <u>astutely</u> drafted a resolution calling another convention to be held in Philadelphia in 1787.

Shays' Rebellion—August 29, 1786 and February 3, 1787

In Concord, Mass., three times as many men were in prison for debt than any other crime, and in Worcester, Mass. that number was even larger (twenty times). The prisoners were mostly small farmers. Daniel Shays, a former army captain, led a mob of farmers in a rebellion against the government of Massachusetts. The purpose was to prevent foreclosures on debt-ridden land by keeping the county courts of Massachusetts from sitting until the next election. In early 1787, Shays' Army seized control of the county courthouse disrupting the trials of debtors and attacking the federal arsenal. The state appealed to the federal government for assistance, but the federal government was powerless because it lacked the power to create a standing army. The state eventually regained control when a private army of 5400 men put down Shays' Army of 2000 men on February 3, 1787. Shays was sentenced to death for treason but pardoned by Governor Hancock. This illustrated the government's inability to deal with insurrection. Property owners began calling for a strong national government that could deal with radicalism.

Constitutional Convention

The Constitutional Convention began on May, 25, 1787, and lasted until September 17, 1787. Twelve of thirteen states met in Philadelphia, and Rhode Island was absent, sometimes referred to as Rogue Island. Seventy-three delegates were named, but only fifty-five delegates attended and generally no more than thirty were in attendance each day. Most delegates were well educated and successful with 50% being college graduates. Here is a list of their colleges and their religious affiliations.

- Harvard College–Congregational
- Yale College–Congregational
- College of New Jersey (Princeton)–Presbyterian
- William & Mary–Episcopal
- Kings College (Columbia)–Episcopal
- Queens College (Rutgers)–Dutch Reformed
- Pennsylvania–Congregational/Presbyterian
- Dartmouth–Congregational
- College of Rhode Island (Brown)–Baptist

Thirty-three delegates were lawyers, three were physicians, seven were former chief executives of their states, eight were prominent businessmen, and six were large plantation owners. However, the only thing they had in common was the fact that they were all men and all white.

Conflict in Philadelphia

Representation in government was the most hotly debated issue at the convention. One State–One Vote was used under the Articles of Confederation. Population-based representation was proposed by Virginia.

With regard to representation and slaves, the debate was primarily over how to count the slaves with regard to representation in the House of Representatives. Abolition was met with objections by southern delegates who threatened to leave the convention. Northerners conceded in exchange for a Constitution. Concerning voting qualifications, the question was whether to consider property ownership or universal male suffrage. Voting in many of the states was universal or property ownership was so widespread that voting was essentially universal. The

Founders were fearful that any restriction on voting would lead to a rejection of the Constitution by states with universal male suffrage. The debate over representation centered on three proposals; the Virginia Plan, New Jersey Plan, and the Connecticut Plan. Hamilton had a plan as well; however, it was not seriously considered.

The Virginia Plan

The Virginia Plan was presented first on May 29, 1787. This was based on James Madison's, from the College of New Jersey (now Princeton), review of European political favored states with large populations by basing representation on population or taxes paid. It proposed a bicameral legislature with a house chosen by the people and an upper house chosen by the lower house from nominees named by state legislatures. There would be an unspecified national executive elected by the legislature and a national judiciary appointed by the legislature.

The New Jersey Plan

The New Jersey Plan was presented on June 15, 1787, by William Patterson, who was educated at the College of New Jersey (now Princeton). It favored states with smaller populations by retaining a fundamental principle of the Articles of Confederation—one state, one vote. Congress would be able to regulate trade and impose taxes. Acts of Congress would be the supreme law of the land. There would be an executive committee elected by Congress, and the executive committee would appoint a Supreme Court.

The "Great Compromise" or the Connecticut Plan

The Connecticut Plan was presented by Roger Sherman (self-taught attorney) of Connecticut on June 11, 1787. It contained a bicameral legislature with a House of Representatives, which would be apportioned according to the number of free inhabitants in each state, and a Senate, which would have two members from each state elected by the state legislatures. This was an attempt to chart a middle path between those advocating a strong national government and those supporters of state sovereignty.

The Hamilton Plan

Hamilton proposed a British-style monarchy on June 18, 1787, and this may have been enough to move the convention to compromise. However, some thought it signaled a warning to stay away from an authoritarian style of government. In another words, it sent the Convention in the other direction.

The concessions on slavery illustrate the power of the southern delegates. There was some debate over banning slavery, but Southerners opposed ban and threatened to leave the convention. Slaves would be counted as 3/5 a person for purposes of representation. They agreed that the slave trade could be limited by Congress after 1808, and that runaway slaves would be returned to their owners. Slaves are referred to as other persons. Accordingly, slavery was never actually addressed in Constitution.

Compromise on the Chief Executive

The delegates agreed on a one-person executive that would be called President. Other possible titles included governor, or His Excellency. George Washington would serve as a model for the office. The Framers had complete faith in Washington's abilities and his honor. The Framers wanted to create a strong central government but also guard against misuse of power, so they employed three specific techniques.

Separation of Powers

The separation of powers was deemed critical to good government. Montesquieu, the French political theorist, believed that the balance was an indispensable defense against tyranny, and his *The Spirit of the Laws* was taken as political gospel in Philadelphia. The elements of separation of powers, the American Model, would have three branches: legislative, executive, judicial. There would be different election or selection methods with each branch responsible to a different constituency—checks and balances (i.e., veto, judicial review).

Federalism

More power granted to the central government. Retained essential police powers at the state level and created a system of two sovereigns—national and states.

The Bill of Rights

The motion for a Bill of Rights was defeated at the convention. Hamilton and Madison believed the newly created federal government was limited in power. Madison feared debate over the Bill of Rights would derail ratification of the Constitution. Madison agreed to raise the issue after ratification.

Chapter 2

FEDERALISM: FEDERAL VERSUS STATE POWER, TWO HUNDRED YEARS OF DEBATE

PENNSYLVANIA NEBRASKA IDAHO OKLAHOMA MISSISSIPPI INDIANA FLORIDA NEW MEXICO DELAWARE WASHINGTON ILLINOIS WYOMING VIRGINIA NORTH DAKOTA KANSAS SOUTH CAROLINA OREGON TEXAS ARIZONA NEW JERSEY VERMONT CONNECTICUT ARKANSAS NEW HAMPSHIRE KENTUCKY NORTH CAROLINA NEVADA WEST VIRGINIA UTAH HAWAII MICHIGAN ALASKA MASSACHUSETTS CALIFORNIA IOWA LOUISIANA MONTANA RHODE ISLAND WISCONSIN MAINE MINNESOTA MARYLAND SOUTH DAKOTA GEORGIA OHIO MISSOURI TENNESSEE NEW YORK COLORADO ALABAMA

THE RISE OF THE FEDERAL GOVERNMENT: A BRIEF OVERVIEW

Federalism is a system of government whereby there are two levels or layers of government that divide and sometimes share power. The debates regarding the ratification over the Constitution focused on the allocation of power between the newly formed national government and the states. Anti-Federalists feared centralized government and preferred local self-government. Federalists recognized a role for the national government given the deficiencies of the states. The Constitution can be read as specifying certain enumerated or delegated powers of the national government found in Article I, Section 8, and other powers which are reserved for the state governments by the Tenth Amendment. Accordingly, state and local government provide most of the services utilized by Americans through police powers. Considerable variance exists in the manner in which these services are provided. For example, state tax rates and the type of taxes are very different. Beginning with the Great Depression and the election for Franklin D. Roosevelt (FDR), the federal government has intervened in areas traditionally reserved to the states.

THE 1930S: FDR AND THE GREAT DEPRESSION

Federalism under Franklin D. Roosevelt changed with the creation of his New Deal programs. Such programs included the Social Security Act of 1935. These programs were designed to alleviate the difficulties faced by Americans as a result of the Stock Market crash and the economy; however, many were ruled unconstitutional because they went beyond the power given to Congress by the Constitution.

THE 1950S AND 1960S: THE CIVIL RIGHTS MOVEMENT

During the Civil Rights Movement, several important changes came from legislation such as the Civil Rights Act of 1964, the Voting Rights Act of 1965, and the Civil Rights Act of 1968.

THE 1960S AND 1970S: THE REGULATORY ERA

As with the previous changes to federalism, the effects are long-lasting. That was no different for the regulatory era. Many laws were passed that brought about significant changes to the economy and the environment. For example, there were Clean Air and Water Acts, the Endangered Species Act, the creation of the EPA in 1970, OSHA in 1971, Housing and Urban Development (HUD) in 1965, and urban renewal. Yet Americans have become distrustful and resentful of government intervention and regulation, and trust in government has dropped. It appears that the public wants to have their cake and eat it too. The public wants clean air and water; however, that brings more government and cost. Republicans began challenging the size and scope of the national government by arguing for New Federalism and Devolution. This reflects the long-standing debate over federal versus state power that was raised by the Federalists and the Anti-Federalists.

NEW FEDERALISM AND DEVOLUTION

New Federalism was advocated by the Republicans in the early 1970s through the 1980s with Nixon and Reagan. Devolution was advocated by the Republicans in the 1990s with Newt Gingrich and the Republican Revolution of 1994. However, the Republicans did not take control until 1995. At the center of the debate was national versus state power. Republicans and Democrats debate two basic questions. 1) Do we need national standards? 2) Which level of government should ultimately be in control? Democrats support a stronger national government to provide national standards for social programs and environmental programs. The following list represents those programs.

- The New Deal (Roosevelt)
- The Fair Deal (Truman)
- The New Frontier (Kennedy)
- The Great Society (Johnson)

Republicans favor a return of power to the states arguing that over sixty years of federal programs have yielded few results and that states should be treated as laboratories for new policies and programs. A good example is welfare reform passed under the Clinton administration. As mentioned before, the New Federalism of Richard Nixon and Ronald Reagan, and Devolution under Newt Gingrich are the hallmarks of Republican efforts to limit the size and scope of the federal government.

UNDERSTANDING THE FEDERAL FRAMEWORK

There are at least three types of governing systems. The first is a unitary system, which is a constitutional arrangement whereby formal authority resides with the federal or national government and the states are subservient. England and the American Colonies are examples of this system. The second is a confederation, which is a constitutional arrangement whereby the national government relies on the states for its authority. The European Union (EU) and United Nations (UN) are examples of this system. Finally, federalism is the division of powers and functions between the national and state governments.

THE DESIGN OF FEDERALISM

The powers of the national government are found in Article I, Section 8 of the Constitution. The federal government is given seventeen specific or enumerated powers. In addition, the Necessary and Proper Clause, at the end of Article I, Section 8, allows the federal government to do what is necessary and proper to carry out the enumerated powers. This is often referred to as Implied Powers or the Elastic Clause. Couple these enumerated or expressed powers of the national government with the Supremacy Clause found in Article VI and it makes the U.S. Constitution and the laws of the federal government the supreme law of the land.

THE POWERS OF STATE GOVERNMENT

The Tenth Amendment reserves to the states all powers not delegated to the federal government by the Constitution or denied to the states. States retain the police powers, which include the power to regulate the health, safety, welfare, and morality of the state. However, many laws once thought to be reserved to the states have been ruled unconstitutional if they violate the U.S. Constitution.

CONCURRENT POWERS

Certain powers are shared by the states and the federal government. Those include the power to charter banks, borrow money, and tax.

STATE OBLIGATIONS TO ONE ANOTHER

Article IV provides that each state must give full faith and credit to public acts, records, and judicial proceedings. This is often referred to as comity, or the Golden Rule. Do unto others as you would have others do unto you. For example, marriage in one state is binding in all other states. This provision is at the center of the same-sex marriage debate. States cannot give preferences to their own residents under the privileges and immunities provision of Article IV. Alaska attempted to give hiring preferences to Alaska residents, but the Supreme Court declared such action unconstitutional. However, out-of-state residents can be made to pay higher tuition costs.

LOCAL GOVERNMENT AND THE CONSTITUTION

There is no provision in the American Constitution for local government; however, state legislatures can create local governments. In many ways, the District of Columbia acts as a local government with oversight by Congress. State constitutions and laws permit local governments to take on some of the responsibilities of state government. In Texas, for example, counties are considered the administrative arms of the state government. Larger cities are given home-rule status, which allows them to set tax policy and engage in greater self-government.

THE DEVELOPMENT OF FEDERALISM, 1789–1937: RESTRAINING NATIONAL POWER

The early years of the republic were marked by division in public policy authority with each level of government responsible for different areas. Federalists and Jefferson's Republicans continued to debate the appropriate role of the federal government. National government was quite small by comparison both to the state governments and to governments of other western nations.

The Departments of State, Treasury, and War, and the Attorney General were conflicted over federal policy to aid commerce and promote economic development. Alexander Hamilton established the framework for national economic development. Tariffs would provide income as a form of tax on imported goods. There would be a report on public credit, the Mint, The National Bank, and a Report on Manufacturing. Jefferson and James Madison opposed Hamilton's economic policies and attempted to discredit him. President James Monroe vetoed a bill passed by Congress that would have funded the Erie Canal because he believed it to be unconstitutional. State governments were dominant from the 1800s until 1937, as the state legislatures were actively involved in social and economic regulation—for example, Texas Statutes, Texas Code, and Texas Common Law. In addition, the following list relates to state power:

- Property law
- Contract law
- Criminal law
- Commercial transactions
- Corporate law

- Insurance law
- Banking
- Education
- Water and mineral rights
- Morality
- Wills, trusts, and estates
- Public health
- Public safety
- Transportation
- Family law

Marriage, divorce, and child custody/support are regulated by states. For example, states adopt different laws regarding divorce. California recognizes alimony, Texas recognizes community property, and child custody and child support orders are issued by the state. The Texas Attorney General enforces the law. The state regulates and licenses professions such as law and medicine.

DEFINING THE EXTENT OF THE NATIONAL GOVERNMENT'S POWER

Despite attempts to constrain the national government, the Federalists began expanding the political reach of the new national government. The U.S. Supreme Court recognized national powers under Article I, Section 8, as economic forces pushed for more national power. In *McCulloch v. Maryland* (1819) the Court expanded federal power by adopting a liberal reading of the Necessary and Proper Clause (Art. I, Sec. 8) and preventing state interference with federal laws pursuant to the Supremacy Clause (Article VI). Congress created the National Bank in 1791 as part of Alexander Hamilton's economic plan for the new nation to serve as a depository for federal funds and to assist the national government in borrowing funds. Jefferson and Hamilton debated whether Congress had the power to create the bank. Jefferson and his supporters opposed the creation of the bank as an unconstitutional expansion of national powers in that the bank was not indispensably necessary in carrying out Congress's delegated powers. Hamilton argued for a more liberal reading of the Necessary and Proper Clause. Jefferson and Madison conceded the issue when Hamilton agreed to put the national capitol on the Potomac. However, opposition to the bank was not eliminated. Jefferson did not renew the charter for the bank during his presidency. Madison, recognizing the usefulness of the bank, chartered the Second Bank of the United States (1816) during his presidency. Maryland, as many states did, opposed the bank because it competed with state banks, and there was a concern regarding the power the national bank gave to the federal government over the states. Maryland levied a $15,000 tax with the intent of closing the bank and McCulloch, who worked at the bank, refused to pay the tax. The U.S. Supreme Court adopted a liberal reading of the Necessary and Proper Clause and applied to the Supremacy Clause to reject Maryland's attempt to tax the bank. Chief Justice Marshall, a Federalist, ruled that the Necessary and Proper Clause in conjunction with the powers over borrowing and taxing provided the constitutional authority for the bank. Congress is not limited to only those means that are absolutely necessary but may use any appropriate means to achieve the ends specified in the enumerated powers. In other words, any means not prohibited by the Constitution. Furthermore, the State of Maryland could not tax the bank because such a policy would interfere with the constitutional power of the federal government in violation of the national supremacy clause.

Gibbons v. Ogden (1824) established the supremacy of the federal government in areas involving interstate commerce pursuant to Article I, Sec. 8. The New York legislature granted a monopoly to Robert Livingston and Robert Fulton to engage in steamship trade between New York and New Jersey, and this right was ultimately transferred to Ogden. Thomas Gibbons had been given federal authority pursuant to a federal law to engage in steamship trade between New York and New Jersey. The Supreme Court held that the State of New York did not have the power to grant a monopoly because the commerce involved was interstate, not intrastate, and therefore fell under the control of the federal government pursuant to Art. I, Sec. 8.

RETRENCHMENT: THE CRY OF STATE'S RIGHTS

Debate concerning the powers of the federal government continued despite the rulings in *McCulloch* and *Gibbons*. States' rights issues dominated American politics from the founding through the Civil War and for years thereafter. Chief Justice Taney recognized the limits of federal power in the *Dred Scott* case in which the Supreme Court held that the federal government could not prohibit slavery in the territories. South Carolina's John Calhoun argued that the Constitution was a compact between the states rather than with the people. The federal government is an agent of the states. States retained their sovereign nature, and the states had the right to nullify or secede from the union. Lincoln's election in 1860, and a fear in the South that the new Republican government would abolish slavery led to secession and ultimately the Civil War. The exercise of federal authority during Reconstruction created new conflicts over the use of federal power.

EXPANSION OF FEDERAL POWER: THE SUPREME COURT AND INTERSTATE COMMERCE

During the latter part of the 1800s and early 1900s, the U.S. Supreme Court permitted the expansion of federal police powers where the acts clearly crossed state lines and became interstate acts. In *Champion v. Ames* (1903), the U.S. Supreme Court in a 5-4 decision upheld a conviction under an 1895 statute prohibiting interstate traffic in lottery tickets. The defendant used Wells Fargo to move lottery tickets from Texas to California. On appeal, the defendant argued that he was not engaged in interstate commerce. The court concluded that moving goods from one state to another constituted interstate commerce. The dissent argued that the law was really targeting gambling, which was a state matter. The Mann Act or White Slave Act was upheld in *Hoke v. U.S.* (1913). The defendants appealed a federal conviction under the law for enticing two young women to go from New Orleans to Beaumont, Texas for purposes of prostitution. The court held that Congress had the power to regulate interstate commerce even though it had the quality of police regulation (girls crossed state lines). The U.S. Supreme Court, however, refused to uphold federal laws when the activity regulated did not involve crossing state lines.

In *Hammer v. Dagenhart* (1918), the Keating-Owen Act regulating the use of child labor was invalidated on the grounds that the law attempted to regulate child labor and not commerce. The Act prohibited the interstate shipment of goods made with child labor. The child's father sued to challenge the law so that his fourteen-year-old son could work in the textile mill. Police regulations relating to the internal trade and affairs of the states have been uniformly recognized as within such control. This has been so frequently declared by this court, results so obviously from the terms of the Constitution, and has been so fully explained and supported on former occasions, that we think it unnecessary to enter again upon the discussion. The court held that production was not commerce and that regulations pertaining to the production of goods were reserved to the states.

In *Bailey v. Drexel Furniture Co.* (1922), the U.S. Supreme Court declared the federal Child Labor Tax law unconstitutional. In *Adkins v. Children's Hospital* (1923), the U.S. Supreme Court declared a federal minimum wage law for women unconstitutional.

THE DEPRESSION, FDR, AND THE SUPREME COURT– REDEFINING INTERSTATE COMMERCE

The crash of the stock market and the beginning of the Great Depression overwhelmed the capacities of the state governments. Many lost everything in the aftermath of the Stock Market Crash and subsequent bank and business failures. By 1932, 25% of the workforce was unemployed. Hoover (1928–1932) did little to remedy the situation. Franklin Roosevelt (1932–1945) argued that the federal government should and could do something to deal with the Great Depression. After his election in 1932, FDR pushed through Congress a number of measures designed to stimulate the economy under the New Deal. These include:

- Works Progress Administration (WPA) created 8.5 million jobs
- Civilian Conservation Corp (CCC) created 250,000 jobs
- Civil Works Administration (CWA) created 4 million jobs
- Public Works Administration (PWA) provided $3.3 billion

The U.S. Supreme Court declared several of FDR's New Deal programs unconstitutional between 1932 and 1937.

Schecter Poultry Corp. v. United States (1935)

Schecter, a NY Co., sold bad chickens to a butcher in New York. The federal government tried to regulate the sale of sick chickens under the National Industrial Recovery Act. Schecter argued that the law was unconstitutional since both parties were engaged in intrastate commerce. The

Supreme Court (citing *Gibbons v. Ogden*) struck down the National Industrial Recovery Act (NIRA) on the grounds that no act of interstate commerce was involved.

United States v. Butler (1936)

The Agricultural Adjustment Act (AAA) provided payments to farmers to curtail production. It was funded by a tax on processors with the revenue being redistributed directly to the farmers. Butler, a processor, argued that the tax was unconstitutional because it redistributed wealth directly from one individual to another. The Supreme Court struck down the AAA because it attempted to regulate agriculture, which is a state issue. In the New Deal cases, the U.S. Supreme Court objected to the legislation on the grounds that jurisdiction resided with the states or was beyond the reach of either state or federal power. Roosevelt threatened to increase the size of the Supreme Court in a blatant attempt to pack the court with sympathetic allies.

N.L.R.B. v. Jones & Laughlin Steel Company (1937)

In the landmark decision of *N.L.R.B. v. Jones & Laughlin Steel Company* (1937), the Supreme Court performed an about-face with regard to interstate commerce and supported congressional efforts to regulate the economy. The National Labor Relations Board (NLRB) was established pursuant to the National Labor Relations Act (NLRA) in 1935 to protect workers' rights to organize unions and bargain collectively. The NLRB found that Jones & Laughlin had violated the NLRA by engaging in unfair labor practices at its Pittsburgh facility by discharging employees active in the labor union. Jones & Laughlin argued that the Act was unconstitutional on the grounds that it attempted to regulate all commerce (interstate and intrastate), which is in conflict with Article I, Section 8 and the Reserved Powers Clause of the Tenth Amendment. Jones & Laughlin argued that the plant was engaged in intrastate production and not interstate commerce.

The Supreme Court found that even though Jones & Laughlin was located in Pittsburgh, it was actually the hub of interstate activity. Congress has the power to regulate interstate commerce—no matter what the source of the dangers that threaten it. Accordingly, the NLRA is constitutional as is the NLRB. Jones & Laughlin's labor relations in Pittsburgh are subject to federal regulation under the NLRA. Under the *Jones & Laughlin* ruling, Congress has the power to legislate over the channels or facilities of interstate commerce and activities that have a national economic effect. Interstate carriers, roads, and transmissions are channels or facilities of interstate commerce. Activities that affect more than one state:

- An intrastate railroad that blocks competition from interstate railroads
- An intrastate business sells goods that impact the sale of goods in other states or blocks goods entering a state
- A motel that serves interstate travelers
- A restaurant that purchases supplies from other states

TOOLS FOR EXPANDING FEDERAL AUTHORITY OVER THE STATES: SEGREGATION, *BROWN V. BOARD OF EDUCATION* AND THE SUPREMACY CLAUSE

The school desegregation issue firmly established the supremacy of the national government. In 1954, the U.S. Supreme Court issued the *Brown v. Board of Education* decision overruling *Plessy v. Ferguson* and ended segregation in public schools. President Eisenhower and President Kennedy used federal troops pursuant to their power to ensure that the laws of the United States (Article VI) were faithfully executed to force desegregation. Arkansas Governor Orval Faubus called in the National Guard to prevent desegregation of Little Rock High School in 1957, but President Eisenhower responded by recalling the National Guard and sending in the U.S. Army to enforce the desegregation order. President Kennedy followed a similar course of action in 1962 when he enforced desegregation of the University of Mississippi over the direct opposition of Governor Ross Barnett. Alabama Governor George Wallace blocked the entrance of the University of Alabama in 1963 until forced aside by a United States Marshall. U.S. federal courts mandated school desegregation through a number of tools:

- Court-ordered busing
- Court-mandated attendance zones
- Court-management of school districts
- Federal Grants and Federal Rules

Roosevelt created many programs that allowed the states to maintain control over programs through the use of federal dollars or grants-in-aid. Grants-in-aid offer states federal funds to undertake certain activities. Early grants were designed to improve agriculture and farm-related education by funneling cash to the farmers through the states, which avoided conflict with interstate commerce provision. Roosevelt expanded grant programs to include social programs such as Aid to Dependent Children (later AFDC). Congress added new grants after World War II to fund school lunches and highways.

Types of Grants

Categorical grants specify the purpose funds are issued. Here are some examples.

- Head Start
- Asbestos School Hazards Abatement Program
- Federal highway grants for highway construction
- *Click it or Ticket* program for seat belt enforcement

Block grants could be used for a variety of projects. For example, Community Development Block Grants provide funds for infrastructure and social programs in low-income urban areas. An Alcohol, Drug Abuse, and Mental Health Services Block Grant provides funds for a variety of mental health programs. The Local Law Enforcement Block Grant Program provides funds for programs that reduce crime and improve public safety. Federal programs required matching funds or other strings. The Local Law Enforcement Block Grant required a 10% match of the total cost of the program. Highway funds were tied to:

- Drinking age (18 to 21)
- Legal intoxication limit (.10 to .08)
- Speed limit (70 to 55)
- Motorcycle helmets

The states were also required to assist in the delivery of the federal funds (i.e., AFDC, Medicaid, and Food Stamps).

THE ASSUMPTION OF POWER AND FEDERAL DICTATES

Preemption occurs when the federal government takes over areas of regulation previously overseen by state and local governments or, more commonly, ignored by state and local governments. The preemption doctrine derives from the Supremacy Clause of Article VI, which provides that the laws of the United States are the supreme law of the land. Preemption occurs when a statute explicitly preempts state action. Implied preemption occurs when Congress has occupied the field and state regulation would conflict with or frustrate federal law in violation of Article VI. Congress began legislating tobacco in the mid-1960s following a report by the U.S. Surgeon General regarding the health risks related to smoking. In 1965, Congress enacted the Federal Cigarette Labeling Act, which required a warning label on cigarette packages. In 1969, Congress enacted the Public Health Cigarette Smoking Act, which strengthened the warning label and banned cigarette advertising on TV and radio. In *Lorillard Tobacco Co. v. Reilly* (2001), the U.S. Supreme Court ruled that congressional action in the 1960s preempts the states' attempt to restrict tobacco advertising. Unfunded mandates require the states to comply with federal standards or regulations without the funding necessary to carry out the activity. Programs not completely funded include:

- Environmental regulations
- Medicaid
- Food stamps
- Election reform

In 2004, the National Conference of State Legislatures identified $29 billion in unfunded costs imposed on the states.

REPUBLICANS AND THE NEW STATES RIGHTS MOVEMENT: NEW FEDERALISM AND STATE CONTROL

In the 1970s, many began calling for a shift in power back to the states. Block grants were introduced to increase state control over the use of federal grants-in-aid by allowing states to pick projects that were funded. Nixon also implemented revenue sharing to allow states and local governments to exercise greater control over program design. New Federalism suggests that states rather than the federal government are in a better position to solve the nation's problems. New Federalism reappeared in the Reagan Administration. Reagan suggested that federal programs should be shifted to the states and proposed cutting federal spending. The federal share of state operating budgets has dropped since the late 1970s as states have been asked to assume more of the costs.

DEVOLUTION AND THE GINGRICH REVOLUTION

In 1994, the Republicans, under Newt Gingrich, won control of the House and Senate with its platform–The Contract with America. Beginning in 1995, the new Republican Congress took several major steps to achieve Devolution (formally New Federalism). The Unfunded Mandates Reform Act of 1995 attempted to curb unfunded mandates by requiring Congress to provide funding for new programs imposed on the states.

The Welfare Reform Act of 1996 shifted administration to the states under Temporary Assistance to Needy Families (TANF). Congress also reduced federal funding to state and local governments. The Supreme Court's ruling in *United States v. Lopez* in 1995 added further support for the importance of the Tenth Amendment. Congress enacted the Gun Free School Zone Act, which prohibited the carrying of firearms on school grounds. Lopez, a twelfth-grade student in a San Antonio school, was caught carrying a concealed .38 caliber handgun to school. He was initially charged under Texas Penal Code, but charges were dropped after Feds filed charges under the Federal Gun Free School Zone Act. The defendant was indicted by a federal grand jury. A motion to dismiss was made on grounds that the federal act was unconstitutional was overruled. He was convicted following a bench trial and sentenced to six months imprisonment and two years supervised release. The Fifth Circuit reversed the conviction on grounds the statute was unconstitutional and beyond the interstate commerce clause. The Supreme Court granted Writ of Certiorari and analyzed the history of the interstate commerce clause. The government argument was that the Gun Free School Zone Act was related to interstate commerce in three ways.

1. Costs of violent crime impact the national economy
2. Violent crime would deter travel to area affected
3. Guns impact learning, thus creating a handicapped educational process producing a less productive citizenry

The Supreme Court rejected these arguments fearing the proverbial slippery slope. Rehnquist, writing for the court, noted that "accepting the government's argument the Court would have to pile inference upon inference in a manner that would . . . convert congressional authority under the Commerce Clause to a general police power of the sort retained by the States" (O'Conner, Kennedy, Thomas and Scalia joined). The defendant's conviction was overturned as he should have been prosecuted in state court under the Texas Penal Code.

IS THERE A RIGHT ANSWER?

The Robb-Evans Commission, a bipartisan group, proposed in a 1985 report, says states should concentrate on economic development programs, the national government should take care of serving the poor. States do not have it in their interest to serve the poor because they want to keep taxes low and spend money on items that promote economic growth. The controversy exists over the race to the bottom.

Chapter 3

SEPARATION OF POWERS AND CHECKS AND BALANCES IN BOTH THEORY AND PRACTICE

© 2012 Zoran Karapancev. Used under license with Shutterstock, Inc.

The term *trias politica,* or separation of powers, originated with the eighteenth-century French enlightenment writer, social and political philosopher, Baron de Montesquieu. His publication, *Spirit of the Laws,* is considered one of the great works in the history of political theory and jurisprudence. However, the actual separation of powers among different branches of government can be traced to ancient Greece, and it inspired the Declaration of the Rights of Man and the Constitution of the United States. Under his model, the political authority of the state is divided into legislative, executive, and judicial powers. He asserted that, to most effectively promote liberty, these three powers must be separate and act independently. Separation of powers, therefore, refers to the division of government responsibilities into distinct branches to limit any one branch from exercising the core functions of another. However, there is an inherent measure of competition and conflict among the branches of government. Throughout American history, there also has been an ebb and flow of preeminence among the governmental branches. The intent is to prevent the concentration of power and provide for checks and balances.

In theory, the separation of powers and checks and balances seeks to protect liberty by limiting government; it is critical to good government. Montesquieu believed that a balance of power was an essential defense against tyranny. From Madison's notes, we know Montesquieu was cited by delegates attending the Constitutional Convention in Philadelphia. Montesquieu not only discussed the "three sorts of power" that were necessarily exercised by any government but also gave examples of how, in some nations, certain checks on these powers had arisen and had been effective in preventing tyranny. Clearly, our system of separated powers is not designed to maximize efficiency; it is designed to maximize freedom.

Madison, after the Convention, in Federalist Paper No. 47, says, "No political truth is certainly of greater intrinsic value, or is stamped with the authority of more enlightened patrons of liberty, than that on which the objection is founded. The accumulation of all powers, legislative, executive, and judiciary, in the same hands, whether of one, a few, or many, and whether hereditary, self appointed, or elective, may justly be pronounced the very definition of tyranny." It is clear from this statement that avoiding tyranny is the objective of separation of powers. According to Madison, in Federalist Paper No. 51, "the great security against a gradual concentration of the several powers in the same department consists in giving to those who administer each department the necessary constitutional means and person motives to resist encroachments of others." Many political scientists believe that separation of powers is a decisive factor in what they see as a limited degree of American exceptionalism. For example, John Kingdon claimed that separation of powers contributed to the development of a unique political structure in the United States. He attributes the unusually large number of interest groups active in the United States, in part, to separation of powers. It gives groups more places to try to influence and creates more potential group activity. He also cites its complexity as one of the reasons for lower citizen participation.

The Constitution was informed by both reason and experience. The purpose of the Constitution was to frame the government, grant the government power, and limit the power of the government. Madison says, "Justice is the end of government. It is the end of civil society. It ever has been and ever will be pursued until it be obtained, or until liberty be lost in the pursuit." Although not expressly stated, the separation of powers is implied by the first three articles, which create the three branches of the government with each having a particular function. Essentially, the separation of powers is a political doctrine in which the legislative, executive, and judicial branches of the U.S. government are kept distinct in order to prevent an abuse of power. This is also a system of checks and balances in which these institutions share power. In other words, they check and balance each other. The result is that no one branch can exercise power decisively without the support or agreement of the others. However, the founders did not think of or express the concern that one political party might dominate two or more branches. This essentially reduces the effectiveness of separating powers. Madison says in Federalist Paper

Ambition of man

No. 52, "But the great security against a gradual concentration of the several powers in the same department, consists in giving to those who administer each department the necessary constitutional means and personal motives to resist encroachments of the others. The provision for defense must in this, as in all other cases, be made commensurate to the danger of attack. Ambition must be made to counteract ambition. The interest of the man must be connected with the constitutional rights of the place. It may be a reflection on human nature, that such devices should be necessary to control the abuses of government." In other words, the frame of government alone is not enough because of the ambition of men. A classic example of this occurred during the administrations of Bill Clinton and Barack Obama. In the first two years of their administrations, the Democratic Party controlled both houses of Congress. This was a ticket for each president to do pretty much whatever they wanted. The response by the public in both cases was to return Republicans to control in the House. In the case of Clinton, Republicans had not been in control in the previous forty years.

Proportional

FRAME THE GOVERNMENT: THREE BRANCHES

Legislative

The legislative branch makes law and is called Congress. People often remark that this president or that president made a law; however, presidents do not make law. Presidents often get blame or praise for laws that are made while they are in office. For example, LBJ gets credit for the Civil Rights Act of 1964, and George W. Bush gets blame for the Patriot Act. It is important to know who makes law because they must be held accountable. For example, as of this writing, the constitutionality of "Obamacare" is being considered by the Supreme Court. This law carries, in common parlance, the name of the president; however, it is the result of Congress. Yes, the president can propose law and veto law, but only Congress can make law. Since each branch may or may not seek to limit the other branches, the responsibility is left with the people.

Executive

The purpose of the executive is to execute the laws made by Congress. The executive branch is a large institution today; however, when provisions for it were written into the Constitution at the convention in Philadelphia in 1787, the branch consisted of a president. The president serves as the chief executive in that he alone is responsible for executing the laws. Over many years, the Congress has added institutions and people to the executive branch that have the power to implement laws with authority. This section will only consider those powers embodied in the position of the president and the presidential office. Much more is discussed in the section on bureaucracy. There are at least two cases dealing with the breadth of executive power. _Youngstown Sheet and Tube Co. v Sawyer_ (1952) arose when Harry Truman was president. He was responding to labor unrest at the nation's steel mills during the Korean War, and he seized control of the mills. Although a six-member majority of the Court concluded that Truman's action exceeded his authority under the Constitution, seven justices indicated that the power of the President is not

SCOTUS
6 EXC agree but 7

Youngstown v. Sawyer   did not

limited to those powers expressly granted in Article II. Had the Congress not by implication or expressly disapproved of Truman's seizure of the mills, the action would have been upheld.

Judicial

The constitutional function of the judiciary was not judicial review as defined by the U.S. Supreme Court with the case, *Marbury v. Madison.* In the early national period, the judiciary was the weakest of the three branches of government. When Chief Justice John Marshall established the principle of judicial review in *Marbury v. Madison* by declaring an act of Congress unconstitutional, he greatly strengthened the judiciary. However, the Constitution did make it clear that the role of the court was to decide cases involving the U.S. Constitution, laws made by the Congress, and treaties made by the government. How, precisely, that would be done was left to interpretation. Members of the federal judiciary were given lifetime tenure with a guarantee that their compensation would not be reduced.

GRANT THE GOVERNMENT POWER

Legislative: Article I

Article I Section 8 enumerates the powers of Congress as well as the Necessary and Proper Clause, which gives Congress the flexibility to answer the question "how." For example, Congress has the power to regulate commerce among several states; however, the Constitution is not clear about how it can regulate. The Necessary and Proper Clause simply says Congress may do whatever is necessary and proper to carry out the enumerated powers. The enumerated powers are discussed in more detail in the chapters on the Constitution and Congress.

Congress has the power to impeach. The House brings charges of impeachment, indicts, and the Senate convicts. Congress has the power of oversight in that it can conduct investigations of the executive and judicial branches. In addition, Article IV, Section 3 states that "New States may be admitted by the Congress into this Union; but no new State shall be formed or erected within the Jurisdiction of any other State; nor any State be formed by the Junction of two or more States, or Parts of States, without the Consent of the Legislatures of the States concerned as well as of the Congress." This has been an issue of controversy with regard to Texas. The governor, Rick Perry, hinted during the presidential campaign that Texas may need to succeed from the Union. This seems very unlikely given Article IV, Section 3 and Article VI, which indicates that the national government is supreme over the states. In addition, Article IV, Section 3 states, "The Congress shall have Power to dispose of and make all needful Rules and Regulations respecting the Territory or other Property belonging to the United States; and nothing in this Constitution shall be so construed as to Prejudice any Claims of the United States, or of any particular State." This raises the questions of whether President Jefferson, for example, had the power to purchase land for the nation. Another rather important grant of power the Congress has is the ability to tax individual incomes. The Sixteenth Amendment was ratified on February 3, 1913. It simply states that, "The Congress shall have power to lay and collect taxes on incomes, from whatever source derived, without apportionment among the several States, and without regard to any census or enumeration." This one amendment radically changed the country and gave Congress and the president enormous powers over the American people and the states.

Executive: Article II

The powers of the president are not similarly enumerated. They are more general and less specific. For example, the president is the Commander in Chief; however, the president does not have the power to declare war. The president has the power to make war, and Congress has the power to declare war. This illustrates the tension between the two branches. Since Congress funds the military, there is a limit to how much the president can do with the military. Since the military is within the executive branch with the president as its leader, only the president can direct the activities of the military. The powers of the president are articulated in the section on the president; however, it is worth noting that the president can expand his powers to the extent that Congress is willing to allow it. In other words, many presidents have used the military without Congressional authority and without a clear danger to America or Americans. This expansion of power has not produced a significant check on the president. For the most part, Congress can only limit the funds for the military, which would be highly unpopular today. The president was protected against criminal prosecutions while in office, answerable only in an impeachment trial with a super-majority required to convict.

Judicial: Article III

Article III establishes a judicial system with two levels—one Supreme Court and one inferior court. Congress has the power to create the inferior courts and did so with the Judiciary Act of 1789. This is another form of checks and balances because the judiciary cannot grow itself or pay itself. However, the power of the judiciary is somewhat suspect because it may hear cases and may not enforce its rulings. It is safe to say that a respect for the principle of separation of powers is deeply ingrained in every American. The nation subscribes to the original premise of the framers of the Constitution that the way to safeguard against tyranny is to separate the powers of government among three branches so that each branch checks the other two. Even when this system thwarts the public will and paralyzes the processes of government, Americans have rallied to its defense. There was no time in this century when the devotion to that principle was more strongly witnessed than when Franklin Roosevelt introduced a plan to increase the number of Justices on the Supreme Court in 1937. The conflict set off by the President's plan to expand judicial power was in the context of the battle for his New Deal politics.

LIMIT THE POWER OF THE GOVERNMENT

The legislature is limited by the First Amendment by stating that "Congress shall make no law respecting an establishment of religion, or prohibiting the free exercise thereof; or abridging the

Executive limits
2nd D
3rd
4th

freedom of speech, or of the press; or the right of the people peaceably to assemble, and to petition the government for a redress of grievances." One might not think of the Bill of Rights and separation of powers at the same time; however, it is noteworthy for the simple fact that the founders wanted to limit the power of the government. To give one of the other branches the power to limit Congress would mean giving that branch additional power; therefore, the Bill of Rights serves to limit each branch independent of the other. The executive is limited by the Second, Third, and Fourth Amendments. The judiciary is limited by the Fifth, Sixth, Seventh, and Eight Amendments. A discussion of the role of the Bill of Rights can be found in the section on civil liberties.

5th 6th 7th 8th
Limit. of Judicial

DENIALS OF POWER

Congress is denied certain powers in the Constitution. These are found in Article I, Section 9. It says that "the privilege of the writ of habeas corpus shall not be suspended, unless when in cases of rebellion or invasion the public safety may require it." This has been used in recent years to free prisoners when DNA testing was not completed to determine guilt or innocence. In addition, "No bill of attainder or ex post facto law shall be passed." A bill of attainder is a legislative act that singles out an individual or group for punishment without a trial. An ex post facto law means that Congress cannot pass a law today to punish you for what you did yesterday. The following item was superseded by the Sixteenth Amendment. It says, "No capitation, or other direct, tax shall be laid, unless in proportion to the census or enumeration herein before directed to be taken." It also says that "No tax or duty shall be laid on articles exported from any state." This is clearly not a limit on the power of the other branches. Nevertheless, it is important to recognize the limits of Congress. Likewise, "No preference shall be given by any regulation of commerce or revenue to the ports of one state over those of another: nor shall vessels bound to, or from, one state, be obliged to enter, clear or pay duties in another." This clearly was designed to prevent a bias toward one or more states. This may not appear to deal with separation of powers on the surface; however, one of the concerns raised in recent years is that the president, along with a Congress controlled by his party, may take action to help or hinder states. Next, the Constitution says, "No money shall be drawn from the treasury, but in consequence of appropriations made by law; and a regular statement and account of receipts and expenditures of all public money shall be published from time to time." This plays an important role with regard to the political rhetoric that occurs between the president and Congress over debt, deficits, spending, and taxes.

Finally, "No title of nobility shall be granted by the United States: and no person holding any office of profit or trust under them, shall, without the consent of the Congress, accept of any present, emolument, office, or title, of any kind whatever, from any king, prince, or foreign state." This seems outrageous today; however, there has been a development in the current administration of Czars. These Czars are picked by the president and paid by the Congress. They are only accountable to the president. These are advisors to the president and considered part of his executive privilege.

SHARED LEGISLATIVE POWERS

- Pass bills that may be vetoed by the president
- Vetoes may be overridden with a two-thirds vote of both houses
- Provides oversight and rules for the government and its officers
- Creates the jurisdiction of the federal judiciary in cases not specified by the Constitution
- The Senate ratifies treaties signed by the president
- The Senate gives advice and consent to presidential appointments to the federal judiciary, federal executive departments, and other posts

SHARED EXECUTIVE POWERS

- Veto bills passed by Congress, and the veto may be overridden by a two-thirds majority of both houses
- Can only spend what Congress authorizes
- Declares states of emergency
- Issues executive orders
- Makes executive agreements
- Signs treaties with ratification requiring two-thirds of the Senate
- Makes appointments to the judiciary, executive departments, and other posts with advice and consent of the Senate
- Makes temporary appointments during the recess of the Senate
- Grant reprieves and pardons, except in cases of impeachment

SHARED JUDICIAL POWERS

- Decides which laws Congress intended to apply to a given case
- Decides how Congress intended the law to apply to disputes
- Decides how a law determines the disposition of prisoners
- Decides how a law compels testimony and the production of evidence
- Interprets laws to assure uniform treatment by the appeals process

Different election or selection methods with each branch are responsible to a different constituency checks and balances

The president is elected to a four-year term by electors chosen by the states. Presidents can only serve two terms or ten years as a result of the Twenty-Second Amendment. Originally, the president could serve unlimited terms. House members are elected by the voting eligible population to two-years terms with no limits from districts. Senators are elected to six-year terms by the voting eligible population from their state. Originally, state lawmakers elected senators.

As James Madison argued in the Federalist Paper No. 51, "Ambition must be made to counteract ambition." To the extent that government will not limit itself, the power to limit the government is in the hands of the people. Along these lines, for example, there are two opposing views of executive power that have been articulated by past presidents. One, the "strong president" view, was favored by presidents such as Theodore Roosevelt who believed that presidents may do anything not specifically prohibited by the Constitution. Richard Nixon was not far from this point of view. The second, the "weak president" view, was preferred by Howard Taft who believed that presidents may only exercise powers specifically granted by the Constitution or delegated to the president by Congress under one of its enumerated powers.

One way presidents execute power is through the executive order. *Dames and More v. Regan* (1981) considered the constitutionality of executive orders issued by President Jimmy Carter. The Court found executive orders to be a constitutional exercise of the President's Article II powers. The Court noted that similar action had been made at various times by prior presidents and the Congress had never in those incidents, or the present one, indicated its objection to the practice.

Another example is executive privilege, the right of the President to withhold certain information sought by another branch of government, was first claimed by President Jefferson in response to a subpoena from John Marshall in the famous treason trial of Aaron Burr. The Supreme Court's first major pronouncement on the issue, however, did not come until 1974 in *U.S. v. Nixon*. Although the Court unanimously concluded that the Constitution does indeed contain an executive privilege, the Court said the privilege was "presumptive" and not absolute. More recently, *Clinton v. Jones* (1997), the Court rejected President Clinton's argument that the Constitution immunizes him from suits for money damages for acts committed before assuming the presidency. However, to ensure free discussion of controversial issues in Congress, the framers immunized members of Congress from liability for statements made in House or Senate debate.

Chapter 4

THE LEGISLATURE, PRESIDENCY, BUREAUCRACY, AND THE COURTS

© 2012 Brandon Bourdages. Used under license with Shutterstock, Inc.

CONGRESS: REPRESENTING THE AMERICAN PEOPLE

Legislative Assemblies–Historical Origins

A legislative body is a group of individuals elected or chosen to represent the interests of the community from which they are selected. The creation of legislative assemblies in the United States was strongly influenced by traditions established by the Greeks, Romans, and British.

The Greek City State of Athens is believed to have been one of the first representative democracies. Solon created the Council of Four Hundred to represent the city as a whole. These aristocrats would be empowered to act in the best interest of the population. Solon's reforms were dismantled when autocratic rule was established. Cleisthenes established democracy in Athens around 507 B.C. A general assembly of all free men was established to govern the city whereby each man had one vote. The assembly legislated over all aspects of the city's management. Pericles then presided over the continued democratization of Athens. Greek government existed in autocratic, oligarchic, and democratic forms throughout time, but it was the democratic principles that seemed to influence the emergence of Rome.

THE ROMAN REPUBLIC AND THE SENATE: EARLY ROME WAS RULED BY KINGS

About 509 B.C., the Romans overthrew their dynasty of kings and transformed Rome into an aristocratic republic. The king was replaced by two magistrates known as Consuls who were elected from the aristocratic Senate. The Consuls governed, with the advice of the Senate, in the name of the people but in the interests of the aristocratic landowners. The masses (or plebeians) were denied political rights until around 494 B.C. when they wrested power from the patricians and elected their own "tribunes" to represent their interests. About 450 B.C., Rome committed its legal customs to writing—known as the Twelve Tables. Conflict between the patricians and the plebeians led to the institution of elections, the separation of powers, and a system of checks and balances. The Roman Republic collapsed around 100 B.C. and was replaced by imperial leadership under the Caesars as the reach of the Roman Empire expanded throughout Europe, including what is now Great Britain. Julius Caesar seized power in 49 B.C. and was assassinated while in the Senate by Brutus in 44 B.C. Marcus Aurelius (31 B.C.–A.D. 180) greatly extended the borders of the empire. He was succeeded by his son, Commodus, under whose reign the fall of Rome began. The fall of Rome was complete by 480 A.D.

England Expands the Concept of Representative Democracy

England did not become unified until the tenth century and would take the Norman invasion of Anglo-Saxon England to establish the foundation for what we now know as Great Britain. England was ruled by a Monarchy from 1066 until 1215 when the Magna Carta conferred legal rights on the feudal lords. An uprising of English barons against King John (1199 to 1216) culminated on the field of Runnymeade where King John was forced to sign the Magna Carta. The Magna Carta, or Great Charter, established the principle of a constitutional monarchy. The King was limited in power by legal constraints. It created a committee of twenty-five barons to "advise" the King. Henry III (1216–1272) gradually transferred the royal council into Parliament. Under Edward I (1272–1307), Parliament included barons, shire knights, and townspeople. During the fourteenth century, the townspeople and shire gentry split off into a separate House of Commons. Parliament seized power in the mid-1600s as Oliver Cromwell led a civil war that resulted in the beheading of King Charles I in 1649. Cromwell's government (1649–1660) is generally considered to have been a military dictatorship. England returned to a constitutional monarchy following the restoration of Charles II in 1660 and the conflict between <u>absolutism</u> and representative government intensified into the reign of James II (1685–1689). Parliament deposed James II, a Catholic, and replaced him with William and Mary (1689–1694), who were Protestant, in what is known as the "Glorious Revolution," which was intended to preserve the Anglican Church, traditional institutions of Parliament, and decentralized local government. The Glorious Revolution gave us John Locke's *Two Treatises of Government* (1690). It is out of this political history that we arrive at the American Revolution in 1776, the Declaration of Independence, the Articles of Confederation, and finally the United States Constitution.

THE UNITED STATES CONGRESS: HISTORY, PURPOSE, AND STRUCTURE

The first national legislative assembly created following the Revolutionary War was the Congress of the Confederation. Each state sent a number of ambassadors to the Congress. Each state had the power to recall their ambassadors. Each state had one vote, regardless of the state's population. The Congress of the Confederation lacked any real legislative power, which had been retained by the state governments. Problems associated with this lack of power led to calls for reform, a stronger national government. Framers created a **bicameral legislature,** a legislative body with two chambers—the House of Representatives and the Senate. This was a compromise between the large and small states. The small states wanted equal representation, and the large states wanted representation based on population. Each chamber was designed to serve a different constituency. The constituency consists of the individuals who reside in the district or the state from which an official is elected. Members of the House of Representatives are elected by the voters of their congressional districts and are expected to represent the interests of the voting public. One representative is elected from each congressional district as apportioned according to state population, which is established following the decennial census. Congress established the current number of seats at 435 in 1913 pursuant to Public Law 62-5. Senators were initially appointed by the state legislatures for six-year terms and were expected to represent national or state interests. Each state is represented by two Senators for a total of 100 giving each state equal power in the Senate. The seventeenth amendment, which was ratified in 1913, provided for the direct election of Senators.

IMPEACHMENT AND CONVICTION POWERS

The House has the power to impeach an executive or judicial official on the grounds of treason, bribery, or other high crimes or misdemeanors. Articles of Impeachment are presented to the full House from the House Judiciary Committee and are issued on a simple majority vote of the House. Articles of Impeachment are equivalent to a civil indictment. A conviction does not result in criminal punishment. The offender is removed from office and cannot hold future office. Note that a criminal indictment may be issued in addition to Articles of Impeachment. Gerald Ford pardoned Richard Nixon for any crimes he may have committed. A Special Prosecutor agreed not to prosecute Bill Clinton after a formal *mea culpa*. Articles of Impeachment have been issued against two sitting presidents. Andrew Johnson was impeached following his attempt to remove a disloyal Secretary of War in defiance of the Tenure of Office Act, which required Senate concurrence of the removal. The House Judiciary Committee voted to impeach Richard Nixon, but he resigned prior to the House vote. The House Judiciary Committee voted four Articles of Impeachment against William Jefferson Clinton, and a majority of the House concurred. The Senate has the power to convict. The House appoints managers or prosecutors to present the case to the Senate. The Chief Justice of the Supreme Court presides over the case. The Senate sits as a jury and must vote by a two-thirds vote to convict, which is final with no right to appeal. Andrew Johnson, former president of the United States, was acquitted May 26, 1868. William Jefferson Clinton was acquitted February 12, 1999. A number of federal judges have been impeached and removed from office.

ADVICE AND CONSENT ON TREATIES AND PRESIDENTIAL APPOINTMENTS

The Senate has the power of advice and consent on treaties with approval by two-thirds of the Senate and the power of advice and consent over presidential appointments by a simple majority vote. A filibuster has been used increasingly over the past few years to block presidential appointments. One Senator may prevent a vote on a nominee by engaging in a filibuster. However, the threat of a filibuster is usually enough to stall the nominee in committee. Senate Majority Leader Bill Frist threatened to go "nuclear" and change the rules allowing for filibusters if Democrats did not give President Bush's nominees an up or down vote. Senator John McCain and a group of moderate Republicans attempted to reach a compromise that would limit the use of the filibuster to "extraordinary cases." Congress dominated American politics between 1789 and 1932 with regard to both military and economic policy.

CONGRESS AND THE WAR POWERS

Congress has the expressed powers of the purse and the power to declare war and raise an army and navy. However, power has shifted to the president as Commander in Chief during war time. Power would shift back to Congress after the conclusion of the war. The Cold War (1946–1990) created a perpetual state of "war." Accordingly, the president continued to exercise more and more power over foreign policy. Congress formally delegated its war powers to the president beginning with Vietnam and the Gulf of Tonkin Resolution. On August 5, 1964, President Johnson reported that there had been an attack by North Vietnam forces on several U.S. military vessels that were patrolling in international waters. Congress passed the Gulf of Tonkin Resolution on August 7, 1964, allowing the president, as Commander in Chief, to take all necessary measures to repel any armed attack against the forces of the United States and to prevent further aggression. The resolution was to expire when the president determined that the peace and security of the area is reasonably assured by international conditions. The War Powers Act of 1973 attempted to regain congressional control over military involvement. The purpose was to fulfill the intent of the framers of the Constitution to insure that the collective judgment of both Congress and the president will apply to the introduction of troops into hostilities. The president reports to the Speaker and President Pro Tempore within 48 hours. The president will terminate involvement after sixty days has expired unless Congress has declared war, enacted specific authorization extending such sixty-day period (but not for more than thirty days), or is physically unable to meet because of an attack. However, the War Powers Act is probably unconstitutional and has never been invoked.

CONGRESS AND ECONOMIC POWERS

From 1789 to 1932, congressional leaders controlled economic policy. Since the depression, we have looked to the president for economic policy particularly during economic recessions and depressions. FDR proposed and Congress approved the New Deal programs. Lyndon Johnson proposed and Congress approved the Great Society programs. Congress became more reactionary—responding to the demands of the White House. The president submits the annual budget and Congress approves the budget within a few percentage points. The president receives budget requests from the various federal agencies through the Office of Management and Budget (OMB). The OMB prepares an analysis of the budget in conjunction with analysis of the economy provided by the Council of Economic Advisors (CEA). Congress lacked an in-house analysis of the budget and had to rely on the president's economic and budgetary forecasts. The Budget and Impoundment Control Act of 1974 attempted to regain control of the budget process. Congress then created the Congressional Budget Office (CBO) that provides economic forecasts and information to Congress. This information counters the pro-administration information provided by the president by the OMB and CEA.

THE NATURE OF REPRESENTATION: SOCIOLOGICAL VS. AGENCY REPRESENTATION

A representative claims to act or speak for another. The question arises as to how one person can be trusted to speak for another or to speak for many. One can be trusted to speak for another if the two individuals are similar in background; character, interests, and perspectives or the representative's employment is controlled by those represented.

Sociological representation takes place when the representative has the same racial, ethnic, religious, or educational backgrounds as their constituents. This assumes that sociological similarities promote good representation. A legislative body that is expected to provide good representation should mirror the society it represents.

Agency representation occurs when constituents have the power to hire and fire their representatives thereby holding them accountable.

SOCIOLOGICAL REPRESENTATION:
THE SOCIAL COMPOSITION OF THE 112TH CONGRESS

A Snapshot of the 112th Congress demonstrates that the typical member of Congress is a White, Anglo-Saxon, Protestant, Male, and an Attorney. Like the U.S. public, the majority is Protestant and about a quarter Catholic. Baptists and Methodists are the largest Protestant denominations in the new Congress, just as they are in the country as a whole.

Of the 535 members of the new Congress, 304, or 57%, are Protestants, which is slightly higher than the share of Protestants in the U.S. adult population at 51%. Compared with the previous Congress, the 112th Congress has added twelve protestants, an increase of roughly two percentage points.

Baptists remain the largest Protestant denominational family in Congress, essentially unchanged from the 111th Congress, though there are somewhat fewer self-described Baptists on Capitol Hill (13%) than in the national population (17%). Methodists have declined slightly in their proportion of Congress, dropping by six members, or about one percentage point. Nonetheless, Methodists still comprise a larger share of Congress (10%) than of the public (6%).

The composition of Congress along racial and ethnic lines looks like this for the Congress of 2011. Whites are the largest group with 363 in the House and 97 in the Senate. Blacks make up 44 in the House and none in the Senate. Hispanics make up 23 in the House and one in the Senate. There are 5 Asian, Pacific Islander, and/or Native Americans in the House and two in the Senate.

In terms of education, there are 397 members of the House have bachelor's degrees compared to 97 members of the Senate. There are 121 members of the House who have master's degrees compared to 20 members of the Senate. There are 172 members of the House and 57 members of the Senate who hold law degrees.

In terms of occupations, most members of Congress list law or business as their prior occupation, and 39% of House members list law as their prior occupation compared to 57% of the Senate. As for the House, 38% of members list business as their prior occupation compared to 30% of the Senate. There are 14 physicians serving in the 112th Congress. As for prior political experience, 274 members of the 112th Congress served in their state legislatures, and 107 members of the 112th Congress were congressional staffers. With regard to the military, 25% of the House members report military service compared to 31% of the Senate. The average length of service in the House is 9 years, but Rep. John Dingell had served 55 years. The average length of service for the Senate is 12 years, but Sen. Daniel Inouye has served 51 years in the House and Senate combined. Patrick Leahy has served 36 in just the Senate. Protestants constitute the majority of the 112th Congress, but Catholics make up the largest single denomination at 30% of the House and 24% of the Senate. Finally, 9 members of the 112th Congress are foreign-born.

The 112th Congress brought 94 freshman, of which 85 were Republicans and 9 Democrats. In total, 242 House members are Republicans while 193 are Democrats. As for sex, there are 78 women in the House: 25 Republican, 53 Democrat. African Americans comprised 44 members in the House: 2 Republican, 42 Democrat. Of the freshman, 34 affiliated with the Tea Party; 29 in the House, and 5 in the Senate.

The Senate has 51 Democrats—2 independents who vote with Democrats and 47 Republicans. They include 18 women senators—5 Republican and 13 Democrat—and 34 freshmen affiliated with the Tea Parties—29 in the House, and 5 in the Senate.

Of the freshman lawmakers, 43 never held elected office before—3 Senate Republicans, 39 House Republicans, and 1 House Democrat. There are 209 lawmakers who came from the business arena—28 in the Senate and 181 in the House. There are 29 freshmen in the House and Senate who had at one time been a small business owner. There are 200 members who have practiced law as a profession—52 in the Senate and 148 in the House. There are 24 members in the medical profession who were doctors—5 in the Senate and 19 in the House. There are 26 members in the Senate who are military veterans—12 Democrats and 14 Republicans. Finally, there are 92 members in the House who are military veterans—26 Democrats and 66 Republicans.

Party alignment favors the Republicans in the House and Democrats in the Senate with 242 Republicans in the House and 53 Democrats in the Senate. There are 47 Republicans in the Senate and 190 Democrats in the House.

AGENCY REPRESENTATION

Clearly, Congress does not and probably cannot accurately reflect the heterogeneity of the American political community. Accordingly, agency representation becomes much more important. In this case, there are approximately 720,000 clients for a member of the House and an entire state for a U.S. Senator. Members of Congress spend a great deal of time and effort determining the demands of their constituents, pursuing those interests, and reporting back to the constituents. Approximately 25% of a member's time is spent on constituent service. Nearly two-thirds of staff time is spent on **case work;** that is, writing letters, talking to constituents, providing ser-vices, presenting special bills, and attempting to influence decisions of regulatory commissions. On issues of major importance to the constituents, the member is usually bound to act in accordance to their desires. More independence is allowed on issues of lesser importance. The parties recognize the importance of constituent satisfaction and do not require members to vote against their constituents' interests.

THE ELECTORAL CONNECTION—
FACTORS INFLUENCING MEMBERSHIP

Three factors influence the composition of Congress—who decides to run for office, the advantage of incumbency, and the way congressional district lines are drawn.

WHO DECIDES TO RUN FOR OFFICE

Voters' choices are restricted by who decides to run for office. Traditionally, these choices were made by local party officials. Today, candidates are self-selected. Ambition is an important factor.

Money, the ability to raise campaign contributions, is also an important consideration. Political Action Committees (PACs) can minimize the concern over campaign funds, but this may also create a dependency on PAC money. Also, a potential candidate must consider characteristics of the congressional district.

THE ADVANTAGE OF INCUMBENCY

An **incumbent** seeks reelection for an office that he or she already holds. Once in office, incumbents engage in **home-style politics** to enhance their reelection chances. Constituent service includes taking care of the problems and requests of individual voters, establishing personal relationships with constituents through mailings and visits home and through direct patronage.

Then there are Pork Barrel projects, which are specific projects or funding for a district. Projects for a specific district that are inserted into otherwise pork-free bills are called **earmarks.** A line-item veto would have allowed the president to eliminate such **earmarks** from appropriation bills, but the line-item veto was declared unconstitutional.

Intervention plays a role as well by pursuing constituent interests in the bureaucracy. In other words, members have the ability to cut through red tape and solve conflicts or other problems that a constituent may have with one of the agencies.

Members may submit Private Bills, which are proposals to grant some kind of relief, special privilege, or exemption to a specific person. Many of these bills provide relief to foreign nationals who cannot get permanent visas.

Moreover, incumbents have a tremendous advantage in raising money. Constituents believe the incumbent is taking care of the district and supports "their" Representative or Senator financially.

The advantage of incumbency results in 90–98% reelection rate for House members and 75–90% reelection rate for Senators. The **"sophomore surge"** describes this tendency for candidates to win a higher percentage of the vote when seeking reelection. Some candidates are unopposed and contested elections are rarely close. The winning margin has grown, which is referred to as a **diminished marginal.** The district is referred to as a **safe seat.** This was particularly true in the South from 1865 to 1980 when the Democratic Party dominated in a "one-party" system.

This advantage scares off potential challengers who cannot raise enough money to seriously challenge the incumbent. Some candidates lack name recognition, a history of case work, and Political Action Committee (PAC) connections. Therefore, incumbency preserves the status quo of the sociological makeup of Congress and most incumbents are men. Women who run for open seats are just as likely to win as the male candidate. Also, Southern Democrat incumbents rose to positions of power because of their *safe seats and the use of seniority.*

In 1992 and 1994, there were new faces added to Congress, not because of a decline in incumbency advantage but due to a high number of retirements. In 1992, there was a rash of retirements with 65 House members that did not seek reelection. The average retirement rate is approximately 10% for the House and Senate.

Why the hurry to retire? In 1992, Federal Election Commission (FEC) reforms no longer allowed retiring congressmen to convert campaign funds to personal accounts. However, members of Congress who were elected before 1980 and retired before January 3, 1993, were allowed to transfer campaign money to personal accounts. *Roll Call* Magazine reported that nine members of Congress converted almost $1.54 million to personal accounts. Ten members of Congress shifted more than $2.75 million in leftover funds to their own charitable trusts in 1993. The FEC reported that 39 of the 1994 retiring members of Congress who are not currently seeking other elected office had $5,689,633 in campaign accounts.

CONGRESSIONAL REDISTRICTING

Apportionment (or sometimes referred to as **reapportionment**) refers to the allocation of House seats to the states after each ten-year census. The Constitution does not establish a formula, but Congress adopted a formula in 1913 that it continues to follow to this day.

Following reapportionment, the various state legislatures must redraw congressional districts to reflect changes in population in a process known as **redistricting.** Until the 1960s, states legislatures created districts with unequal numbers resulting in inequality of voter representation specifically between rural and urban districts. For example, one Georgia rural district had a population of 272,154 while an urban district had 823,860, thereby diluting the value of the urban vote. Prior to 1962, the United States Supreme Court refused to hear such matters ruling that district boundaries were state matters. In *Baker v. Carr* (1962), the court ruled that inequalities in state representative districts violated equal protection provisions of the fourteenth amendment. The court later ruled in *Wesbury v. Sanders* (1964) that the principle of one person–one vote applies to congressional districts.

The state legislatures engage in a highly political process of drawing district lines for both the U.S. Congress and the state legislature to the advantage of the state's majority party. This process is referred to as **partisan gerrymandering.** Partisan gerrymandering is not illegal unless it consistently degrades a voters' or a group of voters' (i.e., minorities) influence on the political process as a whole. The way the district is drawn determines the political, ideological and ethnic makeup of the district. The power of minorities can be enhanced or minimized. Gerrymandering techniques can include dividing and concentrating. Dividing concentrated political opposition among several districts is known as splintering. Concentrating political opposition into one district to minimize influence is known as packing. In addition, there is the practice of pairing two incumbents in one district to ensure the defeat of one. This is known as a form of punishment.

In the early 1990s, the Department of Justice mandated the use of **racial gerrymandering** to maximize minority representation in Congress through the creation of majority-minority districts. The Voting Rights Act of 1965 specifies that redistricting must be pre-approved by the Department of Justice in states with a history of discrimination or low minority voter turnout. This protects African American, Hispanic, Native American, and Asian voters. In 1982, Congress outlawed any arrangement that has the effect of weakening minority voting power. Some suggest that states must redistrict to maximize minority representation in Congress and state legislatures.

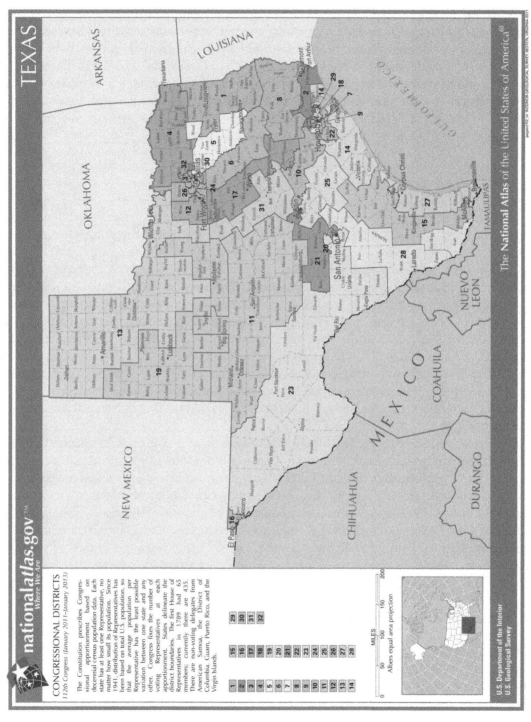

The Department of Justice used the Voting Rights Act to promote affirmative racial gerrymandering, creating predominately African American and minority districts whenever possible; however, the United States Supreme Court later struck down affirmative racial gerrymandering as violating the Equal Protection Clause of the fourteenth amendment. The U.S. Supreme Court first gave notice of its concerns regarding affirmative racial gerrymandering in *Shaw v. Reno* in 1993 by questioning bizarre district patterns utilized to create minority majority districts.

In *Miller v. Johnson* (1995), the United States Supreme Court struck down Georgia's new Eleventh District, which was created under supervision of the Department of Justice. The plaintiffs were white residents of the Eleventh District and claimed that the racial gerrymandering utilized to create the district violated the equal protection clause of the fourteenth amendment, which provides that no state shall deny any person within its jurisdiction the equal protection of the laws. The court noted that racial neutrality in governmental decision making is the central mandate of the fourteenth amendment. Racial distinctions are inherently suspect. In 1965, Georgia was designated as a jurisdiction covered under Sec. 4(b) of the Voting Rights Act of 1965, which concerns states that had discriminated against minorities with regard to voting rights. As a consequence, Georgia was required to get pre-clearance on all redistricting plans. Between 1980 and 1990, only one of Georgia's congressional districts was a majority-black district. The 1990 census indicated Georgia's population had grown to approximately 6.5 million (27% African American), which entitled Georgia to an additional eleventh Congressional seat. The Georgia legislature created two new majority-black districts, which were rejected by the Department of Justice because only two majority-black districts were created. The legislature then created a third majority-black district, which received Department of Justice approval. Accordingly, the Supreme Court determined that race was the overriding and predominant force in the district determination.

In *Bush v. Vera* (1996), the United States Supreme Court declared that the Texas 18th, 29th, and 30th congressional districts were unconstitutional. The Supreme Court noted that the design of the districts were bizarre and utterly ignored city limits, local election precincts, and lacked any sense of continuity. Obviously, the Court found that the Texas Legislature utilized race as "the factor" in drawing district lines following the 1990 census.

THE ORGANIZATION OF CONGRESS

Salaries and Benefits

As of 2011, members of Congress make $174,000 per year plus 15% for outside work such as speeches, legal practice, and consulting. The President Pro Tempore of the Senate makes $188,500, and the Majority and Minority Leaders make $183,500. The Speaker of the House makes $212,100. Salaries are adjusted annually for Cost of Living Adjustments (COLA) unless blocked by Congress. Book royalties are unlimited, and they contribute to social security and the Federal Employee Retirement System.

PARTY LEADERSHIP IN THE HOUSE AND SENATE

House of Representatives

Every two years, at the beginning of a new Congress, the members of each party meet to elect new leaders. For the Republicans, this happens in conference and for the Democrats this happens in caucus. The Majority Party selects the Speaker, Majority Leaders, Majority Whips, Rules Committee (nominees come from the Speaker), and the Budget Committee. The Minority Party elects the Minority Leader and the Whip. The elected leader of the majority party is later proposed to the whole House and automatically elected to the position of Speaker of the House. John Boehner (R-OH) is the current Speaker and has been since 2011. The Majority Leader is chosen to assist the Speaker. The leader of the minority party is the Minority Leader. Both parties also elect Whips to line up party members on important votes and relay voting information to party leaders. The Republican Committee on Committees and the Democrats' Steering and Policy Committee assign new legislators to committees and deal with incumbent requests for transfers to new committees. Membership includes the Majority Leader, the Chief and Deputy Whips, caucus chairs, four members appointed by the Speaker, and twelve members chosen by regional caucuses. Traditionally, party leaders controlled committee assignments. Today, party leaders have less control over these assignments.

Senate

The constitutional leader in the Senate is the vice president who is the **President of the Senate,** but has very few powers other than to break ties. The **President Pro Tempore** is a ceremonial position generally given to the Senator from the majority party with the most seniority. In 2000, Senator Robert Byrd (84) replaced Strom Thurmond (99) as President Pro Tempore. A shift occurred when the defection of a Republican Senator shifted the balance of power in the Senate. In 2002, the Republicans won back control of the Senate and the title went to Ted Stevens of Alaska.

Real power lies with the **Majority Leader** and **Minority Leader** who are elected by party conference and control the Senate's calendar or agenda for legislation. The Majority Leader is not as powerful as Speaker of the House. The position of Majority Leader did not exist until the beginning of this century. Massachusetts's Daniel Webster referred to his chamber as a "Senate of equals" who bowed to no master. Legislative business conducted by a shifting cast that included committee chairmen, sectional coalitions pushing for a particular outcome on the issue at hand, and factions loyal to one or another of the Senate's more prominent and influential figures, such as Henry Clay of Kentucky. A colleague once said of Clay, "When that senator shakes his head and says, 'I hope not,' we know how the yeas and nays will stand as well as if they had been taken and counted."

Progressive Democrats organized following the election of Woodrow Wilson in 1912 to push an ambitious legislative agenda. Wilson wanted to push through his New Freedom program before opposition could form. Democrats selected John W. Kern (a prominent progressive) of Indiana as their caucus chairman who would work closely with the White House. Newspaper accounts of Senate action referred to Kern as Majority Leader as the Senate passed landmark legislation on tariffs, taxes, and monetary policy.

By the early 1920s, both parties were selecting formal leaders, and by 1937, the practice was established that the parties' leaders would occupy the opposing front-row center-aisle seats on the Senate Floor. Although party floor leadership posts carry great responsibility, they provide few specific powers. Instead, floor leaders have had to depend on their individual skill, intelligence, and personality. Majority Leaders seek to balance the needs of senators of both parties to express their views fully on a bill with the pressures to move the bill as quickly as possible toward enactment. These conflicting demands have required majority leaders to develop skills in compromise, accommodation, and diplomacy. Lyndon Johnson described the weakness of the office: "the only real power available to the leader is the power of persuasion. There is no patronage, no power to discipline, no authority to fire senators like a president can fire members of his Cabinet." The current Majority Leader is Harry Reid (D-NV). He has served since 2007. Whips, such as the Majority and Minority Whips, and policy committees are also selected.

THE COMMITTEE SYSTEM

Much of the work of Congress is done by committees and subcommittees.

Standing Committees

Standing committees are the most important arenas of congressional policymaking. They exist from one Congress to the next. They have the power to propose and write legislation. Jurisdiction of each committee covers specific subject matter that generally parallels the major departments or agencies in the executive branch. The most important are those that deal with finances. The House Ways and Means Committee and Senate Finance Committee have jurisdiction over taxes, trade, and entitlement programs (i.e., Social Security and Medicare). The Senate and House Appropriations Committees have jurisdiction over program funding.

THE HOUSE RULES COMMITTEE

This is the only standing committee that lacks the power to receive proposals for legislation and process them into official bills. It decides the order in which bills come up for a vote on the House floor and determines the specific rules that govern the length of debate and opportunity for amendments. The House has twenty standing committees (thirty to forty members each), which are then divided into subcommittees that specialize in various areas of operations.

    Agriculture
    Appropriations
        Agriculture, Rural Development, FDA, Related Agencies
        Commerce, Justice, State, and Judiciary

Defense
District of Columbia
Energy and Water Development
Foreign Operations and Export Financing
Interior
Labor, Health and Human Services, and Education
Legislative
Military Construction
Transportation
Treasury, Postal Service, and General Government
VA, HUD, and Independent Agencies
Armed Services
Financial Service
Budget
Commerce
Education and the Workforce
Government Reform
Homeland Security
House Administration
International Relations
Judiciary
National Security
Resources
Rules
Science
Small Business Standards of Official Conduct
Transportation and Infrastructure
Veterans Affairs
Ways and Means

The Senate has seventeen standing committees (fifteen to twenty members each), each with a number of subcommittees.

Agriculture, Nutrition, and Forestry
Appropriations
Armed Services
Banking, Housing, and Urban Affairs
Budget
Commerce, Science, and Transportation
Energy and Natural Resources
Environment and Public Works
Finance
Foreign Relations

Homeland Security and Governmental Affairs
Judiciary
Health, Education, Labor, and Pensions
Indian Affairs
Rules and Administration
Small Business
Veterans Affairs

Subcommittees conduct most of the legislative work in the House and Senate. Assignments to standing committees are made by a "committee on committees" whose members are appointed by Speaker of the House and presiding officer of the Senate. They try to accommodate the requests of individual members; however, seniority plays a major role. Generally, each committee is chaired by the senior member of the majority party, but the rule is not absolute. Status is determined by years of continuous service on a particular committee.

Select Committees

These committees may be permanent and generally do not have the authority to report legislation. Select committees can hold hearings and investigate particular issues that usually fall between the jurisdictions of standing committees.

Senate Watergate Committee of 1973
Whitewater Committee
Senate Select Committee on Aging (permanent)
House Select Committee on Hunger
Select Intelligence Committees (permanent)
Senate Select Committee on Ethics

Joint Committees

These involve members of both the House and Senate. Four such committees are Economic, Taxation, Library, and Printing. They are permanent but do not have the power to report legislation. The Economic and Taxation committees collect information and hold hearings on economic and financial issues and recommend policies. The Joint Committee on Printing oversees the Government Printing Office, which produces 12.2 million copies of government documents per year.

Conference Committees

Conference committees are temporary committees whose members are appointed by the Speaker of the House and presiding officer of the Senate. They are charged with reaching a compromise on legislation that has passed the House and Senate in different forms.

Significant changes in the organizational structure and procedures occurred in the 1970s driven by a desire to weaken the power of committee chairs. Reforms included an increase in the number of subcommittees, greater autonomy for subcommittee chairs, open committee meetings, and multiple referrals of bills allowing several committees to consider the same bill. The result has been fragmented power that interferes with legislative process. Republicans have attempted to reverse this trend by restoring some of the power to committee chairs.

THE STAFF SYSTEM: STAFFERS AND AGENCIES

Each member of Congress employs a large number of staff members. Each House member has a $600,000 budget to hire staffers—eighteen full-time, four part-time. Senators have an annual salary and expense budget of $2 million plus for office space and salaries. These staffers work in either the Washington or district (state) offices (approximately 11,000). They deal with constituents, legislation, and administrative agencies. Salaries range between $21,000 and $117,000 per year; the Chiefs of Staff make between $98,000 to $117,000, the State/District Director earns between $62,000 to $73,000; a Constituent Case Worker earns $30,000; and a Legislative Correspondent earns $25,000. Committee staffers assist the various committees and subcommittees. Staff agencies also assist members of Congress.

Congressional Research Service
General Accounting Office
Congressional Budget Office
Office of Technology Assessment

INFORMAL ORGANIZATION: THE CAUCUSES

Caucuses are groups of senators or representatives who share certain opinions, interests, or social characteristics and seek to advance the interests of their groups. Ideological caucuses include the liberal Democratic Study Group; the conservative Democratic Forum, or "boll weevils"; and the moderate Republican Wednesday Group. Economic or policy caucuses include the Travel and Tourism Caucus, the Steel Caucus, the Mushroom Caucus, and the Concerned Senators for the Arts. Social caucuses include the Congressional Black Caucus, the Congressional Caucus for Women's Issues, and the Hispanic Caucus.

RULES OF LAWMAKING: HOW A BILL BECOMES A LAW

Introduction and Assignment

Proposed legislation is generally prepared by a member of Congress, the White House, or a federal agency. The bill is referred to as H.R. Bill or S. Bill for most legislation. Joint Resolutions are referred to as H.J. Res. or S.J. Res. similar to bill, except for resolutions proposing constitutional amendments. Concurrent resolutions are referred to as H. Con. Res. or S. Con. Res., which regards matters affecting the operation of the House and Senate. Simple resolutions are referred to as H. Res. or S. Res., which regard matters affecting the operation of either the House or Senate. These are submitted officially by a Senator or Representative who is the sponsor of the bill, which may include an unlimited number of co-sponsors to the Clerk of the House or Senate, assigned a number such as H.R. 1 or S. 1, and then referred to the appropriate standing committee by the Speaker or Presiding Officer. The 108th Congress, Second Session can serve as an example. Here are the statistics. From 1/3/2004 to 12/31/2004, the House spent 110 days in session, and the Senate spent 133 days in session. There were 1,732 bills that originated in the House and 1,032 in the Senate. There were 2,338 total measures in the House and 1,318 in the Senate.

STANDING COMMITTEE ACTION

Subcommittee of the Standing Committee

Once assigned to a committee, the bill is referred to a subcommittee. The subcommittee may hold hearings, listen to expert witnesses, and amend the proposed legislation, which is referred to as mark up. The subcommittee may then refer the bill back to the committee for consideration or may simply allow the bill to die in subcommittee.

STANDING COMMITTEES

The committee may accept the recommendations of the subcommittee, hold its own hearings, and make its own changes to the legislation. Generally, 95% of the bills introduced in a typical congressional session die in committee.

A discharge petition may be used if a bill is stuck in committee. It requires 218 votes on discharge petition to get a bill out of committee for floor vote in the House. The Senate requires only a simple majority.

GETTING THE BILL TO THE FLOOR

House Rules Committee

If the bill survives the committee stage it must pass the Rules Committee. Time is allotted for debate, and it determines to what extent amendments to the bill can be proposed from the floor; a closed rule with no amendments, a restricted rule with limits on amendments, or an open rule that permits unlimited amendments. Opponents of a bill prefer an open rule that allows unlimited floor amendment and debate. Proponents of a bill favor a closed rule that places severe limits on amendments and debate. Most bills have fairly restrictive rules with 75% restricted rule and 10–15% closed rule.

SENATE UNANIMOUS CONSENT AGREEMENTS

The Senate requires a unanimous consent to bring a bill to the floor rather than a Rules Committee. This specifies when a bill will be debated, what amendments will be considered, and when the final vote will be taken. A single senator can kill a bill by objecting to a unanimous consent agreement.

DEBATE

House Debate

The Speaker of the House has the power of recognition during debate. In the House, virtually all of the time allocated for debate is controlled by the bill's sponsor and its leading opponent, usually the committee chair and ranking minority member of the committee that processed the bill.

Senate Debate and Amendments

The presiding officer of the Senate has the power of recognition during debate, but generally has less control than does the Speaker of the House. The Senate supports open discussion and, once given the floor, a Senator may speak for as long as he or she desires. This is better known as a **filibuster,** which allows a Senator to talk a bill to death. Strom Thurmond led a twenty-four hour, nineteen minute filibuster against the Civil Rights Act of 1957. Phil Gramm led a successful filibuster against President Clinton's nomination of a U.S. Surgeon General. Through the use of **cloture,** a vote of three-fifths of the chamber will end a filibuster. Typically, this requires 60 Senators out of 100. Senators may also amend a bill to death because unanimous consent is required on all amendments. Senators can also place holds on legislation. Holds are kept secret. These are used when publicly opposing a bill or nomination would be politically damaging. After all deliberation, the bill is scheduled for floor vote of which there are three types—quorum vote, voice vote, and roll call.

CONFERENCE COMMITTEE

Frequently, identical bills will be introduced in the House and Senate but, as result of the legislative process, will be different when passed by each chamber or after passing one chamber will be changed in the second chamber. A conference committee will be named to work out these differences. The membership includes senior members of the referring committees and the subcommittees. Changes must be approved by a majority of the two delegations. The conference report must then be approved by the House and Senate without any changes.

PRESIDENTIAL ACTION

The president may sign the bill into law or veto the legislation. The president may veto a piece of legislation by returning the bill unsigned within ten days to the chamber in which the bill originated, or if Congress is not in session then it is vetoed without any further action. This is called a **pocket veto**. The typical veto may be overridden by a two-thirds vote of both the House and Senate. A veto is unlikely to be overridden (approximately 10%).

OVERSIGHT—MONITORING THE IMPLEMENTATION OF LEGISLATION

Oversight refers to the effort to oversee or to supervise how legislation is carried out by the executive branch. Oversight is carried out by the committees and subcommittees of the House and Senate. They hold hearings, conduct investigations, subpoena witnesses, compel testimony under oath, and bring criminal charges for contempt and perjury. Appropriations is a key step in the oversight process.

HOW CONGRESS DECIDES—INFLUENCES ON THE LEGISLATIVE PROCESS

Constituency

One would expect that constituent influence would have a great impact on the legislative process. Yet, this influence is not all that clear because most Americans have little or no idea as to what it is that members of Congress do and what legislation they are considering. We do know, however, that members of Congress spend a great deal of time concerned about the desires of their constituents because of the potential impact on the next election.

INTEREST GROUPS

Interest groups attempt to influence the legislative process, and those with supporters in a member's district will have a great deal of power. Grassroots pressure places emphasis on members' constituents. In addition, campaign contributions provide a means of access. Therefore, lobbying can influence the language of legislation.

PARTY DISCIPLINE

Party leaders have some influence over members. At the turn of the century, party leaders could command the allegiance of more than 90% of their members and demand party-line votes. A party vote occurs when at least 51% of one party votes one way and 51% of the other party votes the opposite. Party cohesion is influenced by ideology, organization, and leadership. Committee assignments can create great debts if leaders honor committee requests. The leadership has control of access to the floor, which can lead to influence and leadership. Political Action Committees (PACs) control campaign funds. Whips can control information and access to routes for compromise. Logrolling provides an exchange of support for each others' programs.

At the beginning of the twentieth century, nearly half of all roll call votes were party votes. Party unity was generally greater in the House than the Senate because House rules provide more power to the party's leadership contrary to the Senate. Party line votes are now on the rise due to a partisan Congress. The 1994 election that put Newt Gingrich and the Republicans in control of the House and Senate sparked a rise in partisan tensions. The election of George W. Bush intensified the partisan debate over policies and presidential appointments. However, there were a number of moderate Republicans who defected or compromised with the Democrats, thus weakening Republican unity.

The president may also influence legislation by declaring a "mandate" or by using his constitutional powers. For example, he may invoke the will of the people (if popularity is high enough). He may threaten to veto legislation as Clinton did with the Partial Birth Abortion Bill introduced by the Republicans or actually vetoing legislation. However, there are numerous limitations on the president's influence, such as divided government, separation of powers, the independence of Congress, and Congressional power of the purse.

Weighing Diverse Influences

As you can tell, there are many factors that influence the legislative process and how members of Congress will cast their votes. Each will influence the process at different stages. Influence will also depend on the nature of the issue.

THE PRESIDENCY

Article II of the U.S. Constitution: The President of the United States of America

Election of the President—The Electoral College

The president is elected indirectly through the Electoral College with close elections decided by the House of Representatives.

Why an Electoral College?

Framers hoped to create a strong president responsible to state and national legislators rather than the electorate. They feared that the electorate could be swayed by "propaganda" and would not necessarily pick the "correct" candidate.

What does it take to win the presidency?

There are 538 electors and 270 are required to win, a simple majority. Each state has a number of electors equal to the number of Senators and Representatives (D.C. is given three electors). Failure to win the required majority throws the election to the House of Representatives where each state has one vote.

Becoming President

What are the constitutional requirements for office?

There are three de jure or constitutional requirements for the president. The first is that he must be at least thirty-five years of age. John F. Kennedy was the youngest elected president at forty-three. Teddy Roosevelt became president at forty-two upon the assassination of William McKinley. Ronald Reagan was the oldest elected president at sixty-nine. The second requirement is that the president must be a natural-born citizen of the United States. All candidates since Martin Van Buren have been born in the United States rather than the British colonies. Previous presidents were citizens "at the time of the adoption of this Constitution." Legend has it that the rule was written to prevent Alexander Hamilton from assuming the presidency. Barry Goldwater, a presidential candidate in 1964, was born in the Arizona territory, which qualifies as a "natural-born citizen." John McCain was born in the Panama Canal Zone, which was a U.S. territory at the time. There is now a movement to amend the U.S. Constitution so that several prominent "naturalized" politicians could run for the presidency. Finally, the president must be a resident of the United States for fourteen years. This was designed to block loyalists from returning and seizing power. However, many presidents have lived abroad prior to assuming office. Thomas Jefferson lived in France from 1784–1789. Herbert Hoover lived in Europe and Asia for many years prior to running for the presidency in 1928.

Presidential Characteristics

Presidential characteristics are often referred to as de facto qualifications because it appears that certain characteristics are found among the presidents as a matter of fact. All forty-three presidents have been white males. Geraldine Ferraro (NY) was selected as a vice presidential candidate by Walter Mondale in 1984. The Democrats carried only Minnesota in the 1984 election. Twenty-five of the forty-three presidents have been lawyers. Thirty of the forty-three presidents have served in the military. Twenty-five of the forty-three served in Congress. Sixteen of the forty-three and four of the last five served as governors. Fourteen of the forty-three presidents served as vice president. Five were elected in their own right. Four became president by natural death of the president, and four by assassination of the president. Only one became president by resignation of the president. Nine presidents did not attend college: George Washington, Andrew Jackson, Martin Van Buren, Zachary Taylor, Millard Fillmore, Abraham Lincoln, Andrew Johnson, Grover Cleveland, and Harry S. Truman. Presidents have been overwhelmingly Protestant. John Kennedy has been the only Catholic. Jefferson was a Deist. Lincoln considered himself a "Liberal." Andrew Johnson listed no religious affiliation.

Constitutional Term of Office

The president serves a four-year term. There was no initial constitutional limit on the number of terms. Washington established the two-term tradition. Franklin Roosevelt shattered the two-term tradition, running and winning four times. The result is a limit of two terms by the Twenty-Second Amendment (1951). Only five presidents have served two terms since the ratification of the Twenty-Second Amendment, Eisenhower (1952, 1956), Nixon (1968, 1972–1974), Reagan (1980, 1984), Clinton (1992, 1996), and George W. Bush (2000, 2004). Only Lyndon B. Johnson could have served more than eight years had he been able to win in 1968.

The Line of Succession

Pursuant to the Twenty-Fifth Amendment, if the president becomes incapacitated or is unable to complete his term in office, he will be replaced by the vice president, followed by the Speaker of the House, then the President Pro Tempore of the Senate, and the Cabinet departments by the date of creation:

1. State
2. Treasury
3. Defense
4. Attorney General
5. Interior
6. Agriculture
7. Commerce
8. Labor
9. Health and Human Services
10. Housing and Urban Development
11. Transportation
12. Energy
13. Education
14. Veterans Affairs
15. Homeland Security

EXECUTIVE ORDERS ARE USED TO HANDLE SUCCESSION WITHIN EACH CABINET DEPARTMENT

Impeachment and Conviction

The president may be impeached and convicted for treason, bribery, or other high crimes and misdemeanors. They cannot hold office once convicted. Only two presidents have been impeached, but none have been convicted. Andrew Johnson was charged with impeachment but not convicted. William Jefferson Clinton was also impeached but was not convicted. Richard

Nixon would have been impeached and convicted had he not resigned prior to the House vote on impeachment articles.

Overview of Constitutional Powers

The office was to be one of delegated powers. The powers of the national government are defined in Article I, Section 8. The president is to execute the laws as adopted by Congress. Article I powers include the power to veto legislation. One form of veto exists by returning the bill to the chamber in which the bill originated with objections can be overridden by two-thirds vote of both chambers. Another form of veto is a pocket veto in which the bill will be killed if there are less than ten days left in the session and the president holds on to the bill until after Congress adjourns. A line item veto was granted to the president by Congress in 1996, but was subsequently held unconstitutional by the Supreme Court.

Article II Provides for the Constitutional Powers of the President

The powers of the president include the following:

- Commander in chief
- Request opinions of executive department heads
- Grant pardons, except for impeachments
- Appoint executive and judicial positions with the advice and consent of the Senate
- Enter into treaties with the advice and consent of the Senate

The duties of the president include the following:

- Give the State of the Union Address and recommend measures deemed necessary
- Convene and adjourn sessions of Congress
- Receive ambassadors
- Faithfully execute the laws

The president can draw inferences from power delegated by Congress as long as he remains within the scope of the Constitution.

THE TWO ROLES OF THE PRESIDENT: HEAD OF STATE AND HEAD OF GOVERNMENT

The President as Head of State and the Imperial Presidency

There are three constitutional provisions that provide the basis of presidential power as Head of State. The first deals with the military and is found in Article II, Section 2. It provides for the power as "Commander in Chief of the Army and Navy . . . and the Militia of the several states." The second concerns the judiciary and is also found in Article II, Section 2. It provides the power to grant reprieves and pardons for offenses against the United States, except impeachment. Lastly, there is diplomatic power found in Article II, Section 3 that provides the power to receive ambassadors and other public ministers.

MILITARY POWERS

The president's position as commander in chief makes the president the highest military authority even though he is a civilian. The president also heads the government intelligence hierarchy:

1. National Security Agency
2. Department of Homeland Security
3. National Security Council
4. CIA
5. FBI

These powers are in many ways shared with Congress through its power of the purse and the power to declare war. This has led to a long-running conflict between the two branches. For example, President Johnson's experience with the Gulf of Tonkin Resolution and President Nixon's challenge of the War Powers Act of 1973. President Bush also sought explicit congressional authorization for the Gulf War in 1991, and President Clinton had to obtain federal funding for the stationing of troops in Bosnia. Most recently, President Bush needed to obtain funding for the war in Iraq.

JUDICIAL POWERS

The power to grant reprieves, pardons, and amnesties may be applied to individuals or to groups. The use of this power is very controversial, particularly in the cases of Ford, Carter, and Clinton. President Andrew Johnson gave a full amnesty to all southerners who participated in the "Late Rebellion." Ford granted pardons to Richard Nixon and Robert E. Lee. Lee's petition for amnesty had been misfiled after the war. Congress restored Lee's citizenship after his Oath of Allegiance was found in National Archives in 1970. Carter granted a pardon to Vietnam "draft dodgers," and Clinton pardoned Patty Hearst and "others."

DIPLOMATIC POWERS

The president has the power to receive diplomats and foreign leaders and to grant diplomatic recognition of the legitimacy of other countries. Presidential recognition is necessary for beginning diplomatic and economic relations. For example, Nixon recognized Communist China, Carter recognized Nicaragua, and President Clinton recognized Vietnam. However, challenges generally are made to the logic of the decision rather than the power to make the decision.

THE IMPERIAL PRESIDENCY

Franklin D. Roosevelt (FDR) may have initiated what we now refer to as the "Imperial Presidency." (Coined by *Arthur Schlesinger*) FDR expanded the use of executive orders to broaden presidential powers during the Great Depression. The Supreme Court in 1936 supported expansion of the presidency by holding that the Congress could delegate powers to the president. In 1942, the Supreme Court also upheld the power of the president to use executive agreements to conduct foreign policy. An executive agreement is like a treaty in that it is a contract between two countries but lacks Senate approval. Generally, this is used for agreements made in furtherance of a treaty or for matters below the policy level. The advantage to the president is that it avoids conflict with the Senate. Here are a few examples:

> Franklin Roosevelt—131 Treaties and 369 agreements
> William Clinton—209 Treaties and 2,047 agreements
> Ronald Reagan—125 Treaties and 2,840 agreements

The Cold War and the president's role as commander-in-chief propelled the president to national and international prominence. President Truman deployed troops in Europe to combat Soviet expansion and in Korea pursuant to a U.N. resolution. President Eisenhower deployed military advisors in South Vietnam, but warned of the rise of the military-industrial complex. President Kennedy escalated involvement in Vietnam and confronted the Russians in Cuba. President Johnson convinced Congress to adopt the Gulf of Tonkin Resolution authorizing him to expand the American military presence in Vietnam. President Nixon went even further and became the epitome of the abuse of power as an "Imperial President." Nixon expanded U.S. involvement in Vietnam without obtaining congressional approval and bombed Cambodia and Laos. In response to allegations of wrongdoing during the Watergate investigation, Nixon responded that if the president does it, it is not illegal. Reforms in the 1970s attempted to reign in the president. Examples include the Case Act of 1972, the War Powers Act of 1973, and the Budget and Impoundment Control Act of 1974. President Reagan took at least four military actions that could be viewed as violations of the War Powers Act, Grenada, Iran-Contra, and Libya. President Bush similarly challenged the War Powers Act in Panama. President Clinton used the military on a number of occasions including Iraq, Haiti, and Bosnia. President George W. Bush and Barack Hussein Obama have also expanded the powers of the presidency and may have restored the "Imperial Presidency." Some sight the War on Terror and the Patriot Act, which greatly expanded the investigatory powers of the Executive Branch. Of course, the Patriot Act or any other law can only be made by Congress. The Department of Homeland Security was created by Congress shortly after the September 11th terrorist's acts, and it consolidates powers through centralization of command. The War in Afghanistan was supported more than the War in Iraq. Some cite the opposition to the war raised by France, Russia, and Germany; however, each of these countries had their self-interest ahead of the United States. This resistance may be considered a weakening of the "Imperial Presidency" in the international community.

However, the world still calls on the United States and the president to resolve international conflicts as we are the last standing superpower. A good example of this is the situation in Libya, the conflict between Israel and the Palestinians, and North Korea.

THE DOMESTIC PRESIDENCY: THE PRESIDENT AS HEAD OF GOVERNMENT

There are three constitutional provisions that provide the basis of presidential power as Head of Government. The power is vested in the president by Article II, Section 1 to see that the laws are faithfully executed. Article II, Section 3 says the president is to appoint, remove, and supervise all executive officers and to appoint all federal judges. In terms of the military, the president exercises domestic military power, which is derived from Article IV, Section 4 that stipulates that the president has the power to protect every state against invasion and against domestic violence. With regard to the legislature, the president is given the power under various provisions to participate effectively and authoritatively in the legislative process.

When it comes to executive power, the most important basis of power is Article II, Section 3, which stipulates that the president must see that the laws are faithfully executed, and the Constitution seems to recognize the need for an executive with various departments advising the president and executing the laws enacted by Congress.

Department of State
Department of Defense
Department of Justice
Department of Treasury
Department of Agriculture
Department of Interior
Department of Commerce
Department of Labor
Department of Health and Human Services
Department of Housing and Urban Development
Department of Education
Department of Transportation
Department of Energy
Department of Veterans Affairs
Department of Homeland Security

Laws enacted by Congress delegate execution to the president and executive departments and agencies directly responsible to the president. President Truman had a sign on his desk that read "The Buck Stops Here" recognizing that the president is ultimately responsible for his decisions and those decisions made by his appointees. The president has the power to appoint executive department officials as well as federal judges with the advice and consent of the Senate. All federal employees were appointed by the president until 1883 when President Garfield was assassinated by a disgruntled office seeker. Now only about the top 3000 executive branch officials are appointed by the president with the remaining 3 million employees hired through civil service.

Military sources of domestic presidential power are found in Article IV, Section 4. The United States shall guarantee each state a republican form of government and shall protect each of them against invasion and, upon application of the state legislature or of the executive, against domestic violence. Under this rule the president must receive a request from the state legislature or governor before deploying troops in a state. Governors may declare a state of emergency or martial law and request federal assistance. Governors usually request federal assistance following natural disasters such as hurricanes, floods, or tornados. Jeb Bush requested a declaration from President Clinton following the hurricane in 1999. Jeb Bush requested a declaration from President Bush in 2004 following four hurricanes that hit Florida. The president, however, may send in federal troops without request if necessary to faithfully execute federal laws. In 1954, a showdown occurred between Governor Faubus of Arkansas and Eisenhower over the enforcement of the *Brown vs. Board of Education* decision, which ordered the desegregation of public schools. Governor Faubus posted the Arkansas National Guard at the door to prevent the desegregation of Central High School in Little Rock, Arkansas. Eisenhower sent in federal troops and nationalized the Arkansas National Guard to remove them from Governor Faubus' control. Failing to reach a settlement, Eisenhower ordered the federal troops (101st Airborne) to ensure the desegregation of the school. A similar situation occurred involving Governor George Wallace at the University of Alabama in 1963 when Kennedy nationalized the Alabama National Guard.

Legislative power Article II, Section 3 provides that the president shall deliver a State of the Union address and recommend for their consideration such measures as he shall judge necessary and expedient. The president is now viewed as an initiator of legislation. However, the president's power to propose and initiate legislative proposals is limited by the separation of powers and divided government. Article I, Section 7 provides the president with the power to veto legislation passed by Congress. A regular veto occurs when the president signs the veto message and returns the bill to Congress. A regular veto may be overridden by a two-thirds vote of both the House and Senate. Only 107 of the 1485 presidential vetoes have been overridden by Congress. A pocket veto occurs if the president does not sign a bill within ten days and Congress is no longer in session. A pocket veto cannot be overridden because Congress is not in session, but it can be reintroduced the next session. Presidents have carried out 1,068 pocket vetoes since 1789. Lastly, the line-item Veto does not exist. Congress legislatively provided the power to veto specific line-items in the budget in 1996. It was declared unconstitutional in 1998.

MISCELLANEOUS POWERS OF THE PRESIDENT

Executive privilege concerns the power to withhold "confidential" information. Washington was the first to invoke the principle when he refused to provide the House documents related to the Jay Treaty although he provided the documents to the Senate. Jefferson invoked the doctrine when Burr subpoenaed documents, but he then turned the documents over voluntarily. Nixon argued that Oval Office conversations were privileged, but the Supreme Court ordered Nixon to turn over recordings of meetings because they possibly involved criminal acts (*U.S. v. Nixon*).

Clinton argued conversations with his advisors were protected by executive privilege but withdrew the objection in favor of the attorney-client privilege, which was subsequently rejected. Clinton also invoked a Secret Service privilege to block questioning of Secret Service agents who overheard conversations, a claim also rejected by the Supreme Court. Cheney invoked the privilege to protect discussions of an Energy Task Force, which was subsequently supported by the Supreme Court when the court refused to order that the documents be released.

IMPOUNDMENT

The Constitution provides that the federal government cannot spend money without an appropriation of funds by Congress. President submits a budget to Congress who then adds to the budget various expenditures (i.e., pork-barrel projects). The president, lacking a line-item veto, may attempt to use his position as chief executive to impound expenditures to certain departments or agencies. Presidents have used this power since 1789. Jefferson impounded $50,000 for the acquisition of gunboats since there was no imminent threat to national security. Nixon refused to spend $12 billion in funds that had been appropriated to fight inflationary pressures on the economy. Nixon's use of impoundment set off a firestorm in a Congress that was already on edge because of Watergate. Congress enacted the Budget and Impoundment Control Act of 1974, which requires the president to spend all funds that have been appropriated unless Congress agrees to changes proposed by the president.

INSTITUTIONAL RESOURCES OF PRESIDENTIAL POWER

The Cabinet is the informal designation for the fifteen federal government departments. The Cabinet lacks the formal power of constitutional cabinets. Britain's Cabinet is the government. The U.S. Cabinet officials are ultimately responsible to the president. Traditionally, appointments were made for political reasons. This often resulted in the appointment of inept advisors. Andrew Jackson resorted to meeting with trusted advisors in the White House, thus establishing the Kitchen Cabinet. Appointees are now experienced administrators with policy expertise. There is a significant turnover in the second term as Cabinet officials return to a much more lucrative private sector. Cabinet members received a raise in 2010 to $196,700.

The "Inner Cabinet" is an informal designation. It includes the National Security Council (NSC). The NSC was established pursuant to the National Security Act of 1947 to coordinate foreign and defense policy with the influence and control of the council varying by administration. Members of the NSC include the following:

President
Vice-President
Secretary of State
Secretary of Treasury
Secretary of Defense
National Security Advisor

Chairman of the Joint Chiefs of Staff
CIA Director
President's Chief of Staff
Counsel to the President
Assistant to President for Economic Policy
Attorney General
Director of OMB
Other Departments as Needed

THE WHITE HOUSE STAFF

Advisors that are closer allies to the president than the Cabinet include the White House Staff, which grew out of the Kitchen Cabinet and are generally highly trusted, long-time friends of the president. Differences exist among presidents in their management style. President Carter had a tendency to micromanage and left little discretion to the White House staff. President Reagan delegated power to his Chief of Staff, and President Bush centralized power in the White House Staff but continued to deal directly with cabinet-level officials, the press, and key members of Congress. President Clinton preferred competition among equals in his cabinet and White House officials, whereas President George W. Bush appeared to rely heavily on a few key advisors.

THE EXECUTIVE OFFICE OF THE PRESIDENT (EOP)

The EOP was established by FDR in 1939 to oversee his New Deal programs. It includes 1500–2000 employees who are responsible for helping the president administer the Executive Branch. It includes the following:

White House Chief of Staff
White House Press Secretary
Office of Management and Budget
Council of Economic Advisors
Council of Environmental Quality
National Security Council
Office of Science and Technology Policy
Office of the United States Trade Representative
Office of the National Drug Control Policy
Office of Faith-Based and Community Initiatives

THE VICE PRESIDENCY

Constitutionally, the Vice President has two responsibilities, to succeed the president in case of death, resignation, or incapacitation and to preside over the Senate and cast a tie-breaking vote if necessary. The vice president's 2010 salary was $227,300. The vice president is a political resource for the election by bringing something additional to the ticket or balancing the ticket. President Kennedy's victory in 1960 would have been doubtful without the support brought to the ticket by Lyndon Johnson. President Clinton's selection of Al Gore demonstrated a commitment to the political center and the South, which was necessary after electoral victories by President Reagan (1980, 1984) and President Bush (1988). Generally, vice presidents are given very little political responsibility. President Kennedy isolated Lyndon Johnson. President Carter appeared to rely heavily on Walter Mondale, but little can be attributed to Mondale. President Reagan's delegation of authority gave George Bush more access to the decision-making process but again Bush is significantly in the background. President Bush did not include Dan Quayle "in the loop." President Clinton allowed Al Gore to demonstrate his policy prowess in his efforts to reinvent government and protect the environment, but little evidence of any reinvention exists. President George W. Bush relied heavily on advice from Dick Cheney, but Cheney remained in the background. The vice presidency is generally seen as a stepping stone to the presidency, yet only five vice presidents have gone on to become president by winning the presidency in their own right. This is basically a product of the low level of visible activity by the vice president.

THE FIRST LADY

Traditionally, first ladies performed a ceremonial role. Over the last few decades, first ladies have developed their own agendas and have become very influential in their own right. Eleanor Roosevelt promoted social justice and equality. Jackie Kennedy renovated the White House. Lady Bird Johnson supported the environment. Pat Nixon supported volunteerism. Betty Ford supported the Equal Rights Amendment and women's health. Rosalyn Carter rallied for mental health, poverty, and Habitat for Humanity. Nancy Reagan's "Just say No" campaign targeted drug and alcohol abuse. Barbara Bush and Laura Bush promoted literacy. Hillary Clinton formed health care policy. The scrutiny of the first lady has increased as responsibilities have increased with the most negative attention having been directed at Hillary Clinton. Michelle Obama has enjoyed favorable ratings with her support for healthy living.

POLITICAL RESOURCES OF PRESIDENTIAL POWER: THE POWER OF PERSUASION

Elections as a Resource

Presidents claim a mandate after winning the election. The electoral landslides of 1964 and 1980 gave Presidents Johnson and Reagan real strength during their "honeymoon" period (the first 100 days). President Bush won a decisive electoral victory in 1988, but was denied a honeymoon period because it was simply four more years of a Republican administration. President Clinton received only 43% of the popular vote in 1992 and 49% of the vote in 1996, minimizing any claim of a mandate. President George W. Bush's election led to a question of legitimacy and a non-existent honeymoon period. The honeymoon period usually follows electoral victory as Congress and the nation give the president the benefit of the doubt. The president must identify two to three key issues to push through Congress while there is momentum from the election, which should generate more power for the president on subsequent issues. The second term is considered a lame duck term and even members of the president's party break ranks.

Party as a Presidential Resource

Party is a questionable source of power as the president is considered the leader of the national party but must deal with factions within the party. Presidents are hurt by divided government as the majority of one or both chambers of Congress falls under the control of the opposition party. President Clinton enjoyed success from 1993 to 1994 (86%), but suffered significantly in the Republican Congress (35%) on bills publicly supported by the president. Presidents Nixon, Ford, Reagan, and Bush were limited by a Congress controlled by Democrats. Democrats have held control of House except from 1952–54 and 1995–2010. Democrats held control of the Senate except from 1952–54, 1980–86, 1994–2000, and 2002–2006. Legislative output is also affected by divided government and remains stable when Democrats control Congress under a Republican administration. Legislative output drops when Republicans control Congress under a Democratic administration. Unified party government is not necessarily a benefit because the opposition is also likely to be unified. A unified party may result in a more unified opposition as in the 108th and 109th Congress with Democratic opposition to President George W. Bush. President Carter failed to develop strong ties with party members, thus dooming his legislative agenda.

Interest Groups and Coalitions as a Presidential Resource

Presidents utilize interest groups to mobilize the electorate to gain strength. The Christian Coalition was supportive of George W. Bush. The AARP supported Bill Clinton. Coalitions of groups can be mobilized to put pressure on Congress. President Roosevelt's New Deal coalition helped pushed programs through Congress. The New Deal coalition included northern urban liberals, southern white conservatives, organized labor, and African Americans. This coalition dominated national politics until the 1960s. President Reagan's coalition helped build strong public support for his agenda in the 1980s. The New Republican coalition included southern white and northern blue-collar voters, internationalists, religious conservatives, and big business. These groups helped the Republicans to presidential victories in 1980, 1984, and 1988. President Clinton attempted to rebuild the New Deal Coalition by reaching out to southern whites and northern blue-collar workers.

THE POWER OF THE MEDIA

Media is important not only in campaigns, but also during time in office. President Teddy Roosevelt was one of the first presidents to use the presidency as a "bully pulpit" to promote his agenda. President Franklin D. Roosevelt, the first president to try to directly reach the public through the mass media, utilized radio broadcasts known as "fire side chats," press conferences, speeches, and movie newsreels to rally support for his programs and the war. President Reagan was known as the Great Communicator as he utilized direct television addresses to mobilize the public and build a reputation as the "Teflon" president. President Clinton also established himself prominently through the use of the media. President George W. Bush was surprisingly successful with the media as his ability to relate to the public had been underestimated in the early days of his administration.

PUBLIC OPINION AND PUBLIC PRESSURE ON CONGRESS

With the improvement of polling techniques, presidents have an additional source of information to gauge the demands of the public. However, this strategy can leave the president behind the opinion curve. Presidents are asked to be opinion leaders rather than opinion followers. President Reagan took the lead on tax reform/deregulation as well as standing up to the Soviets. President George W. Bush stood by his decision on the War on Iraq as "the right thing to do." President Clinton is often criticized for being a public opinion follower, but this may not be critical in measuring success. The Clinton Administration would measure public opinion utilizing trial balloons and leaks and then revise policy. Clinton's job approval ratings at the end of his administration were as high as Reagan's ratings.

Positive approval ratings translate into power in Congress as the public is more likely to pressure Congress to support the president's proposals. Recent presidents attempt to maintain high levels of public support through public appearances. This is referred to as the "permanent campaign." Clinton's visit to San Jacinto College in Pasadena, Texas, to promote congressional funding for community colleges and the Hope Scholarship serves as an example. George W. Bush's visit to the new National Counter-terrorism Center to promote renewing the Patriot Act is another example. Reagan was particularly effective in mobilizing public support through the use of the media.

Job approval ratings are a constant reminder of public support. The trend is generally downward from the first day in office, which means declining influence on Congress. Domestic events have a greater long-term impact than international events. Foreign affairs and, specifically, a crisis internationally may result in a rallying effect over a short period of time. During periods of low approval ratings, the president may want to look presidential and make a foreign trip. It has been suggested that the president may use the military to divert attention from domestic problems. It has long been rumored that the military was to disregard any order from Nixon during the final days of the Watergate scandal. President Clinton repeatedly used military strikes on Baghdad just before the House was scheduled to vote on his impeachment.

THE FEDERAL BUREAUCRACY

What is a bureaucracy? Bureaucracy, basically defined, is an organization characterized by specialization of functions, adherence to fixed rules, and a hierarchy of authority. Bureaucratic organizations can be found in a variety of institutions; for example, public institutions such as schools and government agencies. Also, there are private institutions like hospitals and businesses. Even military organizations are bureaucracies. A bureaucracy is essentially a way to manage an organization. Max Weber, the German sociologist and political economist, believed bureaucracy was the most rational form of management. Max Weber characterized model bureaucracy as having a division of labor whereby work is apportioned among specialized workers to increase productivity. Workers are to become specialized in their tasks and are individually responsible for the satisfactory completion of the task. No one worker makes the entire product, and workers are dependent upon co-workers to complete the project. Workers become highly skilled and efficient due to repetition. Productivity is increased and the firm is more profitable. There is a chain of command in which authority flows from top to bottom. The organization is hierarchical in structure with clear lines of authority between workers and their superiors. Policies and rules are adopted and applied in an impersonal manner, whereby all employees are treated fairly based on merit and all clients are served equally, without discrimination, according to established rules. The organization is staffed by full-time, lifetime professionals. Full-time employees are given "vested" interest in success and longevity. The goal is to have the employees identify with the organization. There must be mutual loyalty between the employee and the organization. Therefore, a system is developed by rewarding seniority. Part-time employment is kept to a minimum as part-time employees lack skill development and loyalty to the firm. Clearly defined organizational goals and the subsequent evaluation of the organization's performance is also necessary. Finally, documentation to promote accountability is required. A bureaucratic organization stresses written records. The basic rule is that if it's not in writing it did not happen. Documentation ensures that tasks were performed.

The Science of Bureaucratic Behavior

Universities have contributed significantly to our understanding of bureaucratic management through the teaching of business and public administration. The military has also contributed by becoming the most bureaucratic of all organizations. Weber believed that the military of his time had become the model bureaucracy. Military organizations have "perfected" bureaucratic traits. A model bureaucracy will have line-staff divisions. The line function is designed to meet the overall purpose or function of the organizations. The staff functions to support the line. For example, the faculty in a college would represent the line side of the organization and the administrative assistants would represent the staff side of the organization. Specialization of tasks is prevalent in the military. Corporations have developed extensive planning procedures and specialization of tasks. Mission statements and goals are also important. Moreover, there is a need for procedure manuals, job descriptions, and assembly line production.

The Federal Bureaucracy

The Size of the Federal Service

Americans view the federal bureaucracy as an ever-expanding leviathan. Presidents have spent considerable political capital on attempts to reign in the size and scope of the federal bureaucracy.

In the 1980s, President Reagan attempted to deregulate the economy and significantly reduce the size and influence of the federal bureaucracy and even eliminate two Cabinet departments. In 1996, President Clinton declared the end of big government in his State of the Union Address, and Al Gore spent much of his time as vice president "reinventing" government. In reality, the federal bureaucracy has not grown over the last twenty-five years. It reached its peak in 1968 with 2.9 million non-defense and 3.6 million defense personnel. In 1994, employment had dropped to just under 3 million non-defense and defense employees. In 2000, federal employment continued to decline to just over 2.8 million non-defense and defense employees. In 2002, the number of federal employees continued to decline to 670.200 DoD, 1,168,100 thousand civilian (non-postal), and 811,600 thousand USPS. The federal workforce compared to the total workforce or to state and local government employment has declined significantly since the 1980s. Federal spending, however, has increased significantly over the same time period as employment has shifted to contracts and state mandates.

Employee Characteristics of the Federal Bureaucracy

Occupational Groups

A significant number of federal employees are considered professional, administrative, or technical employees such as attorneys, engineers, and computer technicians.

- 24% of the federal bureaucracy is classified as professional with 87% having a bachelor's degree or higher
- 32% of the federal bureaucracy is considered administrative with 47% having a bachelor's degree or higher
- 19% of the federal bureaucracy is classified as technical
- 13% of the federal bureaucracy is considered blue-collar
- 9% of the federal bureaucracy is considered clerical
- 41% of federal employees have a bachelor's degree or higher

The most significant decline in employment since 1985 has been in blue-collar and clerical employment while professional and technical employment has grown.

Race and Gender

Lyndon Johnson issued Executive Order 11246 in 1965 requiring non-discrimination (affirmation action) in government employment. As a result racial groups are well represented in the federal bureaucracy.

- 17% African American
- 7% Hispanic
- 5% Asian/Pacific Islander
- 2% American Indian/Alaska Native

Women are also well represented.

- 45% of the federal workforce is female
- 17% of federal employment is minority female compared to 14% minority male

Americans with Disabilities and Veterans

- 7% are individuals with a disability
- 22% of federal employees are veterans

Employment Status

- 90% of federal employees are permanent appointments
- 87% of federal employees are full-time

Civil Service and Excepted Status

- 75% of federal employees are competitive hires
- 25% of federal employees are excepted and senior

Employment Location

- 16% of federal employees work in the D.C. area
- 81% of federal employees work outside the D.C. area
- 3% of federal employees word abroad

Patronage and the Spoils System

In 1789, the federal government had a total of fifty employees. The Department of Treasury had the largest with thirty-nine employees. The State Department had nine employees. The War Department had two employees. These appointees received their appointments as rewards for political support or loyalty—otherwise known as patronage. Patronage, or the spoils system, dominated Washington politics despite criticism during the Andrew Jackson era. President Garfield was assassinated in 1881 by a disgruntled office seeker, which led to calls for reform.

The Merit System

The Civil Service Reform Act of 1883 (*The Pendleton Act*) replaced the patronage system with the merit system. This requires government employees to demonstrate that they are qualified to hold their positions. Federal employment would be on the basis of open, competitive exams. Over 90% of current federal jobs are covered by the merit system. Just 10% of the federal workforce is not covered by civil service. There are approximately 6000 presidential appointments. There are approximately 100 independent regulatory commissioners. The rest represent low-level, non-policy, patronage positions such as secretarial assistants to policymakers.

BASIC FUNCTIONS OF THE FEDERAL BUREAUCRACY: LEGISLATE, EXECUTE, AND ADJUDICATE

Legislative Powers

The bureaucracy implements federal laws through administrative regulations. Congress and the president enact laws designed to solve particular problems. However, these elected officials are rarely experts in these very technical areas. Accordingly, elected officials delegate the process of working out the details to the "experts" in the federal bureaucracy. Bureaucrats translate the law into specific regulations, which can be found in the *Federal Register* and the *Code of Federal Regulations.* Bureaucrats interpret the law by defining vague and ambiguous terms or concepts. The laws passed by Congress may be very vague and ambiguous to avoid conflicts that might otherwise kill the legislation. As a result, disagreements develop over the precise intent of the legislation after it has been enacted and referred to a federal agency for implementation. Bureaucrats are empowered by statute to resolve conflicts by defining basic principles or procedures. Bureaucrats become lawmakers through their rule-making and administrative adjudication powers. The Supreme Court has done little to correct this apparent abuse of the separation of powers by ruling that the delegation of authority is appropriate and, absent a denial of due process, is constitutional.

Executive Powers

Federal bureaucrats execute the law through the various administrative regulations promulgated by their agencies. Federal agencies, such as Occupation Safety and Health Administration (OSHA) or the Environmental Protection Agency (EPA), have enforcement officers that inspect facilities and issue citations that may carry significant fines.

Judicial Powers

Federal agencies also have the power to adjudicate violations of their administrative regulations. These agencies have their own administrative courts and, absent a denial of due process, their decisions are final. The FCC's Administrative Law Judges conduct hearings ordered by the commission. The EPA's Administrative Law Judges conduct hearings and render decisions in cases brought by the EPA against alleged violators of EPA regulations.

THE ORGANIZATION OF THE EXECUTIVE BRANCH

Organizational Structure

Cabinet departments account for about 60% of the federal workforce. Cabinet departments are headed by secretaries with the exception of the Department of Justice, which is headed by the Attorney General. Cabinet secretaries are directly responsible to the president but must also answer to Congress. The Department of Homeland Security was initially an office that reported only to the president, which created tension between the White House and Congress in the aftermath of 9/11.

The fifteen cabinet departments are as follows:

Department of Treasury (1789) is responsible for the economic and financial well-being and security of the nation.

- Office of the Comptroller of the Currency
- Bureau of the Public Debt
- Office of Thrift Supervision
- United States Mint
- Bureau of Engraving and Print
- Internal Revenue Service
  Alcohol and Tobacco Tax and Trade Bureau

Department of State (1789) is responsible for U.S. foreign affairs by establishing diplomatic relations by maintaining 263 diplomatic posts around the world.

- Bureau of African Affairs
- Bureau of Arms Control
- Bureau of East Asian and Pacific Affairs
- Bureau of European and Eurasian Affairs
- Bureau of Near Eastern Affairs
- Office of War Crimes Issues

Department of Defense (Department of War 1789) is responsible for managing the nation's military and ensuring national security. The Secretary of Defense is a civilian. The military was unified into a single department in 1949. The Chiefs of Staff of each branch make up the Joint Chiefs of Staff (chair is selected by the President, but generally rotates amongst the Chiefs of Staff).

Department of Justice (1870) is responsible for enforcing the laws of the United States.

- Attorney General
- Solicitor General
- U.S. Attorneys
- Criminal Division
- Civil Division
- Antitrust Division
- Civil Rights Division
- Environment and Natural Resources Division
- Tax Division
- Federal Bureau of Investigation
- Drug Enforcement Agency
- Bureau of Alcohol, Tobacco, Firearms, and Explosives
- Bureau of Prisons

Department of Interior (1849) supervises federally owned lands, operates federal hydroelectric facilities, and supervises Native American affairs.

- U.S. Fish and Wildlife
- National Parks Service
- Bureau of Indian Affairs
- Bureau of Land Management
- U.S. Geological Survey

Department of Agriculture (1862) provides assistance to farmers and ranchers and protects the nation's forests.

- Forest Service
- Agricultural Marketing Service
- Center for Nutrition Policy and Promotion
- Food and Nutrition Service
- Women, Infants, and Children Program (WIC)
- Food Stamps
- School Meals
- Food Safety and Inspection Service
- Federal Meat Inspection Act
- Federal Poultry Products Inspection Act
- Federal Egg Products Inspection Act
- Animal and Plant Health Inspection Service

Department of Commerce (1903) promotes and protects the interests of American businesses.

- Patent and Trademark Office (Copyrights are managed by the Office of Copyrights in the Library of Congress)
- Economics and Statistics Administration
- Bureau of the Census
- Bureau of Economic Analysis
- National Oceanographic and Atmospheric Administration
- International Trade Administration
- Minority Business Development Administration

Department of Labor (1913) administers federal labor laws and promotes the interests of workers.

- OSHA
- Wage and Hour
- Bureau of Labor Statistics
- Employment Standards Administration
- Wage and Hour Division
- Office of Workers Compensation Programs
- Office of Labor-Management Standards

Department of Housing and Urban Development (1965) is responsible for addressing the nation's housing needs and promoting urban development.

- Office of Housing
- Section 8 Housing
- FHA insured loans
- Office of Community Planning and Development
- Rural Housing and Economic Development
- Community Development Block Grants
- Fair Housing and Equal Opportunity Office
- Office of Public and Indian Housing
- Public Housing Units (1.3 million households)
- Indian Housing Loan Guarantee Program

Department of Transportation (1967) finances mass transit programs and funds highway projects.

- Federal Highway Administration
- Interstate Highway Funding
- Critter Crossings
- National Traffic Safety Administration
- Federal Aviation Administration
- Federal Railroad Administration
- Federal Transit Administration
- Federal Motor Carrier Safety Administration

Department of Energy (1977) promotes energy development and conservation through funding a variety of energy projects such as alternative fuels and high-efficiency vehicles.

- Office of Nuclear Energy, Science, and Technology
- Office of Fossil Energy
- National Nuclear Security Administration
- Radioactive Waste Management
- Energy Efficiency and Renewable Energy Administration
- Energy Information Administration

Department of Education (1979) coordinates federal education programs and policies.

- Office of Federal Student Aid
- Office of Elementary and Secondary Education
- Office of Post-Secondary Education
- Office of Vocational and Adult Education
- Office of Safe and Drug Free Schools
- No Child Left Behind

Department of Health and Human Services (1979) promotes public health and welfare.

- Food and Drug Administration
- Public Health Service
- Administration for Children and Families
- Adoption and Foster Care
- Temporary Assistance to Needy Families
- Head Start
- Child Support
- Administration on Aging
- National Institutes of Health
- National Cancer Institute
- National Eye Institute
- National Heart, Lung, and Blood Institute
- National Human Genome Research Institute
- Centers for Medicare and Medicaid Services

Department of Veterans Affairs (1989) provides assistance to America's veterans and operates VA Hospitals.

- Veteran's Health Administration
- Veteran's Benefits Administration
- Montgomery GI Bill
- Vocational Rehabilitation and Employment

Department of Homeland Security (2002) is responsible for protecting the homeland in a post-9/11 world.

- Transportation Security Administration
- Federal Emergency Management Administration
- Customs and Border Protection
- Immigration and Customs Enforcement
- U.S. Citizenship and Immigration Services
- U.S. Coast Guard
- U.S. Secret Service

Director of National Intelligence (2004) coordinates the components of the intelligence community. It was created by the Intelligence Reform and Terrorism Prevention Act of 2004.

- The U.S. Intelligence Community (www.intelligence.gov)
- Air Force, Army, Marine Corps, Navy, and Coast Guard
- CIA, FBI, National Security Agency
- Defense, Energy, Homeland Security, Treasury, State
- National Geospatial, National Reconnaissance
- Center for Counter-Terrorism

Government Corporations

Government corporations are entities created by Congress that perform functions that could be provided by private businesses. Government corporations perform services that are commercial in nature, produce revenue, and require greater flexibility than Congress permits cabinet departments. Government corporations include the United States Postal Service (USPS), which was reorganized as a government corporation in 1971. It is administered by the Postmaster General who is appointed by the nine governors of the Postal Service who are appointed by the president with the advice and consent of the Senate. The USPS handles over 200 billion pieces of mail annually. Postage rates are established by the Postal Rate Commission. Amtrak (1971) is a passenger rail service. Service is provided to forty-six states (Alaska, Hawaii, South Dakota, and Wyoming do not have Amtrak service). Each day 68,000 riders use Amtrak's 300 trains. The greatest usage is in the New York, D.C., Chicago, and Philadelphia corridors. Amtrak has requested approximately $2 billion annually over the next five years. The Tennessee Valley Authority (1933) provides electricity at reduced rates to Americans in the Appalachian region. The Appalachian region is extremely low-income. It failed to attract private utility companies. FDR requested Congress create a "corporation clothed with power of government but possessed of the flexibility and initiative of a private enterprise." On May 18, 1933, Congress passed the Tennessee Valley Authority Act creating the TVA. Federal Deposit Insurance Corporation (1933) supervises banks, insures deposits up to $250,000, and helps maintain a stable banking system. The Corporation for Public Broadcasting (1967) is a private, non-profit organization that funds 1000 public television and radio stations. Nearly 26% of the budget comes from members like you. About 22% of the budget comes from businesses and foundations, and the remaining 11% of budget from colleges and universities.

Independent Agencies

Independent agencies are governmental units that closely resemble a cabinet department, but have a narrower area of responsibility. These agencies are created outside the departmental structure and act independently of the cabinet departments. The president appoints and directs the heads of these agencies. Examples include, National Aeronautics and Space Administration (NASA), which is responsible for advancing space exploration. Created by the National Aeronautics and Space Act of 1958 as an independent agency rather than being placed in DoD to avoid "militarization" of space. NASA is led by an administrator who is appointed by the president and confirmed by the Senate. Johnson Space Center (JSC), created in 1961, leads the agency's human space exploration programs. The Central Intelligence Agency (CIA) is responsible for gathering intelligence and providing the president advice regarding potential threats to national security. It was created by the National Security Act of 1947. The CIA Director now reports to the Director of National Intelligence pursuant to the 2004 reorganization. The Federal Reserve Board (the Fed) manages the nation's supply of money and credit, operates as the nation's central bank, serves as the bank for the U.S. government, and administers banking and finance-related consumer laws. It was created by the Federal Reserve Act of 1913. The members of the board are appointed by the president and confirmed by the Senate along with seven governors who serve one fourteen-year term. The chairman is selected from the governors and serves a four-year term. Ben S. Bernanke is the current chairman and has served since 2006. Finally, the Environmental Protection Agency (1970) is responsible for the enforcement of clean air/water and pollution laws.

Independent Regulatory Commissions

Regulatory commissions are given broad discretion to make rules that regulate specific activities. Regulations adopted by these regulatory agencies have the force of law. These agencies also have their own dispute resolution procedures in which they legislate, execute, and adjudicate violations of the very regulations they enacted. Examples include the Securities and Exchange Commission (1934), which is responsible for protecting investors and maintaining the integrity of the securities markets and is headed by five commissioners appointed by the president and confirmed by the Senate. Joseph P. Kennedy was appointed by FDR as the first Chairman of the SEC. The Federal Trade Commission (1914) was established by Woodrow Wilson to ensure that the nation's markets are vigorous and free from restrictions that harm consumers. It was built on Teddy Roosevelt's Bureau of Corporations and enforces federal consumer protection laws and antitrust laws. Five commissioners are appointed by the president and confirmed by the Senate. The Federal Communications Commission (1934) is charged with regulating interstate and international communications by radio, television, wire, satellite, and cable. It has five commissioners appointed by the president and confirmed by the Senate. Only three commissioners may be from the same political party.

Managing the Bureaucracy

Downsizing the Bureaucracy—Termination, Devolution, and Privatization

Termination is the only certain way to reduce the bureaucracy. There have been attempts to eliminate departments or programs. The Department of Education faced possible termination during the Reagan administration. The Department of Energy was targeted for elimination during the Clinton administration. These attempts failed as support groups and constituents organized in support of the agency.

Devolution involves the shifting of programs back to the states. Beginning with New Federalism in the 1970s, Republicans have attempted to shift numerous functions of the federal bureaucracy to state and local governments. Welfare reform and environmental regulation serve as examples. Devolution has met with opposition. Democrats argue that devolution destroys uniformity achieved through national standards and may result in a "race to the bottom." State and local governments may not be able or want to handle new programs or they fear unfunded mandates.

Privatization occurs when government programs are contracted out or turned over to private business. Much of the work of government today is done by contract with private corporations. One such example is research and development in support of NASA. Another example is garbage collection at the local level. The problem is that most of what the government does is not profitable and does not attract private sector interest. A number of states attempted to privatize welfare administration in the 1990s. Gingrich and Republicans have attempted to privatize PBS and National Public Radio since 1995. Another problem with privatization is that the public has grown accustomed to government-provided services that are "free."

Maintaining Accountability

There are presidential tools for maintaining accountability. The president can appoint upper management of the departments and agencies, direct operations by issuing executive orders, and draft the budget of the United States. The OMB requests budget proposals from the agencies and creates a budget pursuant to the president's directives. Carter introduced Zero-Based Budgeting, which would have required justification of every dollar requested. However, incremental budgeting has survived and only the requested increase must be justified.

There are also congressional tools for maintaining accountability. Congress has the constitutional authority to create or abolish agencies. Congress defines the roles and responsibilities of agencies through legislation. Congress also controls the management of the agencies through the Senate's confirmation of presidential appointments and controls agency budgets through the appropriations process. Congressional investigation and oversight is guided by GAO evaluations, CBO budget analysis, and committee and subcommittee hearings. Congress can solve constituent problems with agencies. This is known as casework. Finally, there is legislation to control the bureaucratic process, such as the Administrative Procedures Act (1946), which establishes procedures for enacting new rules and regulations; the Freedom of Information Act (1966), which allows access to agency records and documents; and the Privacy Act (1974), which makes personal records confidential (i.e., Social Security and income tax records).

THE FEDERAL COURTS

The Development of the Legal System

The law is a set of rules or norms implemented by a society to govern the interaction of individuals in that society. The earliest laws were written by kings or god(s). Mesopotamian kings drafted Urukagina's Code around 2350 B.C. Ur-Nammu's Code may have been the first written laws in 2050 B.C. Babylon's Hammurabi's Code was written around 1700 B.C. The Ten Commandments were presented by Moses around 1300 B.C. India's Laws of Manu were written between 1280 and 880 B.C. Lycergus, King of Sparta, established laws in 600 B.C. Emperor Justinian took the foundation of Roman law and codified it into *Corpus Juris Civilis* in 529 B.C., thus establishing the principles of medieval civil and canon law. Laws were also written by individuals. Draco drafted one of the first legal codes for Athens and gives us the phrase Draconian because of the severity of the punishments. Solon refined Draco's code by democratizing the legal system. Ten Romans drafted the Twelve Tables in 449 B.C., which became the foundation for all modern public and private law. Surprisingly, these laws all have striking similarities as they attempt to regulate the behavior of individuals in a society and punish wrongdoers.

Institutions for the Resolution of Conflicts: From Kings to Courts

Kings ruled on conflicts or appointed officials to sit in judgment. The Ur-Nammu's Code established specialized judges. King Solomon resolved a dispute between two "mothers" over a child by offering to cut the child in half knowing that the real mother would refuse. Dispute resolution in England evolved from the village moot, to the hundred moot, the shire moot, the witan, and finally to formal courts. The village, hundred, and shire moot (committees) served as early courts and resolved conflicts arising within the community. Laws were established based on the community's idea of justice. The witan were nobles who advised the king from the seventh century to the eleventh century and approved the selection of Kings, advised the King on important matters, and sat in judgment of local disputes. Henry I established royal justices to replace the moot. Judicial responsibility was eventually transferred to established courts in the twelfth century under the reign of Henry II. Henry II established a unified and powerful court system with a formal jury system in 1154. Henry II also attempted to nationalize local customs and rulings into a national "common" law, and dissatisfied litigants could appeal to the King. Exchequer of Pleas was one of three common law courts in 1190. The Magna Carta (1215) established the Common Bench followed by the King's Bench and Exchequer of Pleas in 1234. The British legal system evolved over the next 600 years into a formalized system of courts. The U.S. adopted the established and modified the British legal system that operated in the colonies until 1776 to suit their needs. Article III of the U.S. Constitution and the various state constitutions establish legal systems for the resolution of civil and criminal disputes. Alexis de Tocqueville (1835) stated in *Democracy in America* that "there is hardly a political question in the United States which does not sooner or later turn into a judicial one."

Dispensing Justice and Making Law

Justice Felix Frankfurter (1930) once stated: "*The meaning of due process and the content of terms like liberty are not revealed by the Constitution, it is the Justices who make the meaning. They read into the neutral language of the Constitution their own economic and social views. Let us face the fact that five Justices of the Supreme Court are the molders of policy rather than the impersonal vehicles of truth.*" The U.S. Supreme Court and the federal judiciary, rather than Congress or the president, has taken the lead in deciding many of the most heated issues of American politics. The following serve as examples:

- Separation of church and state (First Amendment)
- Freedom of speech and press (First Amendment)
- Rights of criminal defendants (Fourth, Fifth, Sixth, and Seventh Amendments)
- Capital punishment (Eighth Amendment)
- Civil rights and affirmative action (Fourteenth Amendment)

It is politically expedient to allow the U.S. Supreme Court to resolve controversial issues because of their political independence. The U.S. Supreme Court is the most "trusted" of the American institutions, and federal judges are insulated from political repercussions of their decisions by their lifetime terms and protected salaries.

Law in the United States

Criminal Law

Congress and the state legislatures enact criminal statutes to protect the public health, safety, welfare, and morality, such as the U.S. Code, Title 18, and the Texas Penal Code. The criminal statutes codified the common law and provide the basic elements of each crime that must be proven at trial such as murder (Texas Penal Code). Murder means intentionally or knowingly causing the death of an individual, or intending to cause serious bodily injury and committing an act clearly dangerous to life causing the death of an individual. Another example is leaving a child in a car (Texas Penal Code). This results from intentionally or knowingly leaving a child in a car for longer than five minutes, knowing that the child is younger than seven years of age, and not attended in the vehicle by someone who is fourteen years of age or older. The government brings charges against the individual charged with violating a criminal statute—the **defendant.** Examples include *State of Texas v. Lawrence* and *United States of America v. Martha Stewart.* Felony cases require an indictment outlining the allegations against the defendant and what acts as constituted criminal violations. The government has the burden of proof. In other words, the government must prove guilt beyond a reasonable doubt. If the defendant is found guilty, the defendant may be fined or sent to prison. Plea bargains, which are an agreement to accept guilt for a lesser sentence, resolves approximately 90% of all cases.

Civil Law

The courts utilize common law or codifications of the common law. The courts have established standards of conduct regarding contracts, torts (assault, battery, negligence, strict liability), and property disputes. This common law has evolved over hundreds of years:

- Southwest Reporters for Texas case law
- Federal Supplement for U.S. District Courts
- Federal Reporter for U.S. Courts of Appeal
- Supreme Court Reporter for U.S. Supreme Court

Codifications of the common law and statutory law

- Vernon's Texas Code for Texas law
- U.S. Code for federal laws

The court applies previous court rulings on the law as precedent through the doctrine of *stare decisis.* The purpose of civil litigation it to make whole an individual who has been injured as a result of another's wrongful conduct. The **plaintiff** is the injured party, and the **defendant** is the person alleged to have caused the injury. Remedies may include strict performance or monetary damages. The plaintiff has the burden of proof and must establish that the defendant's actions caused alleged damages by a preponderance of evidence. Most civil cases are resolved before trial by settlement.

Public Law

Public law defines the relationship between citizens and the state. Examples include Constitutional law and Administrative law. Criminal or civil cases rise to constitutional cases if the defendant alleges protection under the U.S. Constitution.

Federal Judicial System

Constitution Provisions

The United States Constitution grants the judicial power of the United States to the Supreme Court in Article III and other inferior courts that Congress may establish in Article I, Section 8. The founders created an "independent" judiciary. What makes the judiciary independent, in part, is the judicial appointment for life with the exception of impeachment, and salaries cannot be reduced during their time in office. The federal court jurisdiction is defined by the Constitution as those cases arising under the Constitution, the laws of the United States, and treaties made under their authority. In addition, it includes cases affecting ambassadors, other public ministers and consuls, and cases of admiralty and maritime jurisdiction. It further concerns controversies to which the United States is a party, controversies between two or more states, a state and a citizen of another state, citizens of different states, citizens of the same state claiming lands under grants of different states, and a state, or citizens thereof, and foreign states, citizens, or subjects. The U.S. Supreme Court has original jurisdiction over cases involving ambassadors, other public ministers and consuls, and cases in which a state shall be a party.

The Federal Court System

The federal court system consists of 94 District Courts and 667 active judges and 300 retired, 12 Circuit Courts of Appeal, and one Supreme Court. The District Courts are considered courts of original jurisdiction and are responsible for discovering the facts in a case. Each federal judicial district has a U.S. Attorney who is appointed by the president and confirmed by the Senate.

Court Procedures

Federal rules of evidence and rules of procedure apply to criminal cases and civil trials. In criminal cases, federal criminal statutes apply, as well as the right to grand jury indictment to jury trial in states where a crime is committed, a twelve-member jury, and a unanimous verdict. In civil trials there is a diversity jurisdiction with damages exceeding $75,000. Federal courts will interpret state common law, and as a result a separate body of common law has developed.

Texas is divided into four districts:

- Northern District with twelve authorized judgeships
- Eastern District with seven authorized judgeships
- Southern District with eighteen authorized judgeships
  - ▷ Houston Division (Rusk Street)
  - ▷ Galveston Division
  - ▷ Victoria Division

        ▷ Corpus Christi Division
        ▷ Laredo Division
        ▷ McAllen Division
        ▷ Brownsville Division
   ■ Western District with ten authorized judgeships

Courts of Appeal

The Circuit Courts of Appeal have 167 active judges and 80 retired judges. The number of judges depends on workload of the circuit and ranges from six to nearly thirty. Cases are generally heard by a panel of three judges made up of the active judges, retired judges, and visiting judges. Rarely is a case heard *en banc*—by all the circuit judges. The courts have appellate jurisdiction. They hear appeals from U.S. District Courts, both civil and criminal, and appeals from administrative agencies. Decisions are final unless reviewed by the United States Supreme Court. The court's decision is binding on all district courts within the circuit and may be persuasive in the other circuits Texas is in the Fifth Circuit Court of Appeals with Louisiana and Mississippi and is located in New Orleans with sixteen active judges.

Supreme Court

The Supreme Court is America's highest court and truly the court of last resort. The only court created by Article III. The number of justices is determined by Congress not by the Constitution. There were six justices in the early 19th Century and eventually increased to seven and then nine in 1869. In 1937, Roosevelt was angered by the Court's rejection of his New Deal package. He proposed increasing the number of judges to fifteen. The Supreme Court changed its view on Roosevelt's New Deal and ruled the plan constitutional by redefining commerce from intrastate to interstate. The Court is staffed by a Chief Justice and eight Associate Justices. The Chief Justice presides over public sessions and conferences and may be able to influence the direction of the court. Although the court meets annually, the historical periods of the court are referred to by the Chief Justice at the time. For example, the current court is referred to as the Roberts Court because John Roberts is the Chief Justice. The Associate Justices are equal in power to the Chief Justice.

The Nomination Process

Federal judges must first be appointed by the president. They are selected from the more political active members of the legal profession. The appointment of district court judges is influenced by **senatorial courtesy.** U.S. Senators are given senatorial courtesy to nominate individuals to serve as federal judges in their states. This honor may be given to a Representative, governor, or other ranking party official if the state lacks a Senator from the same party as the president. The president has more latitude in selecting nominees for vacancies on a Court of Appeal or U.S. Supreme Court as Appellate court nominations are generally proposed by the Department of Justice because several states are within a circuit's jurisdiction, but Senators from the circuit are still consulted. The president and his closest advisors analyze the list of potential nominees for a vacancy on the Supreme Court, but they generally come from the Courts of Appeals. The appointees at all levels generally share political position with the president. However, there is no guarantee with the "independence" given to the federal judiciary. Earl Warren is the classic example of a surprise nominee. He was tough on crime as a District Attorney, Republican Governor of California, Dewey's VP candidate in 1948, and appointed by Eisenhower in 1953. He moved the court to the left on many issues, such as the rights of criminal defendants in *Miranda v. Arizona* and civil rights in *Brown v. Board of Education.* Many conservatives suggested Warren be impeached. Reagan used a "litmus test" to select nominees in an attempt to avoid the Warren problem. The FBI performs background checks on all nominees. The American Bar Association reviews judicial candidates and rates their judicial qualifications. The appointee must next face the Senate Judiciary Committee and be confirmed by a majority vote of the Senate. This has become a highly politicized procedure. Nominees are scrutinized with regard to their positions on key constitutional issues. The Senate attempts to determine probable leanings of nominees on hypothetical cases. The nominees attempt to remain non-committal until faced with a real legal dispute. The minority party attempts to block nominees that are too conservative or too liberal and may result in a derailed nominee. Democrats criticized Robert Bork for his role in Watergate, strong conservative writings, and anti-abortion position, and his nomination was ultimately withdrawn by Reagan. Democrats opposed Charles Pickering, a nominee for the 5th Circuit, and his nomination was blocked in 2004. The nomination may never get out of the Judiciary Committee or a Senator may block a nomination by use of the filibuster. Democrats blocked a number of Bush nominees beginning in 2001 because they were viewed as too conservative. The nominees were never voted out of the Judiciary Committee and were never given the opportunity for a vote on the Senate floor. The Republican majority threatened to eliminate the right to filibuster in 2005 if Democrats did not agree to an up or down vote on Bush's nominees. A compromise was reached on the use of the filibuster and a number of Bush nominees received an up or down vote. Priscilla Owen was approved 56–43 to serve on the Fifth Circuit after four years of partisan conflict. Janice Rogers Brown was approved 56–43 to serve on the U.S. Circuit Court of Appeals.

Supreme Court Justices—Who is Selected?

Law degrees are not required. As a matter of fact, there are no constitutional requirements. The court includes graduates of Harvard, Yale, Stanford, Chicago, and Columbia law schools. In terms of age, nominees are generally in their fifties at the time of appointment and there is no retirement age. Judicial experience is not required. As a matter of fact, Obama's last appointment, Elena Kagan, had no judicial experience. Over half of the justices have had judicial experience before their appointment to the U.S. Supreme Court, such as Stevens, Scalia, Kennedy, Thomas, Ginsberg, Breyer, and Souter who were justices on the U.S. Court of Appeals. O'Conner served on the Arizona Appeals Court. One-quarter were engaged in private practice or government service. William Rehnquist served as Assistant Attorney General. Clarence Thomas chaired the EEOC. A few of the justices have held elected office. Sandra Day O'Conner served in the Arizona legislature. William Howard Taft had previously served as president. In terms of race and gender, Thurgood Marshall was the first African American on the court and Clarence Thomas the second. Thomas replaced Marshall in 1991. Sandra Day O'Conner was the first woman to serve on the court and was nominated by Reagan. Ruth Bader Ginsberg was appointed by President Clinton in 1993. Sonia Sotomayor became the first Hispanic appointed by Barack Hussein Obama. Elena Kagan became the fourth female in the court's history to be appointed and is one of three women currently sitting on the court. As far as religious background is concerned, historically, the court has been overwhelmingly protestant.

- Protestant 84 out of 108
- Roman Catholic 13
- Jewish 7
- Other 8

The 2004–2005 Supreme Court

- Protestant 4
- Catholic 3
- Jewish 2

SUPREME COURT REVIEW:
HOW CASES REACH THE SUPREME COURT

Controlling the Flow of Cases

The Solicitor General is the third-ranking official in the Justice Department and represents the United States before the U.S. Supreme Court. The Solicitor General screens cases in which the U.S. is a party and determines which cases will be appealed to the Supreme Court. The Supreme Court accepts 70 to 80% of the cases in which the U.S. government is the petitioning party. There may be a filing of an *amicus curiae* brief on behalf of the United States if not a party to the litigation. *Amicus curiae* translates to "friend of the court." It is filed by a non-party interested in the outcome. Interest groups also file *amicus curiae* briefs. Interest group involvement signals to the Supreme Court the societal importance of a particular case. Interest groups also sponsor litigation through financial support or legal assistance. Examples include the NAACP and civil rights cases, the ACLU and civil liberties cases, and the Center for Law and Justice and religious cases. Law clerks review cases filed before the Supreme Court. Each justice is assigned four clerks who are honors graduates from prestigious law schools. They analyze petitions and recommend cases for Court review, conduct legal research, and assist in writing opinions.

PETITIONING FOR REVIEW—THE WRITS

A writ of certiorari occurs when four justices must agree to hear the case. This is called the Rule of Four. The court has discretion to grant review. A case must come from either a U.S. Court of Appeals or a state court of last resort. A case must involve a federal question. It is more likely to be granted of writ of certiorari in certain cases. For example, when the court decision is in conflict with the U.S. Constitution, the court raises a new federal question, conflict exists between the circuits, there are inconsistent rulings between courts or states, and the court departs greatly from judicial procedure. Refusal to grant writ on an appeal from a U.S. Court of Appeals is interpreted as a non-event even though the lower court decision is left standing.

A writ of habeas corpus can be filed by a defendant challenging imprisonment with limitations on use under the Rehnquist court and is discretionary and rarely granted.

The Supreme Court Jurisdictional Checklist

Cases and controversies required by Article III. The court will not hear hypothetical cases. Nor will the court hand down advisory opinion. Actual disputes must exist, and the issue must not be moot. Moot refers to the timeliness of a case. Parties must have standing. Standing refers to the connection between the individual bringing the case and whether or not they in fact are affected directly by the case.

What happens after review is granted? Briefs are filed

Attorneys for the parties file written legal briefs that outline the precedent and legal arguments that support their position. Interested parties may file *amicus* briefs in support of their position. Oral arguments are held. Parties present their cases directly to the Justices in thirty minutes. Attorneys are then questioned directly by the Justices and issues are clarified. Questions may be used to influence other Justices. A conference is held and then a vote is taken. Cases are discussed at the Wednesday closed conference. The proceedings are held in secret. The Chief Justice speaks first followed by others in order of seniority. A number of straw votes may be taken before final vote. The Justices may change their mind prior to the final vote. The majority vote carries the decision and opinions are drafted. The majority opinion states the rule of law and legal justification for the decision. The author of the decision is chosen by the Chief Justice if he is in the majority or the Senior Associate Justice if in the majority. The decision is binding on all the courts and political institutions in the United States. A concurring opinion can be drafted by members of the majority who agree with the legal decision of the majority opinion but disagree with the stated logic or rationale of the majority opinion. There is no real legal effect but may be used to argue future cases. A dissenting opinion will be drafted by the minority who disagrees with the law announced by the majority. There is no real legal effect but may be used to argue future cases.

The Power to Interpret Law

The vagueness of congressional actions requires interpretation by the courts. Phrases like fairness, good faith, equitableness, good cause, and reasonableness are troublesome. Courts have the power to interpret or define the meaning of statutory laws. Judicial review is one of the most important powers of the federal courts. Disputes involve constitutionality of federal, state, and local laws. Federal courts become lawmakers as they interpret the Constitution. Federal courts exercise judicial review over acts of Congress. The power of judicial review is not specifically mentioned in the Constitution. Alexander Hamilton describes the power in Federalist Paper No. 78 this way. "*Limited government . . . can be preserved in practice no other way than through the medium of the courts of justice whose duty it is to declare all acts contrary to the manifest tenor of the Constitution void.*" Chief Justice Marshall enunciated the power of judicial review in *Marbury v. Madison* (1803). John Marshall initially served as secretary of state under Federalist President John Adams. There were numerous conflicts with Democratic-Republicans and Vice-President Thomas Jefferson Jefferson's Democratic Republicans crushed Adam's Federalist Party in the 1800 election. Adams attempted to pack the courts with Federalists between the election and the end of his term in March. Federalists controlled the Senate and confirmed the lame duck appointments, including John Marshall as Chief Justice on February 4, 1801. Many of the appointments came at the last hours of Adams's term—known as "midnight appointments." It was the task of the secretary of state to deliver judicial commissions to new judges, but Marshall had already assumed his duties as Chief Justice. Jefferson and the Democratic Republicans were outraged by the last minute appointments, so when Jefferson assumed office, he ordered his new secretary of state, James Madison, not to deliver the remaining commissions. William Marbury had been appointed to serve as a Justice of the Peace for the District of Columbia, but his commission was not served. Marbury filed a lawsuit in the Supreme Court asking for a *writ of mandamus* ("we command") to James Madison ordering him to do his duty and deliver the valid commission. The Judiciary Act of 1789 established the federal court system and expanded the original jurisdiction of the Supreme Court to issue *writs of mandamus.* Chief Justice Marshall, therefore, hears a case in which he had failed to deliver the commission in the first place. Marshall realizes that if he issues an order to Madison, Madison will probably ignore it and the Court would have no way to enforce the decision causing a constitutional crisis (loss of power and a loss of legitimacy). Marshall declares that Madison is wrong to withhold the commission but that the Supreme Court could not issue the order because Section 13 of the Judiciary Act of 1789 was unconstitutional because it came into conflict with Article III of the Constitution, which gave limited original jurisdiction to the U.S. Supreme Court. The logic of this decision is as follows. The Constitution is the supreme law of the land and is binding on all branches of government. The Constitution establishes a government with limited powers. Any act repugnant to the Constitution is void. Judicial power includes saying what the law is. The Court must decide if laws conflict with the Constitution. The Court must then declare those laws and acts repugnant to the Constitution void to uphold the supremacy of the Constitution. Marshall's decision cleverly avoided a showdown with the executive branch. This left Jefferson and Madison with no court order to disobey. It also forced Jefferson and the Democratic Republicans to acknowledge the Supreme Court's power of judicial review. The court generally upholds actions of Congress as constitutional thereby avoiding a showdown with Congress. Since 1803, the Court has overturned only about 128 (106 since 1900) of the approximately 60,000 federal laws enacted over 200 years. Thus, federal courts exercise judicial review over presidential actions. *Ex Parte Milligan* (1866) is one such example. It represented Lincoln's suspension of writs of habeas corpus in the rebellious states during the Civil War and was declared unconstitutional. *Youngstown Sheet and Tube Co. v. Sawyer* (1952) is another such example. It dealt with Truman's executive order seizing the nation's steel mills during the Korean War to avert harm caused by a strike declared unconstitutional. Federal courts exercise judicial review over state actions as well. Judicial review is used far more frequently to invalidate state laws (1204 times from 1790 to 1990 and 461 times from 1970–1990). The logic of judicial review over state action can be found in the Supremacy Clause of Article VI. The Judiciary Act of 1789 gives the Supreme Court the power to invalidate state actions in violation of the Constitution, federal laws, or treaties. Judges, whether federal or state, are bound to uphold the United States Constitution. *Brown v. Board of Education* (1954) reversed state school segregation laws (Kansas, South Carolina, Virginia, Delaware). *Griswold v. Connecticut* (1965) invalidated a Connecticut statute prohibiting the sale of contraceptives to married couples. Loving v. Virginia (1967) invalidated a Virginia law that prohibited interracial marriages. *Roe v. Wade* (1973) invalidated Texas anti-abortion law or associating with any organization that advocated such action.

Limitations on the Power of Federal Courts

The prevailing view is that the federal courts have unlimited power given the power to interpret legislation and the U.S. Constitution. However, there are limitations on the power of the federal courts. Courts cannot go out and seek cases. Remedies are limited. There are non-existent enforcement capabilities. Also, Congress can alter the size of the courts. The president and Senate can influence the philosophical leanings of the courts through the appointment of liberal, moderate, or conservative judges.

Explaining Supreme Court Decisions

The Role of a Justice

Most Americans think that the law is the law and that is how cases are decided by federal and state courts. However, a close examination of decisions will reveal that not all opinions are based solely on precedent or on a black letter reading of the law. Instead, the law is shaped and reshaped to fit the mores of society or the philosophical or ideological leanings of the judge hearing the case. These changes have been at the center of considerable debate regarding judicial activism and restraint and the proper role of political ideology in judicial decisions.

Judicial Restraint

Judges may advocate judicial restraint, which argues that deference should be given to the legislative body consistent with the intention of the framers. Advocates of restraint are referred to as "strict constructionists" because they look strictly to the words of the Constitution and the intentions of the framers to decide current constitutional questions. The rationale lies in the fact that judges are not elected and should not substitute their own views for the views of those chosen by the electorate. Justice O'Conner states that "the courts should interpret the laws, not make them. . . . I do not believe it is a function of the Court to step in because times have changed or social mores have changed." Chief Justice Rehnquist and Justices Scalia and Thomas are generally considered advocates of judicial restraint.

Judicial Activism

Judicial activists favor a constitutional interpretation that considers the implications of legal decisions to current society. Some believe the Constitution is a living, dynamic document that can be read within the context of today's societal mores. For example, the right to privacy announced in *Roe v. Wade* is not specifically found in the Bill of Rights but is inferred from several of the Amendments. The Supreme Court addressed the current position of the American Medical Association (AMA) and public opinion when it struck down the Texas abortion statute. Justices Stevens, Breyer, and Ginsberg are considered judicial activists. Political ideology seems to dominate current legal debates with conservative versus liberal perspectives that can be found on the current court. Roberts, Alito, Scalia, and Thomas are considered extremely conservative and generally vote as a block. Kennedy is considered moderate. Justices Ginsberg, Kagan, Sotomayor, and Breyer are considered more liberal. Changes in the composition in the Court impact the ideological leanings of the Court and ultimately the Court's decisions.

Chapter 5

THE ROLE OF PUBLIC OPINION, INTEREST GROUPS, AND POLITICAL PARTIES

© 2012 HumbyValdes. Used under license with Shutterstock, Inc.

INTEREST GROUPS IN AMERICAN POLITICS

The Character of Interest Groups

Interest groups are organizations that seek to influence government policy by mobilizing large groups of supporters to put pressure on government officials. The right to organize is recognized in the First Amendment, which states that Congress shall make no law restricting the freedom of speech or the right to assemble and petition the government for a redress of grievances. As long as freedom exists, groups will organize and attempt to exert influence over the political process. Interest groups understand that organization is power in a democracy. The benefits of interest groups are that they serve as a check on majority tyranny and they engage the public in American politics. Interest groups educate their members about issues and lobby members of Congress and the executive branch. They engage in litigation and represent their members' interests in the political arena. They mobilize their members during elections and monitor the activities of government officials.

Of course there are some criticisms of interest groups. Some don't like the fact that they give a voice to special interests. The existence of interest groups produces competition such that it may obstruct the majority will. To silence interest groups would be to silence liberty itself. Refer to Madison in Federalist Paper No. 10.

Interest Groups and American Government

The Framers feared the power that could be wielded by organized interests and also recognized the inherent freedom to organize and that governments should not limit or prohibit organized interests. Madison viewed interest groups as factions and as a necessary evil in politics. The origin of interest groups is found in human nature—"a zeal for different opinions concerning religion, concerning government, and many other points"—and therefore impossible to eliminate from politics. A good Constitution encourages a multitude of interests so that no single interest can ever tyrannize others. Today, this principle of interest group competition is called pluralism. However, one criticism of interest group pluralism is its class bias in favor of those with greater financial resources. As one critic put it, "The flaw in the pluralist heaven is that the heavenly chorus sings with a strong upper class accent."

What Interests are Represented?

Economic Interests

Business and Trade Groups

Business and trade groups account for more than half of the offices in Washington, D.C. For example, business and corporate interests include BP, Shell Oil, GE, General Motors, and Northrup Grumman. There are also trade associations composed of businesses in specific industries such as the U.S. Chamber of Commerce, National Petroleum Refiners Association, American Petroleum Institute, American Hospital Association, National Association of Realtors, and the Pharmaceutical Research & Manufacturers of America. In addition to business, there are professional associations that rival business and trade organizations political influence. Examples include the American Bar Association, American Medical Association (which does not represent all doctors), National Education Association, and the American Bankers Association.

Farm Organizations

Farm organizations have lost some power as the farm population has declined but are still a political force in states with economies tied to agriculture (i.e., Nebraska, Texas, Louisiana, Wisconsin, and North Carolina). Farming groups include the American Farm Bureau Federation, the National Grange, American Milk Producers, and the Tobacco growers.

Organized Labor

Organized labor has also seen a decline in power as union membership has declined. Examples of labor unions include the AFL-CIO, Teamsters, and the American Federation of State, County, and Municipal Employees.

Age, Race, and Gender Interests

Older Americans are represented by groups such as AARP and Generation America. African Americans and Hispanics are represented by a number of groups that advance government policies designed to fight discrimination and provide equal opportunity. For example, the NAACP and Rainbow Coalition/PUSH represent African Americans, and LULAC and MALDEF represent Hispanics. Women are represented by groups on the political left and right, such as the National Organization of Women, Emily's List, and the Eagle Forum.

Public Interest Groups

Public interest groups are differentiated from other groups in that they cannot exclude anyone. If an interest group does something for the good of everyone, then it is serving the public. For example, consumers are represented by groups advocating product safety and protecting consumers from corporate abuses. This benefits everyone who consumes products or services. One such example is Public Citizen, which was founded by Ralph Nader in 1971. Nader gained national acclaim for his book *Unsafe at Any Speed* (1965). Groups like Nader's are often considered consumer watchdogs. An example is the Consumer Federation of America.

Taxpayers and Voters

Taxpayers and voters are another type of public interest group in that they benefit everyone without the ability to exclude anyone if they are successful. Examples include, Common Cause, Center for Responsive Politics, League of Women Voters, and Rock the Vote.

Environmental Protection

Environment protection is another interest that serves everyone. The Sierra Club, National Wildlife Federation, Greenpeace, League of Conservation Voters, the Nature Conservancy, the Wilderness Society, and Ducks Unlimited are examples of environmental protection groups.

Single-Issue Groups

As the name implies, single-issue groups are concerned with one issue. There are many of these groups. Within the category of abortion, there are the pro-life group National Right to Life Committee and the pro-abortion group National Abortion Rights Action League. When it comes to gun rights, the National Rifle Association is in favor of the Second Amendment, and the Coalition to Stop Gun Violence is opposed to it. As far as alcohol, tobacco, and drugs are concerned there are groups such as Mothers Against Drunk Driving (MADD), the Campaign for Tobacco-Free Kids, and the National Organization for Reform of Marijuana Laws (NORML).

The Organization of Interest Groups

The heart of interest group leadership is the entrepreneur. Entrepreneurs are individuals who are willing to take initiative and risk. Most groups are run by a small group of leaders and activists and few are governed democratically. Many revolve around a charismatic entrepreneur. Examine the growth of the United Farm Workers Union and Cesar Chavez. Chavez organized the unlikely group through personal effort. He effectively challenged stronger farm interests. Another classic example of an interest group entrepreneur is Ralph Nader.

Membership associations are another form of interest group organization. They allow greater input from their members. In addition, there are **staff associations** that are managed by a professional staff. Staffs enjoy considerable freedom in adopting policy positions and dealing with policymakers. Members do not renew membership if they do not like the direction the group is taking.

The Free-Rider Problem

Groups generally find it difficult to recruit and retain dues-paying members because the benefits provided by the group are generally collective goods or benefits. This means that members as well as non-members benefit from the group's work. Individuals who receive the benefit of the group's work without contributing financially are known as **free-riders.** Why should an individual join an interest group? The answer is found in benefits. Here are some examples of benefits. **Informational Benefits** are the most widespread and are provided through conferences, training programs, magazines, and newsletters. Another significant benefit is **Material Benefits,** which are special goods, services, or money provided to members of groups to entice them to join. **Solidarity Benefits** are selective benefits of group membership that emphasize friendship, networking, and consciousness-raising. Sometimes individuals join groups because of the purpose. **Purposive Benefits** are selective benefits of group membership that emphasize the purpose and accomplishments of the group.

Class Bias in Membership

Americans are joiners, as a majority of the population belongs to at least one organization, most often a church. Membership in organized interest groups is clearly linked to socioeconomic status with membership highest among professionals and management. Membership is also high for individuals who are college-educated or have high incomes.

Strategies and Techniques for Influencing Government

Lobbying Government

Interest groups attempt to influence legislation through the process of **lobbying,** which is exerting direct pressure on members of Congress and the federal bureaucracy. Lobbying is regulated by a number of laws including the *Lobbying Disclosure Act of 1995* and the *Honest Leadership and Open Government Act of 2007.* The definition of lobbyist is one who devotes 20% of their client's or employer's time to lobbying activities. The lobbyist must register and report how much they spend. In 2008, $2.81 billion was spent on lobbying with over 14,000 registered lobbyists. Generally, the top lobby spenders are the U.S. Chamber of Commerce, American Medical Association, General Electric, American Hospital Association, AARP, and Pharmaceutical Research and Manufacturers of America. Lobbying Congress requires that lobbyists gain influence by developing close relationships with members of Congress. One way to do this is by providing information. Congressmen and their staffs rely on the technical and political expertise of lobbyists in preparing legislation. Lobbyists testify before committees and provide technical reports in support of legislation. Gaining access to lawmakers is essential. Access is achieved through meeting and talking with decision makers, a prerequisite to direct persuasion. They utilize insider connections to open doors. They also attend social events, fundraising dinners, provide dinners, drinks, travel, vacations, and other amenities. Reforms have eliminated payments for speaking engagements by members of the House and limits for Senators.

Lobbying the federal bureaucracy also requires a close working relationship with those employed in federal departments and agencies. Lobbyists monitor agencies for notices of new rules and regulatory changes. They provide reports and testimony in administrative hearings. They submit contract and grant applications, as well as monitor the performance of executive agencies. They can advocate for the creation of a new agency and influence assignment of implementation to a friendly agency. A lobbyist can sponsor or draft the text of regulations and mobilize the public.

Public relations campaigns or institutional advertising are effective ways to lobby by building and maintaining goodwill with the public so as to maintain favorable climate of opinion. Groups can utilize mass media to spread their message either through paid advertising or news stories.

Protests and demonstrations are a negative and effective way to bring attention to an issue. The sponsorship of boycotts, protests, and demonstrations draw attention to the group's objective with minimal cost. This technique utilizes media coverage to sway public opinion. This tactic can prove unsuccessful if the public perception of the event is not covered well.

Grassroots mobilization seeks to influence government decision making by inspiring constituents to contact their representatives. This technique has been around a very long time and is a low-budget operation. Voters are encouraged to write letters, telegrams, e-mails and make phone calls from "the folks back home."

Electoral Politics

Many interest groups realize the importance of electing the right legislators rather than trying to influence the incumbents through lobbying. Interest groups can influence elections by providing financial support through political action committees (PACs) and campaign activism. PACs are separate organizations created to make campaign contributions to political candidates. PACS are regulated by the Federal Elections Commission (FEC). They must register and report their finances and political contributions periodically. The FEC limits PACs (multi-candidate) contributions to $5000 to any candidate (per election), $15,000 to a party's national committee, and $5000 to any other PAC. The FEC also limits individual contributions (2009–2010) to $2400 per candidate; $5000 to any PAC; $10,000 to a state, district, or local party committee; and $30,400 to a national party committee.

Distributing PAC Money

PACs are more important than political parties for campaigns. Interest groups use contributions to gain access to policymakers. Business, trade, and professional PACs contribute to the incumbent regardless of party. Incumbents are rarely defeated, and the group does not want to antagonize even unsympathetic members of Congress. Ideological and issue-oriented PACs are more likely to contribute to a candidate on the basis of policy positions and voting records. Labor PACs give almost all their contributions to Democrats. Ideological and issue-oriented groups contribute to Democrats since they are usually pro-environment or pro-choice.

Campaign Activism

Groups engage in candidate recruitment and endorsements, getting out the vote, and grading the candidates using Report Cards. Examples include EMILY's List which supports pro-choice candidates and the Christian Coalition supports pro-life candidates. MoveOn.org and the Swift Boat Veterans for Truth ran ads designed to educate the public about the candidates and mobilize voters.

Litigation

Interest groups frequently use the courts to pursue political objectives with 72% of Washington-based firms reported having utilized litigation. Many may file briefs in support of parties (amicus curiae), provide legal counsel, or funding litigation. Examples include the NAACP and desegregation, the ACLU and civil liberties, and the American Center for Law and Justice and religious freedom.

Interest Groups and the Making of Public Policy

Iron Triangle versus Policy Networks

An iron triangle is a model or representation of the groups that strive to maintain close working relationships with agencies and Congress. An iron triangle is the mutually supportive relationships among interest groups, government agencies, and legislative committees with jurisdiction over a specific policy area. These are generally formed when little internal conflict, such as between the defense industry, Congress, and the Department of Defense, exists. Policy networks on the other hand are people who regularly interact in a common policy area, including lobbyists, elected officials, staff personnel, bureaucrats, journalists, and private-sector experts. They share knowledge and interest in a policy field such as transportation, energy, or education. Generally, this is a very competitive environment in which compromises are reached on policy objectives.

The Revolving Door

This term, *revolving door,* is used critically to describe movement from government to private sector and using the experience, knowledge, and contacts acquired in government employment for the benefit of themselves or their new employer. There is a concern that government employees may be biased in favor of lucrative job offers in the private sector. Also, the problem of influence peddling (the sale or rental of access) draws criticism.

Legislation Promoting Ethics in Government

The Ethics in Government Act of 1978 attempted to limit post-government employment. Former members of Congress were not permitted to lobby Congress for one year after leaving. However they are permitted to lobby the White House and the federal bureaucracy. Former executive agency employees were not permitted to lobby their former agencies for one year after leaving and two years on matters on which they worked directly.

The Honest Leadership and Good Government Act of 2007

Senators must now wait two years before lobbying Congress. A Representative still must wait one year before lobbying Congress. Senate staff are also required to wait one year before lobbying any Senate office. President Barack Hussein Obama has promised ethics rules designed to limit influence of former government employees as lobbyists.

POLITICAL PARTIES IN AMERICAN POLITICS

A *political party* is an organization that seeks to influence government policy. The party controls the entire government by electing its members to office to implement the party platform. A *party platform* is a document on the various issues known as planks. The platform is written by ideologues at the national convention. It defines what the party would do if elected. The candidates, however, are not bound by the platform. Political parties must nominate candidates structuring the voting choice of constituents. They can propose alternative government programs and coordinate the actions of government officials between branches. They also organize and structure the interaction between groups and forces in society and government officials. Democratic theorists argue there can be no democracy without at least two political parties. Political parties are outgrowths of the policymaking process. Within the government, parties are coalitions of indi- Are viduals with shared or overlapping interests or ideological positions. Hamilton and the Federal- uneasc ists from 1789 to 1800 organized around the goal of a stronger national government. Republicans from 1854 until 1876 organized around the issue of slavery and reconstruction. Coalitions may also be formed between parties to advance shared policy objectives. True party coalitions are much more likely in Europe with its proportional representation electoral system. Informal coalitions are much more likely in the United States. In the 1950s and 1960s, an informal coalition existed between Republicans and Southern Democrats on a number of legislative proposals. In the 1980s, Southern Democrats and Reagan Republicans formed an informal coalition to push a conservative agenda through Congress. However, coalitions are unnecessary as more conservative Southern Democrats defect to the Republican Party. Political parties form as a necessary element of elections. Controlling the apparatus of government requires winning. The desire to win leads to a need to organize or *mobilize* the electorate to ensure victory at the polls.

What are the Types of Party Mobilization?

Internal mobilization refers to government leaders inside the government that may adopt policy positions designed to serve the interests of those in power. Specifically, party leaders adopt defensive policies to weaken attacks from the outside. Examples of internally mobilized parties include:

The Federalist Party (1789–1800) was a faction that grew out of the movement to ratify the U.S. Constitution under the label the Federalists (a misnomer). The party was created inside the House and Senate to organize support for Hamilton's legislative agenda.

The Democratic Party (1932–1952) implemented social reforms to fend off political attacks from the left. Designed to limit or eliminate the rise of Socialists, Communists, and Progressives.

External mobilization refers to groups outside of the government that adopt or pursue policies for those groups left out of the political process. They attempt to gain control of government by mobilizing the electorate to oust those in power. Examples of externally mobilized parties include: Jeffersonian Republicans (1792–1800) and Republican Party (1854–1860).

Dominant Themes: Realignment, Dealignment, and the Two-Party System

Electoral Realignments

An electoral realignment occurs when a party that has dominated the electoral arena for years is replaced by an opposing party or a new party. The replacement of a dominant party in a *critical election* (V.O. Key) occurs approximately every 28 to 36 years.

- 1800–1828 Jeffersonian Republicans (Federalists)
- 1828–1860 Jacksonian Democrats (Democratic Republicans)
- 1860–1876 Republicans (Whigs/Democrats)
- 1896–1932 Republicans align with big business (Democrats)
- 1932–1968 Democrats (Republicans)
- Modern party politics have been characterized by *divided government*
  - ▷ 1969 Nixon versus Democratic House and Senate
  - ▷ 1981 Reagan versus Democratic House and Senate (1986–1988)
  - ▷ 1993 Clinton versus Republican House and Senate (1995–2000)
  - ▷ 2001 Bush versus Democratic Senate until 2003
  - ▷ 2007 Bush versus Democratic House and Senate
  - ▷ 2011 Obama versus Republican House

There are two possible explanations for electoral realignments

Conversion theory is a shift in voter support from one party to another due to new issues and economic crisis. In addition, social and economic issues serve as cleavage issues dividing parties. The Republican Party and the abolition movement of the 1850s serve as an example. The 1850s saw diverse regional, income, and business interests support either Whigs or Democrats. The Whigs and Democrats divided as Republicans ran on the anti-slavery issue. Anti-slavery Whigs and Democrats moved to the Republican Party. Another example is the Republican Party during the Depression of 1893 when there was a cleavage over the Silver versus Gold Standard and industrialization versus agrarian populism.

Mobilization theory involves the mobilization of new voters, either through immigration or the expansion of suffrage, who previously were uninvolved in politics and getting them to align with the new dominant party. The New Deal realignment is believed to have been the product of new voters being brought into the Democratic Party.

Dealignment

An electoral dealignment occurs when voters do not support a specific political party but instead go to the classification of Independent; however, that status will change when the election rolls around because there are only two significant parties to choose from. It has often been argued that in any given election cycle 40% of the likely voters identify as Democrats and 40% identify as Republicans leaving 20% independent voters. This leaves the parties fighting for the independents while holding on to their base of 40%. Attempts to win the independents may translate into a loss of the base.

The Two-Party System

The U.S. is considered a two-party system despite the fact that there have always been minor parties. U.S. parties are not as programmatic or ideological as in Europe. Anthony Downs suggests that parties will move to the center to capture voters. Parties must capture the most voters to win political office and, with the majority voters in the center, the rational party will abandon its programmatic or ideological position and adopt a centrist position. Minor parties represent social and economic protests not voiced by the major party. The Free Soil Party (1848) represented the anti-slavery members of the Whigs and Liberty parties. The American Party–Know Nothings (1850s) represented the nativist movement, which was anti-immigrant and anti-Catholic. The Prohibition Party (1869–1919) advocated the prohibition of alcohol resulting in the Eighteenth Amendment. The Populist Party (1892–1908) represented the interest of farmers while becoming a viable alternative to the Democrats and Republicans flourished with farmers in the Southwest and Great Plains. They achieved the direct election of Senators with ratification of the Seventeenth Amendment in 1913. The States' Rights Party (1948) represented the Dixiecrats' opposition to racial integration. Southern delegates walked out of the Democratic National Convention, nominated Strom Thurmond from South Carolina, and carried Louisiana, Mississippi, Alabama, and South Carolina. The American Independent Party (1968) represented southern opposition to the Civil Rights Act of 1964 and federal intervention in state matters. They nominated George Wallace and carried Alabama, Arkansas, Georgia, Louisiana, and Mississippi. And then there was Ross Perot and the Reform Party (1992–1996). They advocated political reform, ethics in government, a balanced budget, campaign and election reform, term limits, tax system reform, revisions to Medicare and Social Security, and immigration reform. Perot received 19% of the popular vote in 1992 and 9% of the popular vote in 1996. Of course, there was no likelihood of him winning because he would need 270 Electoral College votes, which requires a plurality of the popular vote in 48 states. Ralph Nader and the Green

Party (2000) represented the antiestablishment, pro-environment, pro-reform wing of the Democratic Party. Nader viewed a vote for Gore or Bush as a vote for the status quo. He received less than 3% of the total popular vote in 2000 and 97,488 votes in Florida, which was ultimately decided by 537 votes. It is clear that Nadar made an impact on the election. Nader voters would most likely have voted for Gore in key states like Florida. Gore voters would vote for Nader in less important states like Texas.

Minor parties have been relatively unsuccessful in challenging the two dominant parties but have demonstrated a significant impact on the political debate. The platforms of a relatively successful minor party are co-opted by a major party. Theodore Roosevelt (Republican) co-opted Socialist and Progressive Party platforms in 1912 as the Bull Moose Progressive candidate. Franklin D. Roosevelt co-opted the Socialist platform in the 1930s as part of the New Deal. Republicans and Democrats co-opted Perot's economic ideas in achieving political reform from 1994–2004 with the Contract with America, welfare reform, a balanced budget proposal, and tax reform. Voters view voting for minor parties as throwing your vote away.

Why the Two-Party System?

The electoral system is detrimental to a multi-party system due to single-member districts and a plurality/winner-take-all system. Americans are sociologically opposed to some third-parties such as the Communist Party and the Socialist Party.

The Two-Party System, Electoral Alignments, and De-alignments: Historical Overview

Constitutional Debate and the Absence of Parties

Factions developed out of Constitutional debate between the Federalists who supported a stronger national government and Anti-Federalists who supported a decentralized, state-based government. The Constitution was ultimately ratified following intense debate in the state ratifying conventions. There were no provisions for political parties in the Constitution. A person with the most electoral votes would serve as president. The person finishing second would serve as vice president.

The New Non-partisan Government (1789–1796)

In the election of 1789, Washington, a Federalist, was unopposed and received all 69 of the Electoral College votes. John Adams (Federalist) was vice president, Alexander Hamilton (Federalist) secretary of treasury, Thomas Jefferson (Anti-Federalist) secretary of state, Henry Knox secretary of war, and Edmund Randolph attorney general. The congressional delegation was split but favored the administration—37 pro-administration and 28 anti-administration.

In the Election of 1792, George Washington received a second unanimous victory receiving all 132 Electoral College votes. John Adams was vice president, Hamilton stayed on as secretary of treasury, Jefferson resigned as secretary of state in 1793, and Congress remained divided as the conflict between Hamilton and his political opponents Jefferson and Madison intensified—39 pro-administration, 30 anti-administration. Jefferson funded newspaper attacks on Hamilton and anti-administration forces in Congress initiated investigations into Hamilton's activities.

The attacks even targeted President Washington. Conflict led Washington to urge the nation to shun political parties. Many framers considered partisan attacks on the government as treason. Alexander Hamilton and the Federalist Agenda led to the formation of political parties during the Fourth Congress (1795–1797). The Federalist Party developed out of the internal mobilization of the Federalist faction. Alexander Hamilton advocated a stronger role for the national government in promoting economic development, debt assumption, public credit, national bank, national mint, and manufacturing. He also organized the Federalists in Congress to pass his legislative agenda and became firmly established as a party by 1795. Jefferson and Madison organized the Republicans to oppose Hamilton. The name was chosen to distinguish themselves from the aristocratic tendencies of the Federalists. Federalists renamed the Republicans the "Democratic Republicans" to link them with disorder of "radical democrats" of French Revolution. The Democratic-Republicans lacked the internal power to defeat the policies of the Federalist Party.

Partisanship and the Election of 1796

The election of 1796 was the first partisan election. The Federalists supported John Adams, and the Democratic-Republicans backed Thomas Jefferson. As for the electoral college, 71 votes went for Adams and 68 votes for Jefferson. This obviously created an awkward situation in the executive branch. The Federalists also controlled Congress—57 Federalists and 49 Democratic-Republicans. The Federalists in Congress responded to foreign meddling in American politics (i.e., XYZ affair) with protectionist legislation. Congress passed a series of acts known as the Alien and Sedition Acts (1798). The Sedition Act made it a crime to publish or say anything that might tend to defame or bring into disrepute either the president or the Congress. Targeted at foreigners in the United States, it had a significant impact on Jefferson's Republicans. Fifteen individuals were arrested and convicted. The Supreme Court explicitly refused to rule on the constitutionality of the Sedition Act. The Sedition Act expired in 1801. The Democratic-Republicans who were angered by the actions of the Federalists began mobilizing the electorate (external mobilization) to defeat the Federalists.

Realignment and the Election of 1800

The election of 1800 was the beginning of the end for the Federalists as the Democratic-Republicans would succeed at external mobilization.

The Candidates

Federalists nominated John Adams and Charles Pickney. Republicans nominated Thomas Jefferson and Aaron Burr.

Electoral College

Jefferson and Burr both received 73 votes, Adams received 65, Pickney 64, and Jay 1. The Constitution provides that the House shall choose the president if no candidate receives a majority of the electoral college votes. A split developed between Jefferson supporters, and some believe that Burr encouraged a Burr-for-President movement. After 7 days and 36 ballots, Jefferson won election in the House. The Twelfth Amendment (1804) was ratified to require the electoral college to vote separately for president and vice president. Ultimately, the Federalists lost control of the Congress, and the presidency and would disappear from the political landscape by the 1820s.

Congress

In 1801, there were 68 Democratic-Republicans to 38 Federalists. In 1821, there were 155 Democratic-Republicans to 32 Federalists.

Presidency

- Thomas Jefferson (1800, 1804)
- James Madison (1808, 1812)
- James Monroe (1816, 1820)

Monroe's victory in 1820 is referred to as The Era of Good Feelings because there was no party opposition. Monroe received all but one Electoral College vote. John Q. Adams, the secretary of state, received one electoral vote to spoil a unanimous victory. This ensured that Washington would remain the only unanimously elected president.

An Internal Division Splits the Democratic-Republicans (1824–1828)

The Democratic-Republicans nominated four presidential candidates.

- John Quincy Adams (Mass)
- Andrew Jackson (Tenn)
- Henry Clay (Ky)
- William Crawford (Ga)

Policy Differences

Adams and Clay favored nationalist policies similar to those of Alexander Hamilton. Jackson was a states' rights advocate.

The Election of 1824

Jackson won plurality of both the popular vote and the Electoral College vote but did not win majority of electoral votes necessary to win the presidency. Again, the House was required to decide the presidency. Clay was Speaker of the House and had considerable influence in the chamber. John Adams won the House vote in what is sometimes referred to as the corrupt bargain. Clay is believed to have been offered the secretary of state post in exchange for supporting Adams in the House. John C. Calhoun was briefly a presidential candidate but withdrew and won the vice-presidential race.

The Aftermath

Jackson supporters were angered by the decision of the House and did not support Adams. Adams was described as an elitis who had stolen the election. Adams' policies were challenged by his opponents. Jackson believed the will of the people had been denied. A coalition of supporters of Jackson, Calhoun, Crawford, and Martin Van Buren formed a coalition that would lead to the rise of a new political party.

The Birth of the Democratic Party in 1828

The Jacksonian coalition began calling themselves Democrats and utilized external mobilization for the election of 1828. Jackson pushed for voter reform to allow more citizens to vote (i.e., the elimination of property requirements). Campaigning included stump speeches, parades, rallies, and barbecues all designed to get out the voters. As a result, the election of 1828 is the first mass election with over 1.1 million votes cast in the election. Martin Van Buren (NY Senator) strengthened the Democratic Party by creating a delicate balance between northern and southern Democrats hoping to prevent slavery from becoming divisive issue. Therefore, there was a balance regarding the admission of states with a southern balance on the presidential ticket. The two-thirds rule used for the convention gave the South influence over the nomination. Jackson won the election of 1828 with 56% of the popular vote and 178 electoral votes to 44% and 83 electoral votes for Adams. Jackson's use of presidential powers drew opposition to his "reign," and he refused to renew the charter for the Second Bank of the United States. He also issued an executive order and removed U.S. funds from the Bank of the United States. From 1829–1831, Congress consisted of 136 Jackson, 72 Anti-Jackson, and 5 Anti-Masons. The National Republicans would nominate Henry Clay in 1932, but Jackson would win a second term with 219 electoral votes to Clay's 49.

Jacksonian Politics and the Whigs

The Whig Party was formed in 1834 in opposition to Andrew Jackson. The party attracted a number of groups, such as the National Republicans who had supported Clay, Anti-Masons because Jackson was a Mason, and Jackson Haters who despised Jackson's tyrannical tendencies. They were so named after British Whigs who opposed powers of the throne. The parties would split the White House over the next twenty years. In 1836, Democrat Martin Van Buren won (170; 73). In 1840, Whig William H. Harrison won (234; 60). He gave the inaugural address in a cold rainstorm and died one month after inauguration of pneumonia, becoming the first president to die in office. He was succeeded by John Tyler. In 1844, Democrat James K. Polk won (170; 105), and in 1848, Whig Zachary Taylor won (163; 127). He died in July 1850 of *cholera morbus* from drinking bad milk during the summer and was replaced by Millard Fillmore. In 1852, the Democrat Franklin Pierce won (254; 42).

Slavery and the Birth of the Republican Party

The slavery debate intensifies as Congress reverses positions. The Missouri Compromise of 1820 involved the admission of Missouri as a slave state and Maine as a free state, thereby maintaining balance and establishing a practice with regard to the admission of new states. It prohibited slavery in the Louisiana Territory north of the southern boundary of Missouri. It allowed states to the south of the line to decide the issue of slavery. The Compromise of 1850 was sponsored by Henry Clay. California was admitted as a free state. It created Utah and New Mexico territories and allowed the slavery issue to be determined by popular sovereignty. It ended the slave trade in Washington, D.C. and strengthened fugitive slave laws. The Kansas-Nebraska Act of 1854, sponsored by Stephen Douglas, established Kansas and Nebraska territories. Each territory was to resolve slavery issue by popular sovereignty thereby repealing the prohibition of slavery established in the Missouri Compromise of 1820. The Republican Party is born out of the conflict and debate that followed the passage of the Kansas-Nebraska Act. The congressional abandonment of abolition meant that both the Democrats and the Whigs could not be trusted to end slavery. The Republican Party formed in opposition to the expansion of slavery in July 1854 drew support from a number of factions, such as the anti-slavery Democrats, anti-slavery Whigs, Free-Soilers, and the Know Nothings. In 1856, John C. Fremont, the Republican's first presidential candidate, was defeated by Democrat James Buchanan (174–114). In 1858, the Republicans won control of the House. The Whig Party divided along pro-slavery and anti-slavery lines and ceased to exist after 1852. Anti-slavery Whigs defected to the Republican Party and pro-slavery Whigs defected to the Democratic Party. In the Election of 1860, the issue of slavery and the Civil War took prominence. The *Dred Scot* decision (1857) prevented the U.S. government from prohibiting slavery in the territories which intensified the conflict over slavery. The abolitionist John Brown led an attempted slave revolt in 1859, and the four candidates in the 1860 election exemplified the division in the country on the issue of slavery.

- John Bell (Constitutional Union Party) avoided the slavery issue
- Stephen Douglas (Democrat) supported popular sovereignty on slavery
- John Breckenridge (southern Democrat) was pro-slavery
- Abraham Lincoln (Republican) opposed the expansion of slavery. He was a former Whig member of U.S. House (1847–49). Lincoln and the Republican Party platform stated that the Constitution protected slavery where it existed.

Lincoln won the electoral vote despite a regional split of popular vote, which denied him a majority of the popular vote (turnout exceeded 80%). Lincoln received 180 of the 303 electoral votes but did not receive a single vote in any future Confederate state except Virginia. Breckinridge carried the South and received 72 electoral votes. Bell carried three Border States and received 39 electoral votes. Douglas carried only Missouri and part of New Jersey for 12 votes. South Carolina triggered state succession leading to the formation of the Confederate States of America and the Civil War. In 1864, Abraham Lincoln with Andrew Johnson (Democrat) as his vice president would be reelected with only 25 states voting (212–21). The Civil War ended April 9, 1865 with Lee's surrender at Appomattox.

Reconstruction and the Post-War Period: 1865–1896

Andrew Johnson became the president following Lincoln's assassination on April 14, 1865. Johnson was a Democrat in a Republican administration. Tensions led to an attempted impeaching of President Johnson for violating the Tenure Act. The Civil War and Reconstruction gives rise to the Solid South. Republicans did not carry a Southern state in a presidential election from

1876 until 1928. They won five states in 1928 as the Democrats ran Catholic candidate Al Smith, and would not win again until 1952 when Dwight Eisenhower won presidency. Democrats would also control Southern congressional delegations, which allowed them to control chairmanships on key committees. However, the presidency became a Republican Party institution with Republican Grant (1868–1872, 1872–1876) and Republican Hayes (1876–1880). Democrat Samuel Tilden won the popular vote and probably won the electoral vote. The twenty Florida, Louisiana, and South Carolina electoral votes were disputed as Republican forces were accused of voiding votes for Tilden. Two sets of returns were submitted for the disputed states, and a joint commission was appointed to investigate. The commission voted along party lines awarding the election to Hayes (185–184). Southern states agreed to a compromise accepting the commission's report giving the election to Hayes in exchange for the end of Reconstruction, the appointment of a southern Democrat to the cabinet, and the funding of infrastructure (railroads, bridges, harbors) improvements in the South. The Republican Garfield (1880–1881) was assassinated by a disgruntled office seeker, which led to adoption of the Civil Service Act and the end of widespread patronage. The period from 1881 to 1896 led to the following cycle.

- Republican Arthur (1881–1884)
- Democrat Cleveland (1884–1888)
- Republican Harrison (1888–1892)
- Democrat Cleveland (1892–1896)

Economic Crisis and a Republican Realignment: 1896–1932

The U.S. was in recession/depression in 1893 with 20% unemployment. William J. Bryan was nominated by both the Democrats and the Populists. He advocated free silver and the Silver Standard. It would result in higher prices (inflation) for farm goods. This meant more income for payment of debts. He rallied Democrats with his Cross of Gold speech.

The book, the *Wizard of Oz* could serve as political fable for Populists. It captures the issues of the era with Dorothy as the everyman. Dorothy's house falls on the Wicked Witch of the East who represents the Eastern industrialists and financiers. The Munchkins are the little people enslaved by the Wicked Witch of the East (i.e., the unions or guilds). Dorothy's shoes are silver referring to the Silver Standard. The yellow brick road refers to the Gold Standard. The Wicked Witch of the West is the new power and destroyed by water. Rain is the answer to drought that had plagued Midwestern and Western farmers. Glenda is the Good Witch of the North, and the Tin Man refers to industry, rusted as a result of the Depression of 1893. He has no heart because industry is dehumanizing. The Scarecrow represents farmers who lack brains and as a result does not know what is in their political interests. The Cowardly Lion represents Bryan with a roar but nothing else. The Winged Monkeys represent the plains Indians that have been enslaved by the Wicked Witch of the West. The Emerald City is Washington, D.C. where the Wizard of Oz resides and all their problems will be solved. The Wizard of Oz is the president who, like all politicians, is what one wants him to be. Oz is short for ounce of gold.

Republican McKinley (1896–1900, 1900–1901)

McKinley was assassinated September 6, 1901 by anarchist and Theodore Roosevelt (1901–1904, 1904–1908) succeeded him as president followed by the Republican Taft (1908-1912) and Democrat Wilson (1912–1916, 1916–1920). Theodore Roosevelt had been shunned by the Republican Party and organized the Bull Moose Progressive Party. Roosevelt's candidacy split the Republican vote. Wilson adopted much of the Progressive Party platform causing a collapse of the party by 1921. The Republican Harding (1920–1922) died of a stroke. Rumors persist that Mrs. Harding may have poisoned the president. He was followed by the Republicans Coolidge (1922–1928) and Hoover (1928–1932).

A Democratic Majority: 1932 to 1968

Franklin D. Roosevelt (1932–1945) promised new solutions to problems associated with the Depression. The Democratic base was made up of labor, European ethnic voters, Southern Democrats, urban workers, Catholics, and Jews. African Americans who voted remained loyal to Republicans. Democrats carried the House and Senate. Harry S. Truman (1945–1952) followed FDR. Southern delegates walked out of the 1948 Democratic Convention and Strom Thurmond was nominated by States Rights' (Dixiecrats) Party. They opposed Truman's civil rights policies and affirmed a belief in the segregation of the races. He won Louisiana, Mississippi, Alabama, and South Carolina. The Republicans nominated Thomas Dewey. A newspaper headline stated "Dewey Wins," which was obviously wrong.

Republican Eisenhower (1952–1956, 1956–1960)

The I Like Ike era brought in Eisenhower and Richard M. Nixon as Vice President.

Democrat Kennedy (1960–1963) ran and won against the Republican nominee Richard Nixon. The popular vote split 49.7% for Kennedy and 49.5% for Nixon. Illinois is decided by 8,858 votes, most in Mayor Daley's Cook County. The Republicans questioned the votes in Illinois and Texas, but no legal challenges were made. Records suggest that the election of 1960 was stolen. Kennedy was assassinated in Dallas on November 23, 1963, and followed by Johnson (1963–1964, 1964–1968) who succeeded Kennedy upon his death. The Republicans nominate Barry Goldwater in 1964, considered the father of the conservative Republican movement. The Daisy Girl ad states that "These are the stakes . . . we must love each other or we must die." This meant that a vote for Goldwater was a vote for war because he had given a speech in which he said "Extremism in the defense of liberty is no vice." Johnson defeats Goldwater in a landslide (486–52). Of course, Johnson took the country into war in Vietnam and 58,000 Americans died. He left the troops in Vietnam and did not seek reelection.

1968: A New Republican Realignment?

Two issues dominated the 1960s, the Civil Rights Movement and the Vietnam War. College students, in particular, were at the heart of the anti-war and Civil Rights Movements. The University of California at Berkeley was home of the Free Speech Movement of 1964, and the ROTC Crisis. The Students for Democratic Society (SDS) was formed in 1964. There were Teach-Ins (demonstrations) on college campuses beginning in 1965. There was a March on the Pentagon in 1967 where 70,000 protestors confronted the war-makers. Abbie Hoffman had the protestors sing and chant in an attempt to levitate the Pentagon, turn it orange, and exorcize the war-makers. The Columbia University Administration Building was occupied in April 1968. However, young voters remained relatively loyal to the Democratic Party. Turmoil existed within the Democratic Party throughout the first half of 1968. Eugene McCarthy, the anti-war candidate, challenged Johnson. Johnson narrowly wins the New Hampshire Primary by 1% of the vote. Robert Kennedy declares his candidacy on March 16. President Johnson withdraws March 31. Martin Luther King, Jr. was assassinated April 4. Hubert H. Humphrey becomes Johnson's replacement April 27. Robert Kennedy was assassinated June 5. The 1968 Democratic Party Convention is held in Chicago. Mayor Richard Daley, the last of the bosses, controls Chicago. Hippies, Yippies, and the anti-war group MOBE apply for permits to stay in Lincoln Park and rally at the Convention site, which are denied by Mayor Daley. On Sunday, August 25, the Hippies and Yippies congregate in the park. It becomes Beat a Hippie Night at 11 p.m. curfew. On Monday, August 26, the protests at Grant Park led to arrests. The second night of Beat a Hippie Night took place in Lincoln Park. On Tuesday, August 27, the protests at Grant Park lead to more arrests. Bobby Seale of the Black Panthers speaks at Lincoln Park and a third night of Beat a Hippie Night took place. On Wednesday, August 28, the Hippies and Yippies marched on the convention. The fourth night of the Beat a Hippie Night commenced as police intercept the march at the convention site. The media coverage of the violence obscures Humphry's nomination. The convention ends in complete shambles. The Republicans nominate Richard Nixon as a Law and Order candidate. George Wallace and the American Independent Party score significant victories in the South weakening the Democratic vote. He advocated the continuation of segregation. Wallace was critical of hippies and pointy-headed professors and wins Arkansas, Louisiana, Mississippi, Alabama, and Georgia.

1972–1976: The Party in Crises

The Republican Party nominates Richard Nixon. The Democratic Party dominated by the strong left of anti-war protestors, civil rights, and feminist activists nominate George McGovern. McGovern was from the left faction of the party. Nixon portrayed McGovern as unpatriotic liberal, willing to "crawl to Hanoi" to sacrifice the nation's honor for peace. The Twenty-Sixth Amendment allowing eighteen-year-olds to vote was ratified in 1971 leading to record registration. He lost support of the AFL-CIO, Lyndon Johnson, and many Democrats. He nominated Thomas Eagleton as his running mate, but it was disclosed that Eagleton had been treated for depression (i.e, hospitalizations and electroshock therapy). Eagleton was replaced by Sargent Shriver, Kennedy's brother-in-law. Nixon wins by a landslide despite predictions to the contrary. He carried every state but Massachusetts and the District of Columbia. The electoral vote was 520 for Nixon, 17 for McGovern. The Watergate Scandal leads to Nixon's resignation and the death of the Republican Party. On June 17, 1972, seven men were arrested after breaking into the DNC located at the Watergate Hotel and Office Complex. Spiro T. Agnew, Nixon's vice-president, was forced to resign October 1973 following charges of tax evasion. Gerald Ford, House Minority

Leader, was appointed to serve as vice president (the first under the Twenty-Fifth Amendment). Nixon's top choices were John Connally, Nelson Rockefeller, or Ronald Reagan. They were unlikely to be confirmed under the Twenty-Fifth Amendment, which required approval of both the House and Senate. Ford had served on the Warren Commission (only surviving member) and was a very popular member of Congress. Nixon was forced to resign in 1974 after months of attempts to cover-up the administration's involvement in the incident. Gerald Ford assumed the presidency upon Nixon's resignation and became the only president to not have been elected to serve as president or vice president. Ford pardons Nixon for crimes he may have committed. This probably denied Ford the possibility of reelection.

The Aftermath of Watergate

Democrat Jimmy Carter (1976–1980) won election in 1976 and was not so much a return to Democratic Party politics, but a vote against Washington. Carter ran as an outsider with the promise that he would never lie to the American public. Republican Ronald Reagan (1980–1984, 1984–1988) defeated Carter. Reagan's coalition included economic and social conservatives, religious fundamentalists, southern whites, anticommunists, and neo-conservatives. It marked the beginning of the end for Democrats in the South. Carter won Georgia in 1980, and Mondale did not win a Southern state in 1984, winning only Minnesota and the District of Columbia. A number of Democrats defected (i.e., Phil Gramm) and created a new generation of Republican candidates that would eventually achieve political success in the 1990s (i.e., Newt Gingrich).

Republican Bush (1988–1992)

Democrats stumbles in the nomination process as Gary Hart is hurt by a womanizing issue. He denied the activity and challenged the press to prove it. A photo surfaced of Hart on a boat with Donna Rice. Dukakis, former Governor of Massachusetts, is a Liberal viewed as soft on crime. Dukakis is hurt by the Willie Horton advertisement. An unemotional answer to a hypothetical debate question concerning capital punishment for someone who raped and killed his wife only added to his problems. The image of Dukakis in a tank made him look silly. Lloyd Bentsen, vice-presidential candidate, blasts Dan Quayle for not being John F. Kennedy. Bush wins in another Republican landslide. The electoral vote is 426–111 and one Dukakis elector cast a vote for Bentsen.

Democrat Clinton (1992–1996, 1996–2000)

The 1992 election brought the Man from Hope to defeat George H.W. Bush. Bush was soaring high after Gulf War but was hurt by economic recession in 1991 and 1992. Bush seemed out of touch with America Broke pledge "read my lips, No new taxes." Job approval fell from a high 89% to 33%. He received 37.4% of the popular vote. Perot pulled conservatives away from Bush. Perot campaigned on a promise of fiscal responsibility. He received 19% of the popular vote. Clinton and the Democratic Leadership Council moved Democrats back to center to capture the presidency in 1992. James Carville engineered a campaign strategy focused on "It's the Economy, Stupid." He received 43% of the popular vote and captured a few southern states—Louisiana, Arkansas, Tennessee, and Georgia.

Republican Revolution of 1994

A divided government occurred in the midterm election in which Republicans seized both the House and the Senate for the first time since 1954–1956 and the New Deal. Newt Gingrich organizes Republicans around the Contract with America.

1996 Election: The Clinton Resurgence

Clinton's job approval hit a low point at 37% in the third year; however, Clinton turned things around prior to the election by standing up for children, the elderly, and the environment. He becomes the first two-term Democrat since FDR. The Republicans split between moderates and conservatives. Dole received 40.7% of the vote to Clinton's 49.2%. Perot is a non-factor at 8.4%. Republican control of the House and Senate reaffirmed in the 1996 election despite Clinton's presidential win. Republican suffered a minor setback in the 1998 midterm election and lost five seats in the House and maintained position in the Senate. There was possibly a backlash to the prosecution of Clinton. Paula Jones sues for sexual harassment May 1994. The Monica Lewinsky scandal surfaces in January 1998. Clinton denies the relationship January 1998 and apologizes for his mistake in September 1998. Clinton's approval rating average was 64% in 1998. Clinton is impeached by the House in December 1998 despite an approval rating of 73%. The Senate voted not to convict in February 1999.

Republican Bush (2000–2004, 2004–2008)

Controversy and the 2000 Election

George Bush and Al Gore competed in the closest election in U.S. history. Gore received a plurality of the popular vote but lost the electoral vote. Bush wins Florida's twenty-five electoral votes giving him 271 electoral votes. He wins the state by 537 votes, which triggers automatic recounts. Democrats then attempt hand recounts in strong Democratic counties. Lawsuits are filed by both Gore and Bush. The U.S. Supreme Court refuses to allow continued recounts because different methods and standards were being used in the various counties. Ralph Nader ran as a third party candidate. He refuses to throw his support to Gore. He receives 97,421 votes in Florida effectively denying Gore the presidency. Bush has control of the Congress for approximately five months when he lost control of the Senate due to a party defection of Senator Jim Jeffords of Vermont who declares himself an Independent. The Senate goes from being 50-50 with Cheney the deciding vote to 49 Republicans, 50 Democrats, and 1 Independent. Jeffords had generally voted with the Democrats so the only real impact was on leadership and committee composition. Bush regains control of the House and Senate in 2002 midterm election as he personally stumps for Republican candidates.

Senate: 51 Republicans, 48 Democrats, 1 Independent
House: 229 Republicans, 205 Democrats, 1 Independent

2004 Election: Bush Returns

Despite early exit poll predictions, George W. Bush defeated John Kerry. Early turnout numbers seemed to favor the Democrats; however, the Republican turnout is much higher than expected. Voters are divided on salient issues.

- 22% Values (79% voted for Bush)
- 20% Economy/Jobs (80% voted for Kerry)
- 19% Terrorism (86% voted for Bush)
- 15% Iraq (74% voted for Kerry)

Democrats regain control of House and Senate in 2006. The Iraq War became more unpopular. Bush approval ratings drop to about 38%.

Democrat Barack Hussein Obama (2008–   )

Barack Hussein Obama defeats Hillary Clinton in primaries as the candidate of hope and change and McCain in general election as the economy worsens. Obama campaigns in states tradition-ally considered red and puts pressure on McCain and changes the political landscape. Demo-crats consolidate power in House and Senate for 2009 and 2010. The Democrats lose the House in 2011. It was a referendum on Obama's policies of Obamacare, stimulus spending, nationalizing banks, student loans, and automakers. The Tea Party mobilizes voters for tax cuts, reduces spend-ing, a repeal of Obamacare, and party organization.

The National Party

National Convention

Parties hold televised national conventions every four years to highlight strengths of the party. Traditionally, this was covered from gavel to gavel. Now, it receives less than twenty hours of cov-erage. They are considered to be more flash than news because the candidate is chosen via the primary and caucus process. The attendees at the convention are called delegates. They are party activists from the left or right wings of the party. They are chosen through the primary or cau-cus process. The number of delegates from each state is in proportion to party voters in the state. The Democratic Party delegates generally are more diverse than Republican Party delegates.

The national convention determines the party's operational rules, and the platform is drafted. The party's goals are set. However, these decisions are binding on the nominee. The party's pres-idential candidate is formally nominated. Party bosses once hand-picked the candidate at the conventions. Changes were made to democratize the process. Before these changes the nomi-nees were debated and selecting a nominee may have taken days with multiple ballots. Now the convention affirms the choice made during primaries/caucuses. The presidential candidate names a running mate. This is usually for political purposes, and it is made by the presidential nominee. The convention is one big party to build support and mobilize the base. The presi-dential candidate usually receives a bounce in the polls after the convention.

National Committees between Conventions

Each national political party is headed by its national committee. The Democratic National Committee, and the Republican National Committee.

Congressional Campaign Committees raise funds for House and Senate races. They are the Democratic Congressional Campaign Committee, the Democratic Senatorial Campaign Committee, the National Republican Congressional Committee, and National Republican Senatorial Committee. These may not be coordinated with National Committee as both groups try to raise money from the same contributors.

The state party consists of state political party committees—the Texas Republican Party and the Texas Democratic Party. There is another level at the county, the county political party committees. For example, there is the Harris County Republican Party and the Harris County Democratic Party. The party also has a presence at the precinct level. The precinct is the building block of the process and is designated by a number on your voter registration card.

Parties and the Electorate

Party identification determines which party you belong to, and the party organizations are made up of millions of rank-and-file members. Voters develop party identification with one of the political parties, which is generally a function of ideology. American voters form a bell curve distribution between liberals on the left, conservatives on the right, and moderates in the center. Party activists are strong identifiers and are more likely to vote and contribute time to electoral politics. Democrats battle between moderates and liberals. Republicans battle between moderates and conservatives. Party identification varies over time based on a variety of factors. One such factor is the party in power in the White House. If the president is an unpopular Democrat, then it is more likely that the country will swing to the right. The fact that the country identifies with an ideological position does not necessarily mean that they will vote that way in the election. Ideological and partisan identifiers do not always vote or vote according to their label.

The Partisans—Where are the Parties Strongest?

Democratic Coalition

When it comes to education, Democrats tend to have a high school degree or less (except Whites) and a post-graduate education. With regard to occupation and income, Democrats tend to be union members, blue collar workers, unskilled and semi-skilled workers, and low-income. With regard to gender, race, and relationship status, Democrats tend to be supported by women, African Americans, Hispanics, unmarried singles or divorcees, and gays. In terms of religion, Democrats are likely to be Jews, Catholics, and attend church services infrequently. Concerning society, Democrats tend to be supported by Hollywood elites and members of the music industry. Democrats have the greatest strength from the Northeast, Upper-Midwest, West coast, and urban areas.

Republican Coalition

The Republican coalition looks much different. With regard to education, occupation, and income, Republicans tend to be college graduates, professional, white-collar, management, or small-business owners with high incomes. In terms of gender, race, and relationship status, Republicans are most likely white men, NASCAR dads who are married, from a small town, and blue collar workers. As far as values are concerned, Republicans believe in God, family, and guns. In addition, they may have low income, and low education. Cuban-Americans support the Republicans as opposed to Mexican-Americans. White Protestants, particularly Evangelicals-Southern Baptists and those that attend church services at least once a week, are more likely to support Republicans. Country musicians and their fans follow Republicans. The South traditionally supported Democrats, but swung Republican with Reagan, Gingrich, and Bush. Farm states of the Southwest and West support Republicans. However, suburbanites traditionally thought to be Republican swung Democrat in the 2008 election. The 2008 election may be changing some of these traditional alignments.

Chapter 6

THE ELECTION PROCESS

© 2012 Laura Gangi Pond. Used under license with Shutterstock, Inc.

POLITICAL PARTICIPATION AND ELECTIONS

Voting in America and the Right to Vote

The right to vote is also referred to as *suffrage* or the *franchise.* The word *suffrage* derives from the Latin *suffragium,* which means to support or assist. The word *franchise* derives from the French *franchir* meaning to set free.

Voting Rights in the United States

White Males

Several states provided for universal white male suffrage, but others limited voting to white males who owned property or paid taxes. The property requirement was brought to the colonies from

England. It was believed that property owners had sufficient stake in society to exercise the vote in a responsible fashion. The availability of land during the colonial period created an electorate of between 50% and 80% of adult males. Drafters of the Constitution were concerned that conflicts would arise over the Constitution in states with greater voting rights if restrictions were included. Property requirements for voting remained in some states until just before the Civil War, when suffrage expanded to all white males over twenty-one. The American Revolution brought about a relaxation of the property requirement and the electorate climbed to near 90% of adult males in most states as taxpayer status became more important (along with residency status). By 1790, five states allowed all male (white) taxpayers to vote. North Carolina, Virginia, and Rhode Island were the only states with property requirements as of 1840. Seven states had universal male suffrage. Fifteen states had taxpayer requirements. North Carolina was the last state to abandon property restrictions in 1856. In comparison, voting in England was restricted to approximately 10% of the adult male population from 1688 through 1832.

- First Reform Act (1832) suffrage to 14% of the adult males
- Second Reform Act (1867) suffrage to 32% of adult males
- Secret Ballot Act (1872) suffrage to 56% of adult males

African American Males

The Fifteenth Amendment (1870) established that the right of citizens of the United States to vote shall not be denied or abridged by the United States or any state on account of race, color, or previous condition of servitude. States retained the right to establish voting qualifications so long as they did not discriminate. However, Congress retained the power to pass legislation to ensure African American voting rights. Southern states instituted poll taxes, literacy tests, grandfather requirements, or white primaries. Texas utilized a poll tax from 1902 until it was abolished in the 1960s. Texas utilized white primaries in various forms.

Locally:
- Regulated by Democratic Party (abolished 1923)
- Mandated by State Law (abolished 1927)
- Mandated by State Democratic Executive Committee (abolished 1932)
- Mandated by Democratic State Convention (abolished in 1944 by the U.S. Supreme Court in *Smith v. Allright*)
- Civil Rights workers murdered in Mississippi (June 1964) after attempting to register African American voters (**See *Mississippi Burning***) during Freedom Summer

The Civil Rights Act of 1964 prohibited discrimination in voting, education, and the use of public facilities. LBJ signed the bill into law on July 2, 1964 after months of debate and filibusters, which was defeated by a cloture vote. It required uniform electoral laws and created a presumption of literacy with a sixth-grade education to minimize the effect of literacy tests. A Voting Rights March took place from Selma to Montgomery, Alabama (March 1965), which ended in violence and is known as Bloody Sunday. The Twenty-Fourth Amendment (1964) abolished poll taxes in states for national elections. The Voting Rights Act of 1965 (August 1965) gave the U.S. Attorney General the power to take measures to stop voting discrimination in the states and banned discriminatory voting tests. The U.S. Supreme Court (1966) ruled that poll taxes for elections of state officials were unconstitutional (*Harper v. Virginia Board of Elections* and *Texas v. U.S.*).

Women

The first women's rights convention was held in Seneca Falls, NY in 1848. Elizabeth Cady Stanton and Susan B. Anthony formed the American Equal Rights Association to promote universal suffrage in 1866. Susan B. Anthony was arrested, tried, and fined for attempting to vote for Ulysses S. Grant in 1872.

Women were first granted right to vote in the Western United States:

- Wyoming territory in 1869
- Colorado followed in 1893
- Utah, Idaho in 1896
- Washington in 1910
- California in 1911
- Oregon, Kansas, Arizona in 1912
- Alaska, Illinois in 1913
- Montana, Nevada in 1914
- New York in 1917
- Michigan, South Dakota, Oklahoma in 1918

Teddy Roosevelt's Bull Moose Party adopted a women's suffrage plan in 1912. Jeanette Rankin of Montana became the first woman elected to represent her state in the U.S. House of Representatives in 1916. The Nineteenth Amendment (1920) granted that the right of citizens of the United States shall not be denied or abridged by the United States or any state on account of sex. Meanwhile, in England, representation of the People Act (1918) expanded the right to vote to men over twenty-one and women over thirty (younger women were considered too radical). The Equal Franchise Act (1928) lowered the voting age for women to twenty-one.

Eighteen- to Twenty-Year-Olds

The Twenty-Sixth Amendment (1971) guaranteed that the rights of United States citizens, who are eighteen years of age or older, to vote shall not be denied by the United States or any state on account of age. It was first introduced in 1941 and reintroduced over the years. It was reintroduced in 1971 during the Vietnam War era. Finally, it was ratified by the state legislatures quicker than any previous amendment, 100 days, and signed by Nixon on July 5, 1971. Policy makers hoped to channel the protest movement into acceptable political behavior. Student protests declined, but voting did not increase significantly.

Voter Turnout

Turnout in the United States is low considering universal suffrage. Turnout is approximately 50–60% in presidential elections, although there is an increase in total votes cast over time. Turnout is approximately 30–40% in midterm congressional elections. The factors that could influence turnout are as follows:

- Party strength
- Mandatory voting laws
- National holidays
- Shorter campaigns
- Fewer elections so no burnout
- Parliamentary versus presidential
- Proportional versus plurality

Why is Voter Turnout So Low in the United States?

The Rational Voter Model suggests that the economic cost of voting outweighs the economic benefits of voting and this explains non-voting. Voters are rational and will evaluate the exercise of voting to see if the costs of voting outweigh the expected value. If costs are greater than the benefits, then there will not be a vote. If the costs are less than the benefits, there will be a vote. Because there are so few economic benefits to voting, such as gas, time, and lost wages, turnout should be almost nonexistent. Yet, over 132 million voted in the 2008 presidential election. The psychological benefits outweigh the monetary costs of voting. There is satisfaction in achieving the ethic of voting, patriotism, a sense of duty, and an allegiance to democracy. The burden of registration can depress voter turnout and is viewed as an obstacle to voting. A citizen must register thirty days prior to the election. Texas previously required a January registration. Approximately 66% of the voting age population is registered to vote.

Why Voter Registration

Registration is designed to prevent voter fraud. Progressives pushed for registration to minimize corrupt voting practices and limit immigrant voting. However, we occasionally have an election in which a significant number of dead voters show up at the polls. Who is hurt most by registration requirements? Those with low levels of education, low levels of income, and minorities are hurt by registration. Registration requirements have been relaxed over the last decade despite objections. A few things have been done to improve voting:

- Motor Voter bill (1993)
- Postcard registration
- Jury duty no longer tied to voter registration in Harris Co.
- Military and Overseas Voter Empowerment (MOVE) Act

Lack of competition also depresses turnout as most elections are not close. Turnout improves when the race is more competitive. More competition means more media interest is generated and increases interest in the campaign. Voters believe their votes will count for something. Most congressional races are decided by at least 15 to 20 points. Only a handful of states are considered battleground states in presidential elections. Political alienation depresses turnout as most Americans believe that politics is irrelevant to their lives or that they cannot personally affect public affairs. About 66% of those surveyed believe politicians do not care about their problems.

Therefore, these individuals are less likely to vote. A lack of interest in politics depresses turnout and a strong interest in politics increases the tendency to vote. Extreme liberals or extreme conservatives are more likely to vote. Many Americans are uninterested in politics and lack any real knowledge of the candidates or policies. Other factors contribute to low voter turnout:

- Voter intimidation
- Interfering with registration drives
- Purging voter lists
- Deception regarding election day
- Felony convictions

Who Votes in the United States?

Socioeconomic variables are a good indicator of participation. Individuals with higher levels of education, higher income, and professional occupations are more likely to vote. The contrary is true for unconventional behavior such as protests. However, civil rights protestors were highly educated. Older Americans are more likely to vote. Younger citizens tend to engage in unconventional methods of political participation, such as protests and demonstrations. In addition, voting increases with age.

Race also suggests differences, but other variables explain differences in turnout. Minorities are reported to be less likely to vote, in particular Hispanics. African Americans vote in numbers that approach whites; however, Hispanics generally lag far behind.

Education and income are better predictors than race as college-educated minorities vote at rates equal to or higher than college-educated whites. Minority turnout has traditionally been critical to the success of Democratic candidates. Voter mobilization efforts have targeted minority groups. Get out the vote efforts have been at the forefront of Democratic Party efforts on Election Day.

Traditionally, the turnout for women was lower than that for men, but this is changing. Before 1980, men voted at a higher rate than men. Since 1984, women have reported voting at a higher rate than men. In 1996, women voted at 56% to men at 53%. In 2000, women voted at 60% to men at 58%. As a result, the parties are now paying more attention to issues that are important to women. Women are slightly more likely to vote for Democrats. This gender gap is approximately 10%. A higher turnout of women is expected to benefit Democratic Party candidates.

Elections and Democracy

What purposes do elections serve? Elections provide an opportunity for opposition and for the orderly transfer of power. They reinforce the power and legitimacy of the government and facilitate popular influence. They also promote leadership accountability.

What Is a "Mandate"?

A mandate is the perception of overwhelming support from the people for the candidate's or party's policies and programs. The following criteria must be met for a mandate to occur. Competing candidates must offer clear policy alternatives. Voters cast their ballot on the basis of these alternatives. Election results clearly indicate voters' preferences, and elected officials are bound to their campaign promises.

Do Candidates Really Win Mandates?

Presidents cannot really claim a mandate after winning an election. Candidates rarely offer clear policy alternatives, and voters rarely cast their votes on policy differences. Electoral victories are rarely convincing. Reagan had a mandate in 1984 if you had only looked at the results of the election. Reagan received 525 electoral votes to 13 for Mondale (Minnesota and D.C.). Reagan received 59% of the popular vote to 41% for Mondale. Clinton claimed a mandate in 1992 and 1996, with 43% of the vote in 1992, and 49.9% of the vote in 1996. George W. Bush claimed a mandate or political capital with his win in the 2004 election. Bush received 286 electoral college votes to Kerry's 252 electoral college votes. Bush received 61 million votes to Kerry's 57 million votes. Bush won 31 states to Kerry's 19. Presidents do not have the ability to implement their campaign promises absent help from Congress. Congressional elections do not generally serve as mandates, and candidates usually run independent of the party platform. Candidates are elected to represent a district or a state. Yet, in 1994, Republicans claimed mandate.

The Election Process in the United States

The Nomination Process

The Party Primary

Primaries are used to select the nominees for the general election. Primaries are either closed primaries open to party voters only, or open primaries open to all voters. Texas has mixed with open until ballot cast then closed. Runoffs are used in many states if no candidate wins an absolute majority (51%) of the primary votes.

General Election

The presidential election is every four years and the congressional elections are every two years. There are 435 House seats and one-third of the Senate seats up for election every two years. Incumbents seeking reelection generally win. Open seats are most likely to result in realignment. The midterm or off-year elections usually see the party of the president lose seats. With the 1994 elections, the Republicans took control of both chambers. The 1998 Republicans lost seats in the house leading to Newt Gingrich's departure as Speaker of the House. The 2002 President Bush gained seats in the House and Senate when he personally campaigned for Republican candidates. In 2007, the Democrats took control of both chambers, and in 2011, Republicans took control of the House. It is important to remember that elections are in even-numbered years and the inauguration is in the odd-numbered year. For example, Bill Clinton won in 1992; however, he was inaugurated in 1993.

State Races

State and local elections may not coincide with national elections to minimize the impact of national candidates/issues. The Texas gubernatorial election is held at the midterm to prevent a statewide Republican vote for president from influencing the state races.

Recall Elections

Recall elections are used to remove elected officials. They are available in twenty states. One of the most prominent examples is California. Californians ousted Gray Davis in 2003 and replaced him with the Arnold Schwarzenegger.

The Criteria for Winning

An absolute majority (half plus one) is used in primaries. A plurality system (one more vote than the opponent) is used in the general election. Proportional representation is used in Europe. In other words, parties are represented based on the proportion of the vote they receive.

Congressional/Legislative Districts

States draw congressional and state legislative districts every ten years following the census, which must be an actual count. The Supreme Court mandates that districts follow the one-person one-vote rule. The Supreme Court has also held that districts should be contiguous, compact, and consistent with existing political subdivisions. Partisan gerrymandering creates districts that benefit a particular party. Racial gerrymandering has been ruled unconstitutional.

The Ballot

Prior to the 1890s, voters cast ballots according to political parties. Each party would print its own ballot listing its candidates. Basically, they forced straight ticket voting. The current neutral ballot allows voters to choose among competing parties and candidates. This illustrates the difference between straight-ticket voting versus split-ticket voting. The coattail effect results from straight-ticket voting. The coattail effect means that candidates down the ballot from the candidate at the top—usually the top candidates are the president, a governor, or mayor—will benefit from their popularity. In other words, if the Republican presidential candidate is popular, other Republicans down the ballot will benefit.

Voting Methods Varies by State

Some states have a paper ballot, lever machine, punch card (butterfly ballot), electronic, and optical scan. The electoral college was established by the founding fathers as a compromise between the election of the president by Congress and an election by popular vote. The electoral college consists of 538 electors, one for each of 435 members of the House of Representatives and 100 Senators, and three for the District of Columbia by virtue of the Twenty-Third Amendment. Each State's allotment of electors is equal to the number of House members to which it is entitled plus two Senators. From 1789 to 1832, electors were chosen by the state legislatures. Since 1832, electors have been popularly elected by the States and the District of Columbia on the first Tuesday after the first Monday in November (the general election). The slates of electors are generally chosen by the political parties. State's laws vary on the selection of electors. In some states, the party leaders appoint the electors pledged to support the party's candidate. The electors for Texas are chosen at the state party convention in accordance with the party's rules. Neither the

Constitution nor Federal law prescribe the manner in which each state appoints its electors other than directing that they be appointed on the Tuesday after the first Monday in November. The Constitution forbids a Senator, Representative, or person holding an office of trust or profit under the United States from being appointed as an elector. Generally, the slate of electors for the candidate who receives the most popular votes is appointed in a winner-take-all election. In Maine and Nebraska, two electors are chosen at-large by state-wide popular vote, and the rest are selected by the popular vote in each congressional district. As a result, the electoral procedure in these states permits a split slate of electors to be chosen. This may not actually occur given the partisanship of the respective states. Maine is a Blue State and votes Democratic. Nebraska is a Red State and votes Republican. On the first Monday after the second Wednesday in December the winning state of electors meet in their respective states. The state legislature may designate where in the state the meeting will take place. It usually takes place in the state's capital, often in the capitol building. At this meeting, the electors vote by ballot for president and vice president. There must be distinct ballots for president and vice president. The electors' votes are recorded on a Certificate of Vote. This certificate must contain a list of all persons voted for as president and the number of electors voting for each. It must also contain a list of persons voted for as vice president and the number of electors voting for each. The names of candidates receiving no electoral votes do not appear on the Certificate of Vote. There is no Constitutional provision or federal law requiring electors to vote in accordance with the popular vote in their states. In the 1976 election, a Washington elector pledged to President Gerald Ford voted for Ronald Reagan. In the 1988 election, a West Virginia elector voted for Senator Lloyd Bentsen as president and for Governor Michael Dukakis as vice president. But some state laws require electors to cast their votes according to the popular vote and provide that so-called "faithless electors" may be subject to fines or may be disqualified for casting an invalid vote and be replaced by a substitute elector.

Certification by Congress

The Congress is scheduled to meet in joint session in the House of Representatives at 1:00 p.m. on the ninth day of January to conduct the official tally of electoral votes. The vice president, as president of the Senate, is the presiding officer. Two tellers are appointed to open, present, and record the votes of the states in alphabetical order. The president of the Senate announces the results of the vote and declares which persons, if any, have been elected president and vice president of the United States. The results are entered into the official journals of the House and Senate. The president of the Senate then calls for objections to be made. If any objections are registered, they must be submitted in writing and be signed by at least one member of the House and Senate. The House and Senate would withdraw to their respective chambers to consider the merits of any objections. If no candidate receives a majority (270 votes), the election is thrown to House where the top three candidates are considered. Each state casts one vote. The House rules determine how state votes are decided. There was no clear majority in 1800 and 1824. The popular vote and electoral college vote differed in 1876, 1888, and 2000.

Who are the Candidates?

Power and Ambition

Joseph Schlesinger stated that personal ambition is a driving force. Politics attracts people seeking power and celebrity who usually describe their motivation as "civic duty," "service to community," and "government reform." Political ambition is a distinguishing characteristic of politicians. Politicians are not the smartest, best informed, or wealthiest. They must be willing to give up time, family, and private life to live in fishbowl.

Constitutional Requirements for Office

The president (Art II, Sec. 1) must be a natural born citizen, resident of the nation at least fourteen years, and at least thirty-five years of age. Senators (Art I, Sec. 3) must be a resident of the state from which they are elected, a citizen of the United States for nine years, and at least thirty years of age. A representative must be a resident of the state from which they are elected, a citizen of the United States for at least seven years, and at least twenty-five years old.

Candidate Characteristics

Candidates must possess basic political skills to obtain voter approval. Political entrepreneurial skills include salesmanship, organization, fund raising, and communication. They must also have political temperament and leadership with a vision. They must know why they are running for office. White, Anglo-Saxon, protestant males dominate politics; however, women and minorities are gaining ground. Minority congressional districts were declared unconstitutional in 1996. Businessmen and lawyers are over-represented, and they have parallel skills and training in law and politics. Many go to law school with politics as the ultimate goal. Opportunities arise as a result of legal career.

The Advantages of Incumbency

Elections are an opportunity to "throw the rascals out." Voters rarely vote out the incumbent. Incumbents are candidates currently in office seeking reelection and who generally enjoy a strong advantage. Since the 1950s, between 90–98% of all House incumbents were successful in their reelection bid and generally won by large margins (60% of the vote). U.S. Senate victory rates for incumbents are not as high but are still an impressive 75 to 95% because of the challenger's profile. Between 18 to 30% of Americans believe Congress is doing a good job.

Reasons for Success of Incumbents

Home Style Politics

Incumbents benefit from name recognition as a result of being a congressman. Note that challengers for the Senate seats usually have high-profile positions (e.g., governor, state treasurer, U.S. Representative). This may account for lower Senate incumbency success. Nevertheless, advantages include, media attention, Franking privileges, casework, pork barrel projects, and public relations.

Campaign Finances

Incumbents are stronger at raising funds regardless of party, and challengers have no track record and no position of power. Political Action Committees (PACs) show a strong preference for incumbents.

Campaign Strategies

Campaigns are conducted through mass media. The political parties have little control over campaigns, and campaigns consume a great deal of money. Campaigns are high-tech events focusing more on style than substance. Campaigns are now marked by negative ads or mudslinging, and rumors regarding religion, birth certificates, and terrorist ties.

Evolution of Campaigning

An election campaign is an organized effort to persuade voters to choose one candidate over others competing for the same office. An effective campaign requires sufficient resources (money) to identify and acquire information about voter's interests. They must develop a strategy matching tactics to appeal to those interests and deliver the candidates message. They must hire advisors and campaign staffs to run the campaign.

Strategies and Tactics

The campaign must develop an overall strategy and tactics to convey a message to the voters. The strategy refers to the overall approach used to persuade voters. Tactics refer to the content of messages and the delivery method. They must also be party centered to rally party loyalists and issue oriented to make voters aware of key issues. They can also be image oriented to portray candidates in a positive light. Polling is used to establish or identify issues, and focus groups are used with a small number of people brought together in a comfortable setting to discuss and respond to themes and issues, allowing analysis of tactics and strategies. Tracking polls are used to track candidates and issues. A Debate Reaction Meter allows measurement of performance. They must select a theme that conveys a positive image of the candidate. Finding the right theme or slogan is essential. It is similar to running an ad campaign for a soft drink. A successful theme characterizes the candidate or the electoral choice confronting the voters. This is usually very simple— "A leader you can trust." Another example is the question, "Are you better off today than you were four years ago?" These generally focus on personal issues rather than policy issues. If the candidate must discuss policy issues, they usually leave it as a broad concept tied to image (e.g., tough on crime, fights for the taxpayer). The candidate must define the opponent in negative terms. An example is the 1964 Johnson anti-Goldwater Daisy Girl advertisement. In 1988, Bush portrayed Dukakis as an unpatriotic "Liberal" who furloughed murderers, befouled harbors, spurned the American flag, and looked silly in a tank. Pictures of Dukakis side by side with repeat offender, Willie Horton, who committed a rape while out of prison under a state early release program portrayed Dukakis as soft on crime leading to his defeat in the 1988 Election. Clinton failed to grant a review of a controversial execution during his campaign to avoid being labeled as soft on crime. In 1992, Bush refused to attack Clinton on personal issues, and Bush was hurt by economic issues raised by Clinton. Clinton's theme was: "It's the economy, stupid." In 2004, Bush portrayed Kerry as weak on the War on Terrorism, a flip-flopper on congressional spending and on support for the War in Iraq. Bush helped by running Swift Boat Vet ads critical of Kerry's Vietnam War record. In 2008, Barack Hussein Obama tied John McCain's voting record to Bush in addition to McCain's appearance to be out of control on the economy. The incumbent has a strategic advantage over the challenger in most cases. Generally, the number one issue facing a presidential incumbent is the state of the economy as voters vote pocketbook issues. A good economy means electoral victory. Examples include Reagan in 1984 and G. H. W. Bush in 1988. A bad economy means a lost election for the incumbent party. Examples include Hoover in 1932, G. H. W. Bush in 1992, and McCain in 2008. Congressional incumbents take credit for work done for constituents while challengers attack the record of the incumbent suggesting he is out of touch with constituents. Challengers may depict themselves as outsiders thus capitalizing on distrust and cynicism toward government as Jimmy Carter did in 1976 in the aftermath of Nixon and Watergate. Candidates must receive positive news coverage. Television is the real battleground in modern campaigns. How something is said is probably more important than what is said. Media events are carefully planned to achieve a photo op. They must create short sound bites that are easy to remember, and they must do something newsworthy. Kerry went goose hunting to appease the NRA. Bush landed on an aircraft carrier in a jet fighter. Bush visited the troops in Iraq on Thanksgiving. Network news coverage of the incumbent president tends to be negative while coverage of the challenger is positive. Another example is Dan Rather's report on the Bush Air National Guard Memos, which later were determined to be forgeries. Coverage of the War in Iraq by network news stations ABC, NBC, and CBS focused on casualties rather than accomplishments. Kerry's Vietnam War record was propped up by networks as they became a wing of the campaign. Kerry was critical of Fox coverage in the aftermath of the election and the attention given to the Swift Boat Vets. The must use paid advertising to generate name recognition. Advertising is the most expensive aspect of campaigning. It must achieve name recognition and create a negative image of opponent as a last line of defense. It must utilize free air time through talk shows and debates. Clinton utilized talk shows and MTV in 1992 and 1996. Gore and Bush became regulars on late night TV in 2000. SNL became major force in 2008 with Tina Fey's Sarah Palin impersonation. Another major factor was the emergence of YouTube and social networking in 2008 as new media.

Money in Elections

The Costs of Running a Campaign

Campaigns are expensive, with budgets broken down as follows:

- TV 40–70%
- Polling 5–10%

- Staffing, overhead, and travel 10–20%
- Fundraising 20–25%
- $5.3 billion was spent in 2008 for all federal elections
- $2.6 billion was spent in 2008 on the presidential race

The average spent in 2008 for the House race was $1.1 million, and the average spent for Senate race was $6.5 million ($44 million was spent on the Minnesota Senate race and $11 million for NY House seat). Incumbents spend more because they raise more and attempt to scare off challengers with bank accounts. Generally, a person who spends the most wins.

Regulating Campaign Financing

Campaign funding was unregulated before 1974. Individuals, political parties, and PACs raised and contributed millions of dollars without any regulation on how the money was raised or how the money could be used. The 1972 campaign was rife with campaign abuses. The Committee to Reelect the President (CREEP) spent $65 million in support of Richard Nixon. It received $2 million from one contributor, and money was used to finance the Watergate break-in and cover-up.

The Federal Election Commission (FEC) attempts to regulate campaign financing. It was created in 1974 in response to the 1972 presidential election. It enforces limits on campaign contributions, requires disclosure of spending, and administers public financing of presidential campaigns since 1976.

Sources of Campaign Funds

The FEC Presidential Matching Funds

The candidates of the major parties must qualify for federal funding for their primary and general election campaigns. They must raise $100,000 by raising $5000 plus in private contributions of less than $250 in twenty states. The candidates must also agree to spending limits and keep records and agree to an audit. Third-party candidates receive funding only after the election and only if they receive 5% of the vote. They are also funded by the $3 checkbox on federal income tax form, which is checked by only 19% of the taxpayers. The FEC matches up to half of the spending limit, which rises with inflation for candidates for nomination.

- 1992—$33 million
- 2004—$76 million
- 2008—$84 million

Some talk about expanding it to include congressional races. The decision to accept limits is determined by the ability to raise money. In 1992, all the candidates received FEC funding with the exception of Perot, who did not accept any federal money. In 1996, all the candidates received FEC funding. In 2000, Bush declined matching funds. In 2004, Bush and Kerry both declined matching funds. In 2008, Barack Hussein Obama declined matching funds.

Political Party Organizations

The Democratic Party raised $618 million in 2003–2004

- $299 million DNC
- $76 million DCCC
- $76 million DSCC

The Republican Party raised $744 million in 2003–2004

- $330 million RNC
- $159 million NRCC
- $68 million NRSC

527 Groups

- Spent $400 million in 2003–2004 on issue ads/voter mobilization

MoveOn.org and the Swift Boat Vets are examples and were most effective in 2004. This impact came under scrutiny after the 2004 election and contributed to Barack Hussein Obama's refusal to accept FEC Matching Funds.

- Political Action Committees (PACs) raised $629 million in 2003–2004, and contributed in excess of $200 million to political candidates.
- Labor union contributions go to Democrats (86–98%)
- Trial Lawyers contributions go to Democrats (93%)

Candidates

Candidates must raise and spend money within the FEC limits for individuals and PACs or possibly make personal loans to the campaign. Barack Hussein Obama raised money via the internet. Hillary Clinton loaned millions to her campaign.

2004 Election

Money Raised

- George Bush raised $367 million to John F. Kerry's $325 million
- George Bush spent $310 million to John F. Kerry's $310 million
- Ralph Nader raised and spent $4.5 million

2008 Election

Money Raised

- Barack Hussein Obama raised $750 million
- McCain raised $368 million

Money Spent

- Barack Hussein Obama spent $730 million
- McCain spent $330 million

What Do Contributors Buy?

Money buys access to policymakers, and they expect to be able to call or visit their officeholder to express their views. With the president, they may expect to gain access to assistants or staff. Money also buys assistance. They expect the officeholder to intervene with agencies on their behalf, cut red tape, expedite cases, and procure favorable decisions. They may even bend rules or regulations.

The Politics of Campaign Finance

Campaign Finance Reform is Very Controversial

Reform should minimize opportunity for corruption, inspire voter confidence, and equalize voter influence. Public funding and limits on spending would end constant demand for fundraising activities, but would give unfair advantage to incumbents and increase cost of government to taxpayers. The Supreme Court found in *Citizens United v. Federal Election Commission* (2010) that political spending is a form of speech under the First Amendment, and the government may not keep corporations or unions from spending money to support or denounce individual candidates in elections. While corporations or unions may not give directly to campaigns, they may seek to persuade the voting public through other means, including ads, especially where these ads were not broadcast.

The Presidential Campaign

Identifying Presidential Candidates

Media generally identifies potential candidates years in advance so that viewers can watch the careers of these presidential hopefuls. Political experience (e.g., vice president, U.S. Senator or Representative, governor) is necessary to establish credibility as a leader. John McCain was viewed by some as George W. Bush's successor after the 2000 race. Rudy Giuliani's service as mayor of NY on 9/11 gave him a national stage from which to consider a run in 2008. Hillary Clinton was elected to the Senate with an eye on the 2008 race. Barack Hussein Obama's speech at the Democratic National Convention put him in the media spotlight and made him a viable candidate in 2008. The decision to run generally boils down to campaign finances. The candidate must be successful in appeal to party loyalists in primaries and caucuses and flexible enough to gain support of moderates in general election. Hillary Clinton established the political framework between 2000 and 2008 to secure the nomination by recruiting the old guard. Barack Hussein Obama broke the mold by mobilizing new voters through a system of social networking that mobilized voters and raised money at unprecedented levels. If a candidate meets all of the above, the next step is announcing candidacy.

Campaigning for the Nomination

The selection of convention delegates varies by state and by party. The presidential primaries are used to select a nominee and delegates win based on a formula. Thirty states use this method. The local caucus begins with local meeting of party supporters to choose delegates to attend subsequent meeting (usually at county level). They then select delegates for state convention who then select delegates to attend the national convention (twenty states). Iowa and New Hampshire set the stage. The Iowa caucus measures organizational strength. The New Hampshire primary tests the popularity with voters. New Hampshire is the first test for the presidential election, and media analysis of the candidate's performance will propel the candidate to the White House or become a political graveyard. Since 1952, the eventual president has won New Hampshire except for Bill Clinton, George W. Bush, and Barack Hussein Obama. Since 1960, thirteen of sixteen party convention nominees have won New Hampshire. The front-end strategy is when the candidate focuses available resources on winning the early primaries to build momentum. States have been jockeying to be amongst the first primaries or caucuses. Michigan and Florida violated party rules in 2008 by moving their primaries up on the calendar. A compromise was eventually reached on seating delegates. Super Tuesday and the Southern Strategy is a cluster of primaries held in nine southern and the border states in early March. It was organized by moderate Democrats to offset losses in the general election because nominees were too liberal. They hoped that by holding primaries in more conservative states in the beginning of the primary season, liberal Democrats would be weeded out. It helped Clinton pull ahead of the liberal Paul Tsongas, who had won in New Hampshire. It gives conservative Democrats the lead with Texas and Florida delegates. The candidates next focus on winning big states to gain large numbers of delegates. Usually by late March or early April, contenders drop out of the race, and we know who the party's nominee will be for the general election.

The Convention

The party's candidate is chosen by delegates attending the national convention. The process has evolved into ratification of the victor of the primaries.

The Presidential Campaign: The General Election Battle

Campaign begins in earnest around Labor Day. Candidates spend a bulk of their time and resources in states with large electoral college delegations.

Election Day

The general election is held the first Tuesday after the first Monday in November in even-numbered years. The president is chosen by the electoral college, not by popular vote. The number of electors is based on the number of members of Congress and three for the District of

Columbia (total of 538 with a minimum of 270 needed to win). States are given one elector for each Senator and House member.

- California has 55 (Blue)
- Texas has 38 (Red)
- New York has 29 (Blue)
- Florida has 29 (Battleground)
- Pennsylvania has 20 (Battleground)
- Ohio has 18 (Battleground)
- Michigan has 16 (Battleground)
- Illinois has 20 (Blue)

Voters actually choose electors. The winner of a state receives all electoral votes for the state with the exception of Maine (vote split by congressional district). If no one candidate receives 270 votes, it goes to House where each state gets one vote on top three finishers (1800 and 1824). On four occasions, the candidate who won the popular vote did not win a majority of the electoral college vote and was denied the presidency; Andrew Jackson in 1824 had a plurality of the popular vote (42.2%) and the electoral vote, but he did not receive the required electoral majority. He lost the House vote to John Q. Adams. Samuel Tilden in 1876 received 50.9% of popular vote and lost to Rutherford Hayes 185 to 184 in the electoral vote. Grover Cleveland in 1888 lost to Harrison in the electoral vote (169 to 233) and won the popular vote 48.6% to 47.8%. In 2000, each candidate received approximately 48% of the popular vote, Bush 50,456,169 and Gore 50,996,116. Bush won the electoral college vote 271 to 266. In 1960, Kennedy won the popular vote 49.5% to 49.3%, but won the electoral vote 303 to 219.

Explaining Voting Choice

Party identification and ideology are the best predictors. Democrats voted overwhelmingly for Kerry in 2004 (89%). Republicans voted overwhelmingly for Bush in 2004 (93%). Liberals voted overwhelmingly for Kerry in 2004 (85%). Conservatives voted overwhelmingly for Bush in 2004 (84%). Liberals voted overwhelmingly for Barack Hussein Obama in 2008 (94%). Conservative support for McCain slipped in 2008 (77%). The Retrospective Voter v. the Prospective Voter considers how voters review the behavior or effectiveness of officeholders. If they have done a good job they are reelected, if not out they go (i.e., Throw the Rascals Out). Retrospective voting is heavily influenced by economic factors as voters tend to vote their pocketbooks.

Race and Ethnicity

African Americans vote overwhelmingly Democratic
- 93% voted Gore in 2000
- 89% voted Kerry in 2004
- 99% voted Barack Hussein Obama in 2008

The Hispanic vote splits between Democrat and Republican with Mexican-Americans who tend to vote Democrat and Cuban-Americans who tend to vote Republican, but there was some slippage amongst young Cuban-Americans in 2008.

Republicans Gained Ground with Bush in 2004

2000 Election
- 65% Gore
- 35% Bush

2004 Election
- 55% Kerry
- 45% Bush

Democrats regained support with Hillary Clinton and Barack Hussein Obama in 2008. The 2008 Primary saw significant support for Hillary Clinton amongst Hispanic voters.

2008 Election
- 67% voted Barack Hussein Obama
- 31% voted McCain

White (Not-Hispanic) remain split, but lean Republican

2004 Election
- 41% voted Kerry
- 58% voted Bush

2008 Election
- 43% voted Barack Hussein Obama
- 55% voted McCain

Chapter 7

THE RIGHTS AND RESPONSIBILITIES OF CITIZENS

© 2012 gracious_tiger. Used under license with Shutterstock, Inc.

THE BILL OF RIGHTS AND CIVIL LIBERTIES: A CHARTER OF LIBERTIES

You are born free and you have a right to liberty. To the framers, individual liberty was inherent in the human condition. Liberty is not derived from governments or even from constitutions. On the contrary, governments and constitutions exist to protect liberty. People form governments and endow them with powers to secure peace and self-preservation, avoiding the brutal life of a lawless society. People voluntarily relinquish some of their individual freedom to establish a government that is capable of protecting them from their neighbors as well as foreign aggressors. This, however, requires a delicate balance between authority and liberty. Governments once instituted may be tyrannical. The revolution was fought because the founders believed the British government had deprived them of their constitutional rights. These violations are outlined in the Declaration of Independence.

Madison believed that the great object of the Constitution was to preserve popular government yet at the same time protect individuals from "unjust" majorities. The U.S. Constitution attempted to spell out the limitations of the national government, but many believed that it did not go far enough to insure that government would not infringe on individual liberties. Madison recognized that if a democratic government is conducted by the majority, little can be done to protect the individual liberties of the minority.

THE DRAFTING OF THE BILL OF RIGHTS

A Bill of Rights had been proposed during the Constitutional Convention in 1787, but there was considerable disagreement regarding the need for such protections. Hamilton argued that a specific list of prohibitions was not necessary because the new government was one of limited powers. The Anti-Federalist blocked ratification of the Constitution until an agreement was reached to adopt a Bill of Rights after ratification. On September 25, 1789, the First Congress of the United States proposed to the state legislatures twelve amendments to the Constitution that met the arguments most frequently advanced against it. The first two proposed amendments, which concerned the number of constituents for each Representative and the compensation of Congressmen, were not ratified. Amendments Three to Twelve were ratified by three-fourths of the state legislatures and constitute the first ten amendments of the Constitution, known as the Bill of Rights. Justice Robert Jackson in *West Virginia Bd of Education v. Barnette* (1943) declared:

> *The very purpose of a Bill of Rights was to withdraw certain subjects from the vicissitudes of political controversy, to place them beyond the reach of majorities and officials, and to establish them as legal principles to be applied by the courts. One's right to life, liberty, and property, to free speech, a free press, freedom of worship and assembly, and other fundamental rights may not be submitted to vote: they depend on the outcome of no elections.*

NATIONALIZING THE BILL OF RIGHTS

The Bill of Rights states that "Congress shall make no law. . . ." Accordingly, only the powers of the national government were limited. The Supreme Court recognized this limitation and refused to apply the Bill of Rights to state actions in *Barron v. Baltimore* (1833). Following the Civil War, the Thirteenth, Fourteenth, and Fifteenth Amendments were added to the Constitution. The Thirteenth Amendment prohibits slavery and involuntary servitude except as punishment for crime following conviction. The Fourteenth Amendment grants citizenship to all persons born or naturalized in the United States and provides that **no state shall deprive any person of life, liberty, or property, without due process of law; nor deny to any person within its jurisdiction the equal protection of the laws.** The Fifteenth Amendment provided that the right to vote could

TABLE 1.1   The Nationalization of the Bill of Rights

Year	Amend	Protection	Decision
1897	5th	Eminent Domain	*Chicago et al. v. Chicago*
1925	1st	Freedom of Speech	*Gitlow v. New York*
1931	1st	Freedom of Press	*Near v. Minnesota*
1932	6th	Right to Counsel in Capital Case	*Powell v. Alabama*
1937	1st	Freedom of Assembly	*DeJonge v. Oregon*
1940	1st	Free Exercise of Religion	*Cantwell v. Connecticut*
1947	1st	No Establishment of Religion	*Everson v. Bd. of Education*
1948	6th	Public Trial	*In Re Oliver*
1949	4th	Unreasonable Search and Seizure	*Wolf v. Colorado*
1962	8th	Cruel and Unusual Punishment	*Robinson v. California*
1963	6th	Right to Counsel in Felony Cases	*Gideon v. Wainright*
1964	5th	Freedom from Self-Incrimination	*Malloy v. Hagan*
1965	6th	Right to Confront Witnesses	*Pointer v. Texas*
1967	6th	Speedy Trial	*Klopfer v. North Carolina*
1968	6th	Jury Trial in all criminal cases	*Duncan v. Louisiana*
1969	5th	Double Jeopardy	*Benton v. Maryland*

not be denied on the basis of race. The Supreme Court, however, did not view the wording of the Fourteenth Amendment as extending the protections of the Bill of Rights to the States in the *Slaughterhouse Cases* (1883). In 1897, the Supreme Court extended Fifth Amendment protections against governmental seizure of land to the states in what is considered the beginning of the **nationalization** of the Bill of Rights. However, it would not be until the 1920s that the Supreme Court would apply the Bill of Rights to the states in protecting individual liberties. In *Gitlow,* the Supreme Court adopts the **incorporation doctrine,** which holds that the due process clause of the Fourteenth Amendment requires state and local governments to guarantee the rights defined by the Bill of Rights. The Supreme Court has applied the protections of the Bill of Rights to the states on a case-by-case basis rather than en masse—the principle of **selective incorporation** by which only some of the liberties of the Bill of Rights are applied to the states on a case-by-case, fact situation by fact situation basis.

Supreme Court Building

The Supreme Court established a three-prong test to determine whether a particular action constitutes an establishment of religion in violation of the First Amendment in *Lemon v. Kurtzman* (1971). It must have a secular purpose. The primary effect does not advance or inhibit religion. It must not foster an excessive entanglement with religion.

Assistance to Parochial Schools

Transportation

Reimbursement for the cost of transporting students via public transportation to parochial schools was upheld in *Everson v. Bd. of Education* (1947). However, payment of field trip transportation was ruled unconstitutional in *Wolman v. Walter* (1977).

Textbooks and Supplies

Supplying textbooks (that are also used in public schools) to parochial schools was upheld in *Cochran v. Lousiville Bd. of Education* (1930) and *Bd. of Education v. Allen* (1968). Providing maps, films, and lab equipment for use in parochial schools was held unconstitutional in *Wolman v. Walter* (1977).

Teachers

The state cannot provide salaries for parochial school teachers, as held in *Lemon v. Kurtzman* (1971). Moreover, providing secular courses to non-public school students at public expense in classrooms located in and leased from non-public schools, and using state-paid teachers was upheld as unconstitutional in *Grand Rapids v. Ball* (1985).

Health Services

Public health services are religiously neutral and may be provided by the government to parochial schools in *Lemon v. Kurtzman* (1971). Diagnostic testing for speech, hearing, and psychological services may be provided by non-parochial personnel. The state must provide a sign language interpreter to a deaf student enrolled in a parochial school, as held in *Zobrest v. Catalina Foothills School District* (1993).

Remedial, Guidance, and Therapeutic Services

Remedial education could not be provided on parochial school campus because there was no way to ensure that public school personnel could remain religiously neutral in *Aguilar v. Felton* (1985). The state may provide remedial education to students attending parochial schools per *Agostini v. Felton* (1997).

Tuition Grants and Tax Credits

Reimbursement or grants to parents to assist in payment of parochial school tuition was held unconstitutional in *Committee for Public Education v. Nyquist* (1973). State income tax deductions for tuition, textbooks, and transportation costs for sending a child to school, including parochial school was upheld in *Mueller v. Allen* (1983). Providing vouchers to all students that may be used in selecting public and private schools is constitutional per *Zelman v. Simmons-Harris* (2002).

Aid to Religious Institutions and Direct Financial Aid to Religious Institutions

Federal grants to church-related colleges for construction of facilities deemed secular in nature (e.g., library, music, science, and language buildings) was upheld in *Tilton v. Richardson* (1971). Federal grants to church-related hospitals for construction of new wards and care of indigent patients have a secular purpose and effect and are valid in *Bradfield v. Roberts* (1899). Government aid to public and private agencies to counsel against adolescent sexual relations and to care for teenage pregnancies have been upheld [*Bowen v. Kendrick* (1988)].

Tax Exemption for Religious Property

Tax exempt status of real or personal property used exclusively for religious, educational, or charitable purposes was upheld in *Walz v. Tax Comm. of New York* (1970). Tax exemption for religious publications violates the establishment clause *Texas Monthly Inc. v. Bullock* (1989).

Use of Public Facilities

The use of public facilities by religious organizations does not violate the establishment clause if non-religious groups also use the facility because there is a secular purpose in providing a public forum for the exchange of ideas in *Widmar v. Vincent* (1981).

Public Displays of Religious Symbols

Lynch v. Donnelly (1984) upheld a publicly funded nativity scene on public property where a nativity scene included Santa and other holiday characters as a holiday display—including, Santa, his house, his sleigh and reindeer, candy-striped poles, carolers, Christmas tree, cutouts of a clown, elephant, teddy bear, colored lights, a sign reading "Seasons Greetings," Infant Jesus, Mary, Joseph, angels, kings, animals, and shepherds. The display of a Menorah on the main entrance steps of a government building alongside a Christmas tree and a sign that read "Salute to Liberty" was upheld as a seasonal display in *County of Allegheny v. ACLU* (1989). A publicly funded nativity scene displayed by near the main entrance of the courthouse funded by a local Catholic Church and the message "Glory to God in the Highest," which was in Latin was ruled unconstitutional in *County of Allegheny v. ACLU* (1989). The display of the Ten Commandments at a state courthouse is unconstitutional if it clearly is a religious display in *McCreary County v. ACLU* (2005). The display of the Ten Commandments in front of the Texas Legislature is acceptable as a tribute to the law in *Van Order v. Perry* (2005).

Religion and Public Schools

Religious Instruction

Allowing on-campus religious instruction one hour a week was struck down in *McCollum v. Board. of Education* (1948). Releasing students for off-campus religious instruction was upheld in *Zorach v. Clausen* (1952). Dismissing class for all students to encourage attendance at religious classes held off campus is valid. Religious holidays are also valid.

Religious Meetings at Public Schools

The Equal Access Act that prohibits schools that receive federal funds from prohibiting after-school meetings on school property by student religious or political groups was upheld in *Bd. of Education v. Mergens* (1990). Use of public school buildings after hours to show religious films if other groups in the community are allowed to use school facilities after hours was upheld in *Lambs Chapel v. Center School District* (1993). *In Good News Club v. Milford Central School* (2001), the Supreme Court allowed a parent-initiated religious club to operate on school grounds after school hours despite an initial decision by the school district not to allow the organization to use school facilities because of their religious purpose.

Funding for Religious Activities on Campus

The University of Virginia violated the constitutional rights of a religious group by denying financial support from student fees that are provided to other student groups because the group proposed publishing a newsletter that would be religious in nature in *Rosenberger v. Univ. of Virginia* (1995).

Prayer and Bible Reading in the Classroom

New York State's Board of Regents nondenominational prayer "Almighty God, we acknowledge our dependence upon Thee, and we beg Thy blessings upon us, our teachers, and our country" was declared unconstitutional in *Engle v. Vitale* (1962). The prayer was said aloud in each class in the presence of a teacher at the beginning of class. Those who did not wish to participate were allowed to be excused from the prayer. Daily bible readings conducted during home room between 8:15 and 8:30 a.m. were unconstitutional even if those who did not want to participate were excused in *Abington School District v. Schempp* (1963). In *Wallace v. Jaffree* (1985), the Supreme Court struck down an Alabama statute that provided for a moment of silence for meditation or voluntary prayer. The legislative history of the statute suggested state endorsement and promotion of prayer. Chief Justice Burger in his dissent accused the Court of exhibiting hostility toward religion. Louisiana allowed a teacher to ask for a student volunteer to offer a prayer at the beginning of the school day and if no student volunteered to offer a prayer, but that was struck down in *Edwards v. Aguillard* (1987). Texas legislature passed a statute requiring a minute of silence for reflection/meditation/prayer and recitation of the U.S. and Texas pledge (2003).

Posting of the Ten Commandments

A Kentucky statute requiring a copy of the Ten Commandments, purchased with private contributions, to be posted on the wall of each public classroom in the state was held unconstitutional in *Stone v. Graham* (1980).

The Teaching of Evolution and Creation

Arkansas statute that prohibited the teaching of the Darwinian theory of evolution was struck down in *Epperson v. Arkansas* (1968) (9-0). Louisiana law prohibiting the teaching of evolution unless the theory of creation science was also taught was struck down in *Edwards v. Aguillard*

(1987) (7-2). In 1999, the Kansas Board of Education removed the evolution from its science curriculum but reinstated the teaching of evolution in 2001 with limitations (see Kansas Science Standards). Alabama requires a disclaimer regarding evolution to be inserted in each textbook. The academic study of religion or the bible does not violate the establishment clause because the purpose and effect is secular (i.e., to educate children about their importance, not to indoctrinate religious tenets), as held in *Abington School District v. Schempp* (1963).

Prayer at School Functions

Graduation Prayer

Lee v. Wisman (1992) held as unconstitutional the inclusion of an invocation by a clergyman in public secondary school graduation ceremony. The principal had decided on a prayer. The principal had chosen a rabbi to deliver a nonsectarian prayer during which the students were required to stand as a group. In *Jones v. Clear Creek ISD* (1992) the Fifth Circuit upheld a student-initiated, student-led, non-denominational prayer at graduation and the *writ of certiorari* was denied in 1993. In *Harris v. Joint School District* (1994), the Ninth Circuit rejected the Clear Creek approach, but the decision was vacated and remanded by the Supreme Court as moot. The Ninth Circuit decision left the Fifth Circuit decision the only standing decision on graduation prayer.

Football Games

In *Doe v. Santa Fe ISD* (2000), the U.S. Supreme Court ruled that student-initiated and student-led prayers at high school football games violated the establishment clause, distinguishing such prayers from the more solemn graduation prayer. The District Court permitted the prayer. The Fifth Circuit reversed the District Court. The Supreme Court upheld the Fifth Circuit. Congress and the president responded to court imposed limits on religious activities in public schools. Congress responded with the Religious Freedom Amendment of 1998, which is designed to counter the Court's position on religion in school, but the measure failed on a House vote 224-203. The Clinton Administration and the Department of Education issued guidelines in 1998 to assist schools in dealing with religious issues.

Free Exercise of Religion

The wording of the Free Exercise Clause seems absolute, but the court has never interpreted the phrase to protect all conduct carried on in the name of religion. The general rule is if the purpose of a statute or other governmental action is to single out religion for adverse treatment, or to hinder (or discriminate against) a particular religion, or interferes with a person's beliefs, it violates the Free Exercise Clause. In *West Virginia State Bd. of Education v. Barnette* (1943), the Court reversed a previous decision and struck down compulsory flag salute and pledge of allegiance. In *Sherbert v. Verner* (1963), the Court ruled that Seventh-Day Adventists could not be disqualified from receiving unemployment benefits because of a refusal to work on Saturday, which was their Sabbath. The right of Amish parents to withdraw their children from public school was upheld in *Wisconsin v. Yoder* (1972). States generally require the Amish to use orange traffic signs on their buggies or substitute reflective tape. States are also imposing requirements on the Amish to wear orange vests during hunting season. City ordinances that prohibited animal sacrifices by a religious group violated the Free Exercise Clause in *Church of Lukumi Babalu Aye v. City of Hialeah* (1993). The right to distribute literature in public buildings, parks, etc. is protected but may be limited as to location per *Krishna Consciousness v. Lee* (1992). However, the Free Exercise Clause does not apply to neutral laws that happen to impose a substantial burden on religious practice. The Supreme Court ruled in *Reynolds v. United States* (1879) that polygamy could be outlawed in the Utah territory. Mormons argued that it was part of their religious faith. It distinguished between faith and behavior noting that Congress has the power to legislate violations of social duties. The Supreme Court denied a plea by the Native American Church for an exemption to an Oregon statute that made possession of peyote a crime in *Employment Division v. Smith* (1990). Congress exempted use of peyote by the Native American Church from federal drug laws under the American Indian Religious Freedom Act Amendments (1994). States regulate peyote use. In Texas, the user must be of native descent and a member of the Native American Church. Idaho restricts use to the reservation. The Air Force dress code that prohibits the wearing of yarmulke does not violate the Free Exercise clause given the military's need for order per *Goldman v. Weinberg* (1986). Sacred land used by Native Americans does not prohibit timber cutting for a road-widening project through part of National Forest in *Lyng v. Northwest Indian Cemetery Protection Assoc.* (1988). A requirement that Amish contribute to Social Security was upheld in *U.S. v. Lee* (1982). Sales tax is applicable on the sale of religious material per *Jimmy Swaggart Ministries v. Bd. of Equalization* (1990). The Washington State Promise Scholarship Program prohibiting the use of funds for pursuit of a degree in devotional theology does not violate the Free Exercise Clause in *Locke v. Davey* (2004).

Freedom of Speech

Introduction

The First Amendment provides that Congress shall make no law . . . abridging the freedom of speech. Again the Supreme Court has refused to follow the clear language of the law by interpreting the Constitution as permitting restrictions on some types of speech.

Preferred Position Doctrine

Freedoms of speech, freedom of press, and the freedom of assembly are given a **preferred position** in constitutional law. Under the preferred position doctrine, the government has the burden to justify any restrictions on speech, writing, and assembly. Any speech, writing, or assembly is presumed constitutional unless the government proves that *a serious and immediate danger would ensue.*

Political Speech, Political Correctness, and the First Amendment

Political Speech

Political speech is generally afforded significant protection. However, speech that poses a "clear and present danger" is not protected by the First Amendment. In *Schenck v. United States* (1919), the defendants had been convicted of seeking to disrupt recruitment of military personnel by dissemination of certain leaflets; Justice Holmes formulated the **"clear and present danger"** test. In *Gitlow v. New York* (1925), the majority supported the right of the government to curtail any speech that tended to subvert or imperil the government. Justice Holmes dissented, arguing that *"every idea is an incitement. . . ."* Unless the expression of an idea created a serious and immediate danger, Holmes argued that it should be tolerated and combated or defeated by better ideas. In *Dennis v. United States* (1951), the Supreme Court upheld the convictions of men who had advocated an overthrow of the government on the grounds that the speech posed a *"clear and present danger."* In *Brandenburg v. Ohio* (1969), the Court applied the direct incitement test in defining danger—advocacy directed to inciting or producing imminent lawless action, and likely to incite or produce such action.

Fighting Words

The Supreme Court upheld convictions for the use of "fighting words," which are defined as words that "by their very utterance inflict injury or tend or incite an immediate breach of the peace" in *Chaplinksy v. New Hampshire* (1942). Speech that is offensive to a particular group may be protected or may be subject to criminal or civil liability. The First Amendment protects speech on public issues no matter how hurtful (*Snyder v. Phelps*, 2011 ruling 7-0). This would include racist comments and sexual harassment. However, political correctness has become standard on most universities to avoid speech that tends to offend one group or another.

Commercial Speech

Commercial advertising has not been traditionally protected by the First Amendment. Only recently has the Supreme Court recognized some protections of commercial speech:

- States may not prohibit price advertising by pharmacists
- States may not prohibit advertising handbills on news racks
- States may not prohibit price advertising by liquor store
- States may not prohibit attorney advertising

Restrictions on hard liquor ads have been achieved through agreements within the industry or acceptance of bans on certain types of advertising, as with the tobacco settlement agreement.

Symbolic Speech, Speech Plus, and the Rights of Assembly and Petition

Protected Symbolic Speech

The wearing of black arm bands in protest to the Vietnam War was upheld in *Tinker v. Des Moines Independent Community School District* (1969). In *Cohen v. California* (1971), a conviction for wearing a jacket with the inscription "Fuck the Draft. Stop the War" was overturned as a violation of the First Amendment. State law prohibiting the KKK's activities (wearing hoods and gathering together to burn a cross) as criminal for advocating violence violated the First Amendment in *Brandenburg v. Ohio* (1969). Flag desecration is protected as symbolic speech. In *Street v. New York* (1969), the defendant's conviction for violating a statute punishing desecration was overturned. The defendant burned the flag and uttered contemptuous words. The conviction was set aside because it might have been premised on his words alone or on his words and the act together, and no valid governmental interest supported penalizing verbal contempt for the flag. In *Smith v. Goguen* (1974), a conviction for wearing trousers with a small U.S. flag sewn to the seat under was overturned. The court found the statute overly vague. The language of the statute subjected the defendant to criminal liability under a standard "*so indefinite that police, court, and jury were free to react to nothing more than their own preferences for treatment of the flag.*" In *Spence v. Washington* (1974), a conviction under a statute punishing the display of a United States flag to which something is attached or superimposed was set aside. Spence had hung a flag from his apartment window upside down with a peace symbol taped to the front and back. The Court noted that the flag was privately owned, that it was displayed on private property, and that there was no danger of breach of the peace. The Court rejected a state dese-cration statute designed to protect the flag's symbolic value and held that prosecutions for flag burning at a public demonstration violated the First Amendment in *Texas v. Johnson* (1989). The Court rejected a more limited federal statute purporting to protect only the flag's physical integrity in *United States v. Eichman* (1990). In *United States v. O' Brien* (1968), the defendant's conviction for burning his draft card in violation of a federal statute prohibiting destruction of a military document was upheld on the grounds that the statute served an important and sub-stantial interest in maintaining an orderly military draft. A state can outlaw cross burning as an act of intimidation per *Virginia v. Black* (2003).

The Rights of Assembly and Petition

The First Amendment guarantees the right of the people peaceably to assemble and to petition their government for redress of grievances. The right to organize political parties and interest groups derives from the right of assembly. Freedom of petition protects most lobbying activities. The right to associate with others is also protected. In *NAACP v. Alabama* (1958) the action of the state requiring the NAACP to turn over membership lists was upheld as an infringement of the First Amendment freedom of association. In *Boy Scouts of America v. Dale* (2000) a state anti-discrimination law requiring the Boy Scouts to accept a homosexual scout leader violated the First Amendment freedom of association. The right to engage in protests, parades, and demon-strations is also protected but may be limited. Authorities may, within reasonable limits, enact restrictions regarding time, place, and manner of an assembly so as to preserve public order, smooth traffic flow, freedom of movement, and peace and quiet. The Court must determine whether the regulation is aimed primarily at conduct, as is the case with time, place, and man-ner regulations, or whether instead the aim is to regulate content of speech. Members of the American Nazi Party were allowed to march in Skokie, Illinois (a city with a large number of holocaust survivors) in *National Socialist Party of America v. Skokie* (1977). A city ordinance ban-ning residential demonstrations was upheld in *Frisby v. Schultz* (1988), which involved protests in front of the home of a doctor who worked in an abortion clinic. In *Ward v. Rock Against Racism* (1989), the City of New York's Use Guidelines regulating noise levels were upheld as a rea-sonable regulation of time and manner. In *Thomas v. Chicago Park District* (2002), the process for issuance of permits to demonstrate in the city's parks was upheld after an application by the organization advocating reform of marijuana laws was denied. In *Snyder v. Phelps* (2011), the

First Amendment was upheld as a protection of speech on public issues no matter how hurtful (7-0 ruling).

Sex, Lies, and Videotape

Libel and Slander

False statements causing damage are not protected. Written false statements are considered libel. Oral false statements are considered slander. Individuals must prove two elements, false statement and damage. Public officials must also prove that the statement was made with malice or reckless disregard of the truth. Michael Irvin settled a claim against the Dallas media for $2.2 million for reports stemming from a sexual assault charge. Sylvester Turner's $3.25 verdict was overturned on appeal because there was no malice in the report. Truth is a defense to a claim of libel or slander. Parodies are generally protected no matter how outrageous as in *Hustler Magazine v. Jerry Falwell* (1988).

Art, Pornography, Obscenity, and the First Amendment

Obscene materials of all kinds—words, publications, photos, drawings, films—are not protected by the First Amendment. Examples include *Ulysses* by James Joyce, *Candide* by Voltaire, the *Naked Lunch* by William Burroughs, the Hard Rock Café billboard in Las Vegas, the 2 Live Crew album "*As Nasty As They Wanna Be.*" Most states banned the publication, sale, or possession of obscene material, and Congress bans its shipment in the mail (Texas Penal Code, Chapter 43 and United States Code, 18 U.S.C. Chapter 71).

Defining Obscenity

Defining obscenity is difficult, but as Justice Stewart wrote "I know it when I see it." In *Roth v. United States* (1957) the Supreme Court upheld Roth's conviction for distributing pornographic magazines through the mail by defining obscenity narrowly. "*Whether to the average person applying the contemporary community standards, the dominant theme of the material, taken as a whole appeals to prurient interests.*" The material must be utterly without redeeming social or literary merit. Sex and obscenity are not synonymous.

In *Miller v. California* (1973) obscenity was redefined by a community standard and a reasonable person. Taken as a whole the work appeals to one's prurient interest, which is a tendency to excite lustful thoughts, portrays sexual conduct in a patently offensive way, and the work lacks serious literary, artistic, political, or scientific value.

In the 1980s, cities adopted bans on pornography to reduce violence against women. Indianapolis defined pornography as material that depicts the sexually explicit subordination of women, in words or pictures, or presents women as sexual objects of domination, conquest, violation, exploitation, possession, or use, or through postures or positions of servility, submission, or display.

Cincinnati bans the "display, description or representation of any material that contains sex, masturbation, sexual arousal, nudity, bestiality, extreme or bizarre violence, cruelty or brutality, repeated use of foul language, physical torture, dismemberment, destruction or death of human beings or criminal activity that tends to glorify or glamorize the activity."

The Cincinnati Contemporary Art Museum and the Robert Mapplethorpe Exhibit

The museum director was charged with pandering obscenity for displaying an exhibit by photographer Robert Mapplethorpe. The photographs were generally sadomasochistic and homoerotic. The jury found that the work met the first two prongs of *Miller,* but they could not say that the work lacked artistic value. Theater productions of *Hair* and *Oh Calcutta!* were also challenged. Bookstores were targeted for displaying *Playboy.*

Live Shows

In *Barnes v. Glen Theatre, Inc.* (1991), the Court upheld application of Indiana's public indecency statute to require that dancers in public performances of nude, non-obscene erotic dancing wear "pasties" and a "G-string" rather than be totally nude. In *New York State Liquor Authority v. Bellanca,* (1981) and *California v. LaRue,* (1972), the Court held that states may regulate nude dancing in establishments licensed to serve liquor by virtue of the power conferred under the Twenty-First Amendment. *Schad v. Mount Ephraim* (1981) noted that nude dancing is not without its First Amendment protections from official regulation. A city zoning ordinance was upheld in *Renton v. Playtime Theaters* (1988) as means of controlling secondary effects of prostitution and drugs associated with adult-oriented businesses.

Internet Obscenity

The Communications Decency Act of 1996, which prohibited the transmission of obscene material to anyone under the age of eighteen, was declared unconstitutional in *Reno v. ACLU* (1997). In *U.S. v. American Libraries Assoc.* (2003), the Children's Internet Protection Act, which required libraries to utilize anti-pornography filters or lose funding, was upheld.

Child Pornography

Material depicting children engaged in sexual conduct regardless of whether the material is obscene is not protected by the First Amendment. Such conduct includes any visual depiction of children performing sexual acts or lewdly exhibiting their genitals. The existence of the material itself is evidence that a crime has been committed. However, a federal statute banning virtual child porn—Child Online Protection Act (1998)—was declared unconstitutional in *Ashcroft v. The Free Speech Coalition* (2002).

Film

Initially, the Supreme Court did not extend First Amendment protection to the new film industry. As films grew in importance, the Supreme Court extended some protection under the First

Amendment. To avoid government censorship, the motion picture industry adopted its own voluntary system of rating films:

- G—Suitable for all audiences
- PG—Parental guidance suggested
- PG13—Parental guidance strongly suggested for those under 13
- R—Restricted to those 17 or older unless accompanied by a parent or guardian
- NC17—No one under 17 admitted

Attempts to restrict the showing of adult films have been upheld in *Young v. American Mini Theaters, Inc.* 427 U.S. 50 (1976), which involved a city zoning anti-skid row ordinance.

Radio and Television Censorship

The FCC was created in 1934 to allocate broadcast frequencies and license stations. In *FCC v. Pacifica Foundation* (1978) the Supreme Court upheld the power of the FCC to regulate **patently offensive** words such as George Carlin's Seven Dirty Words skit from radio broadcasts. The FCC has increased its enforcement of indecency standards in the aftermath of the Super Bowl wardrobe malfunction.

Freedom of the Press

Democracy and a Free Press

Democracy depends upon the free expression of ideas. Authoritarian regimes either monopolize press, radio, and television facilities or subject them to strict regulation.

Doctrine of Prior Restraint

English law protected newspapers from government restrictions or licensing prior to publication—a practice called prior restraint. In *Near v. Minnesota* (1931), the Court struck down a Minnesota law that prohibited the publication of a malicious, scandalous, or defamatory newspaper affirming the *doctrine of no prior restraint.* The local county attorney sought a permanent injunction against muckraking publication accusing local officials of trafficking with gangsters under the Minnesota law. Prior restraint is possible if the information threatens the country's safety during times of war. . . . The Supreme Court upheld the right of the newspaper to publish secret documents that had been stolen from the files of the State and Defense Departments in *New York Times v. United States* (1971). Any attempt by the government to prevent expression carries "a heavy presumption against its constitutionality" in *Nebraska Press Assoc. v. Stuart* (1976). This does not exempt publishers from subsequent punishment for libelous, obscene, or other illegal publications.

The Second Amendment and the Right to Bear Arms

Conflict over the Rationale for the Amendment

The Second Amendment provides that a well-regulated militia, being necessary to the security of the state, the right of the people to keep and bear arms, shall not be abridged. There is considerable debate over the meaning of this provision. Some contend that the amendment was only intended for militias. Others contend it secures the right to rebel against tyranny.

The Supreme Court has observed that "with obvious purpose to assure the continuation and render possible the effectiveness of [the militia] the declaration and guarantee of the Second Amendment were made."

Federal Restrictions on Gun Ownership

The Court sustained a statute requiring registration under the National Firearms Act of sawed-off shotguns in *United States v. Miller.* "In the absence of any evidence tending to show that possession or use of a shotgun having a barrel of less than 18 inches in length' at this time has some reasonable relationship to the preservation or efficiency of a well-regulated militia, we cannot say that the Second Amendment guarantees the right to keep and bear such an instrument." Since this decision, Congress has placed greater limitations on the receipt, possession, and transportation of firearms, and proposals for national registration or prohibition of firearms altogether have been made.

The Brady Act (Handgun Violence Prevention Act of 1993) imposed background checks on prospective handgun purchasers to be carried out by local enforcement agencies, which was subsequently declared unconstitutional in *Printz v. United States* (1997) because Congress lacked the authority to compel the states to act.

Until 2010, the Second Amendment had been interpreted with regard to a state action as the Supreme Court refused to review a lower court ruling upholding the constitutionality of a local ordinance banning handguns in *Quilici v. Village of Morton Grove* (1983).

McDonald v. City of Chicago Illinois (2010) followed the ruling of *District of Columbia vs. Heller* (2008) holding that Second Amendment protects the right to keep and bear arms for purposes of self-defense. The Court struck down a District of Columbia law that banned the possession of handguns in the home. The *McDonald* ruling held that the ban and several related city ordinances violated the Second Amendment as well as the Fourteenth Amendment's *Privileges or Immunities Clause.*

Rights of Criminal Defendants

The Role of Police

We generally recognize that society needs the protection of the police. Many suggest that it is equally important to protect society from the police.

The Guarantee of the Writ of Habeas Corpus

A writ of habeas corpus requires a hearing to explain why a person in custody is being confined. If a judge finds that the prisoner is being unlawfully detained, or finds that there is insufficient evidence that a crime has been committed or that the prisoner committed the crime, the judge must order the prisoner's release. The Supreme Court has never sanctioned the suspension of writs of habeas corpus even during wartime. In *Ex Parte Milligan* (1866), Lincoln suspended the writ in several areas during the Civil War, and the Supreme Court held the action unconstitutional. The military had no right to substitute military courts for ordinary courts in Hawaii during WWII, even though Hawaii was an active theater of war.

Prohibition of Bills of Attainder and Ex Post Facto Laws

A bill of attainder is a legislative act inflicting punishment without judicial trial and is forbidden under Article I of the Constitution. An ex post facto law is a retroactive criminal law that makes an act criminal after the act is committed or a law that increases the punishment for a crime and applies it retroactively.

Unreasonable Searches and Seizures

Individuals are protected by the Fourth Amendment from unreasonable searches and seizures of their private persons, houses, papers, and effects. The Supreme Court notes that *"A search compromises the individual interest in privacy; a search deprives the individual of dominion over his or her person or property."* Generally, a search warrant must be issued before conducting a search. No warrant shall be issued without probable cause, supported by oath or affirmation, and particularly describing the place to be searched, and the persons or things to be seized. The indiscriminate searching of whole neighborhoods or groups of people is unconstitutional. The police may require an individual to give "credible and reliable" identification and to account for his or her presence. When may the police conduct a search without a warrant?

- In connection with a valid arrest
- Protection and safety of a police officer
- Evidence is in the immediate vicinity and in the suspect's control
- Preserve evidence in danger of being destroyed
- With the consent of the individual

Thermal imaging searches are unconstitutional, but fly-overs are permissible because evidence is in plain view. Citizens have limited privacy rights while operating a motor vehicle because there is a reduced expectancy of privacy while operating a motor vehicle, which has broadened police powers to conduct searches. The police must have some "reasonable suspicion" of criminal activity in order to make random stops of vehicles on the roads. Fixed-checkpoint stops in the absence of any individualized suspicion have been upheld. A valid stop may be based on a traffic violation. After a valid stop and with a reasonable belief that weapons may be present, the police may conduct a search of those portions of the passenger compartment in which a weapon could be placed or hidden to ensure their own safety. Police may seize contraband and suspicious items "in plain view." Police may search with your consent. Private employers can require drug tests without violating the Fourth Amendment, but not a state government.

Arrests

A person can be arrested without a warrant when a crime is committed in the presence of an officer and when an arrest is supported by probable cause to believe a crime has been committed by the person apprehended. Police may not enter a home to arrest its occupant without either a warrant for the arrest or the consent of the owner.

Grand Juries and the Right to Indictment

The Fifth Amendment requires that an indictment be issued by a grand jury before a person may be brought to trial on a felony offense. Grand juries are usually under the control of the prosecutor. Proceedings are secret and the right to an attorney does not apply.

Double Jeopardy

The Fifth Amendment also proves that no person shall be tried twice for the same offense. The rationale behind the double jeopardy clause is that the State with all its resources and power should not be allowed to make repeated attempts to convict an individual for an alleged offense, thereby enhancing the possibility that even though innocent be may be found guilty. Little or no controversy accompanies the rule that once a jury has acquitted a defendant, government may not, through appeal of the verdict or institution of a new prosecution, place the defendant on trial again. The double jeopardy clause does not limit the legislative power to split a single transaction into separate crimes so as to give the prosecution a choice of charges that may be tried in one proceeding.

Self-Incrimination

The Fifth Amendment protects individuals from being compelled to testify against themselves. The Fifth Amendment is not applicable if immunity is granted. In *Miranda v. Arizona* (1966) the Court held that before questioning suspects, a police officer must inform them of all their constitutional rights. On March 3, 1963, an 18-year-old girl was kidnapped and raped. Miranda, a poor, mentally disturbed man with a ninth-grade education was arrested ten days later. The victim identified Miranda in a line-up and Miranda signed a written confession after a two-hour interrogation. Miranda was never told of his constitutional right to an attorney or that he had the protection against self-incrimination. The Supreme Court overturned the conviction on the grounds that Miranda had not been told of his right against self-incrimination and remanded the case for a new trial without the confession. After Miranda, the police began reading an accused the Miranda Rights.

> *You have the right to remain silent. Anything you say can and will be used against you in a court of law. You have the right to talk to an attorney and have him present while you are being questioned. If you cannot afford to hire a lawyer, one will be appointed to represent you before any questioning, if you wish one.*

Miranda rights may be waived by the accused. The Burger and Rehnquist courts have relaxed the Miranda requirements, but the police must still inform a defendant of the Miranda rights if a confession is to be used at trial.

The Right to Counsel

The Sixth Amendment provides that the accused shall have the assistance of counsel for his defense. In *Gideon v. Wainwright* (1963), the Court held that equal protection under the Fourteenth Amendment requires that free legal counsel be appointed for all indigent defendants in all criminal cases.

In *Escobedo v. Illinois* (1964), the Court held that suspects are entitled to confer with counsel as soon as police investigation focuses on them or once the process shifts from investigatory to accusatory.

In *Brewer v. Williams* (1967), the right to counsel was found violated when police elicited from the defendant incriminating admissions not through formal questioning but rather through a series of conversational openings designed to play on the defendant's known weakness. The police conduct occurred in the post-arraignment period in the absence of defense counsel and despite assurances to the attorney that the defendant would not be questioned in his absence. Lineups are a critical stage and that in-court identification of defendants based on out-of-court lineups or show-ups without the presence of defendant's counsel was held to be inadmissible in *United States v. Wade* (1967). The Sixth Amendment also guarantees the right to represent yourself.

The Right to a Jury Trial

Defendants are entitled to a speedy trial, a right to confront their accuser, and a trial by an impartial jury. Prosecutors may not use their peremptory strikes to exclude African Americans especially when the defendant is African American, as found in *Boston v. Kentucky* (1986) or men in paternity suits, rape trials, or domestic violence cases, as in *J. E. B. v. Alabama* (1994).

The Exclusionary Rule

Evidence obtained illegally by a federal official may not be used in the subsequent federal criminal trial per *Weeks v. U.S.* (1914). This exclusionary rule is one of the more controversial procedural rights that the Supreme Court has extended to criminal defendants. The rule is a means to enforce the protections of the Fourth and Fifth Amendments. To allow the police to use the "fruits of a poisonous tree" would only encourage such activity. The exclusionary rule applied to all criminal cases in *Mapp v. Ohio* (1961). Mapp was suspected of harboring a suspect in a bombing incident. Police forcibly entered her home claiming they had a warrant. Police did not have a warrant only a piece of paper. Police found evidence of gambling and obscene materials. Mapp was convicted for possession of obscene materials. Exclusionary rule applied as the search and seizure violated the 4th Amendment. A good faith exception applies if the officers have acted in objective good faith or their transgressions have been minor (see *U.S. v. Leon* (1984)). The warrant was issued by a neutral magistrate. The officer was not dishonest or reckless. The officer had a reasonable belief that the warrant was valid. The evidence would have been discovered inevitably.

Bail Requirements

The Eighth Amendment provides that excessive bail shall not be required. Pretrial release is not available to all criminal defendants. Pretrial release can be limited based on the seriousness of the crime or the probability that the accused will flee the jurisdiction or the accused poses a threat to the community. Otherwise bail must fit the crime.

The Death Penalty

Opponents of the death penalty claim it violates the Eight Amendment's prohibition against cruel and unusual punishment. In contrast, most Americans see capital punishment as an appropriate retribution for heinous crimes. The Supreme Court has stated that given society's longstanding acceptance of the death penalty, it cannot say that the penalty violates the prohibition against cruel and unusual punishment. Prior to 1971, the death penalty was officially sanctioned by about half the states and federal law.

Reforming the Death Penalty Process

In *Furman v. Georgia* (1972), the Supreme Court ruled that capital punishment, as then imposed, violated the Eighth and Fourteenth Amendment prohibitions against cruel and unusual punishment and due process of law. States rewrote their death penalty laws to try to ensure fairness and uniformity of application. Some have mandated the death penalty for murders committed during rape, robbery, hijacking or kidnapping, murders of law enforcement officials, or multiple murders. Trial is bifurcated with the first phase dealing with guilt or innocence and the second phase dealing with punishment during which aggravating or mitigating factors can be considered. In *Gregg v. Georgia* (1976), the Supreme Court upheld these changes and ruled that the punishment of death does not invariably violate the Constitution. The Court noted that the framers of the Constitution had accepted death as a common penalty for crime.

Current social values continued to support death as a means of punishment in that juries were willing to order the death penalty and legislators passed death penalty legislation. The social purposes of retribution and deterrence justified the use of the death penalty. The Court did require that death penalty sentences be reviewed automatically by the state's Supreme Court and disapproved provisions that mandated the death penalty for all first-degree murder cases, holding that such laws were unduly harsh and unworkably rigid.

In *Atkins v. Virginia* (2002), the Court ruled that the Eighth and Fourteenth Amendments forbid the imposition of the death penalty on defendants determined to be mentally retarded (an IQ of 70 is the approximate threshold). Oddly enough Atkins raised his IQ and may be retried.

In *Roper v. Simmons* (2004), the Court ruled that the Eighth and Fourteenth Amendments forbid imposition of capital punishment on a defendant under the age of eighteen at the time the crime was committed.

Current Challenges to the Death Penalty

- Racial imbalance in conviction rates
- Defendant lacked competent counsel
- Defendant innocent

Over the past thirteen years, over 100 persons have been released from prison after DNA confirmed innocence. New York found twenty innocent based on new evidence.

The Right to Privacy

Privacy in the Bedroom

The Supreme Court recognized that a zone of privacy exists in the Constitution in *Griswald v. Connecticut* (1965). An 1879 Connecticut law made it illegal to provide information about birth control or provide contraceptives. Planned Parenthood employees were convicted of providing information to married couples. The Court was repulsed over the thought of the police searching a couple's home for evidence of the use of contraceptives. The Supreme Court found that a zone of privacy was created by the First, Third, Fourth, and Fifth Amendments and protected by the Ninth Amendment and applicable to the states through the 14th Amendment. A few years later, the Court utilized privacy rights to overturn a conviction of George Stanley for the possession of obscene materials in *Stanley v. Georgia* (1969). The defendant's home was being searched pursuant to a warrant issued for alleged bookmaking items. While searching the house, police came across a number of 8mm films that were determined to be obscene. The defendant was arrested and convicted under a Georgia statute that made it illegal to possess obscene material. Stanley argued that he has the right to view what he pleases in the privacy of his home. Supreme Court held that statute to be unconstitutional because it made mere possession illegal without any intent to sale or distribute obscene material. The Court reasoned that a man has the right to privacy in his home and the state does not have the right to control the moral content of his personal thoughts solely because it may lead to antisocial conduct.

In *Carey v. Population Services* (1977), a New York law banning the sale of birth control devices to those under sixteen and requiring the sale of birth control devices by a pharmacist to those over sixteen was held unconstitutional. The statute applied to nonprescription birth control devices. Population Planning Associates (PPA) sold mail-order contraceptives by advertising in periodicals sold in New York. PPA was threatened with legal action for advertising in magazines distributed on college campuses and selling to those under sixteen. The Court noted that the state demonstrated no compelling interest even if the desire was to eliminate sex by minors. The right to privacy extends to minors as well as adults. The Court upheld a sodomy conviction in *Bowers v. Hardwick* (1986) refusing to apply the zone of privacy for homosexual conduct. A number of states had Sodomy Statues on the books that prohibited sexual acts not designed to produce babies. The defendant was charged with violating the Georgia Sodomy Statute for having sex with another adult male in the bedroom of his home. The Court found no constitutional right to engage in sodomy. Homosexual conduct is not related to previously recognized rights of family relationships, marriage, and procreation. Court reasoned that there is no right to use illegal drugs in the privacy of your home or bedroom and the law is based on morality. The Georgia Supreme Court subsequently declared the Georgia Sodomy Statute unconstitutional on the grounds of being over broad. Texas rewrote the Texas Sodomy Statute to narrow its application to "deviant sexual acts," which basically meant homosexual conduct.

In *Lawrence v. Texas* (2003), the Supreme Court extended the zone of privacy to the bedroom for homosexual conduct. HPD was dispatched to a Houston apartment in response to a reported weapons disturbance. HPD entered the apartment and found two men, Lawrence and Garner, engaging in a sexual act. The men were arrested for violating the Texas Penal Code provisions relating to deviate sex and convicted before a JP Defendants appealed de novo to the Harris County Criminal Court, and after their constitutional claims were rejected the defendants plead "no contest" and paid a $200 fine and court costs. Kennedy, writing for the majority, reversed Bowers and found that the defendants as adults were entitled to privacy in the bedroom. Scalia's dissent is worth reading for his attack on the majority.

Abortion Rights

In *Roe v. Wade* (1973) a Texas Abortion Statute made it a crime to obtain abortion except on medical advice to save the life of the mother. The Court found that abortion was legal in the United States until mid-1800s and then state legislatures began imposing restrictions. The AMA lobbied to outlaw abortions. In 1967, 87% of physicians favored liberalizing abortion laws. Public opinion also moved to support legalized abortions. The Texas statute violates a woman's right to privacy/procreation. The Court noted that at some point (viability) the right of the fetus must be considered, which is the third trimester. There are no restrictions during the first trimester and limited restrictions allowed to safeguard women during the second trimester. Since *Roe,* the states have attempted to restrict abortion rights.

In *Planned Parenthood v. Danforth* (1976), a Missouri law that defined viability through use of artificial means was upheld, but the Supreme Court struck down requirements for consent from the spouse or parents.

In *Beal v. Doe* (1977), the Supreme Court held that a state can refuse to fund abortions under Medicaid where the procedure is not medically necessary as determined by physician. The Court noted that states have broad discretion to fund medical procedures under federal Title XIX of Social Security Act. Therefore, there is no requirement to fund abortions under Medicaid. The State has important and legitimate interest in childbirth.

In *Harris v. McRae* (1980), a federal statute prohibiting federal funding of abortions under Medicaid was found not to violate the equal protection component of due process clause of the Fifth Amendment.

In *City of Akron v. Akron Center for Reproductive Health* (1983), an Akron ordinance requiring hospitals, after the 1st trimester, to obtain parental consent, informed consent, and require a waiting period was found to be overly restrictive and, therefore, unconstitutional. In *Webster v. Reproductive Health Services* (1989), the Supreme Court upheld restrictions on public funding of abortions, parental notification laws, and state-required fetal viability tests in the second trimester.

In *Planned Parenthood v. Casey* (1992), a 5-4 majority upheld Roe, but narrowed its scope by refusing to invalidate a Pennsylvania statute restricting abortion rights by upholding. The statute held that a woman seeking an abortion must give her informed consent prior to the procedure, that she be provided with certain information at least 24 hours before the abortion is performed, and it mandates the informed consent of one parent for a minor to obtain an abortion. The Court in *Casey* struck down a requirement that a married woman seeking an abortion must sign a statement indicating that she has notified her husband. Congress enacted the Partial Birth Abortion Ban Act in 2003 and lower federal courts have already declared the law unconstitutional. It violates the right to privacy, and does not contain an exception for the health of the mother.

Chapter 8

ISSUES AND POLICIES IN U.S. POLITICS

© 2012 Jorge Salcedo. Used under license with Shutterstock, Inc.

PUBLIC POLICY

Public policy can be defined as an intentional course of action by the government in dealing with some problem or matter of concern. Public policy can also be defined as an officially expressed purpose or intention backed by sanction, which can be either a reward or punishment. All public policies are coercive in that the goal is to get you to do less of something or more of something by either rewarding or punishing actions. Issuing traffic tickets for speeding is an example of punishment. Crime Stoppers giving rewards for reporting on criminals is an example of an incentive.

The Public Policy Process

David Easton adopted a systems theory approach to public policymaking. There is public input through citizen and/or group demands. Decision making is conducted by government institutions; this represents the black box. The output represents the adoption of public policy. The feedback is the public response to that output and evaluation measured against input. An expanded or modernized version of Easton's model has been developed as a stages process.

Stages of the policymaking process:

- Problem recognition and definition
- Agenda setting
- Policy formulation
- Policy adoption
- Budgeting
- Policy implementation
- Policy evaluation

Techniques of Control: How Government Manipulates Behavior

Promotional Techniques: Rewarding Behavior

Subsidies are government grants of cash or other valuable commodities, such as land to individuals or organizations, to promote activities. Hamilton promoted the use of subsidies to encourage manufacturing. Land grants were used to promote expansion into the Western United States and the development of state colleges. Using a crop subsidy to a farmer is a technique of promoting crop production or a shift to new crops. The recipients of subsidies can include corporations and farms.

Contracting can be used to encourage development. The government can encourage or require certain activities by purchasing goods and services from the private sector. Government contracts also support research and development.

Privatization occurs when an activity is contracted out to a private business under government supervision.

Licensing is a privilege granted by the government to engage in an activity that would otherwise be illegal. State laws require licensing for practicing medicine, law, or driving. Licensing can be both promotional and regulatory.

Regulatory Techniques: Punishing Behavior

Police Regulation

Police powers are generally reserved to the states as they are permitted to regulate health, safety, welfare, and morality. Civil penalties are regulatory techniques in which fines or other forms of material restitution are imposed for violating civil laws or common law principles, such as negligence. Criminal penalties are regulatory techniques in which imprisonment or heavy fines and the loss of certain civil rights and liberties are imposed.

Administrative Regulation

Administrative regulations are rules made by regulatory agencies and commissions. This includes environmental, communications, and workplace safety. Examples include the EPA, FCC, and OSHA.

Regulatory Taxation

Sin taxes are heavy taxes on certain activities to discourage participation by increasing the cost and decreasing demand. Sin taxes can be found on alcohol and cigarettes. There has also been a proposed sin tax on fast food as a way of discouraging consumption of fatty foods and subsidizing future health care costs.

Expropriation of property is the confiscation of property with or without compensation. Eminent domain involves confiscation based on public use and just compensation. Seizure of property used in commission of a crime is one example. Expropriation of labor is yet another example.

Economic Policy

In *The Wealth of Nations* (1776), Adam Smith argued that the government should maintain a limited role in the economy. This has led to a debate over the past 200 years as to what the government should do with regard to promoting, regulating, or stabilizing the economy.

Generally, the government is expected to achieve two objectives: 1) maintain order and protect the rights of individuals to allow them to achieve economic growth; and 2) stabilize the economy, lower unemployment, and protect those who are unable to prosper. Historically, Americans have been unsure as to which level of government should be responsible for promoting, regulating, or stabilizing the economy.

Defining Economic Problems

First, the state of the economy must be determined before a policy is adopted. One measure of the economy is Gross Domestic Product (GDP), which is the market value of all final goods and services within a nation's borders in a given period. GDP is used to determine economic growth, which is an increase in output (real GDP). Real GDP is the value of final output produced in a given period, adjusted for changing prices. The U.S. economy has grown at about 3% (real GDP) since 1900 while the population has increased by only 1%. A higher per capita GDP results in a higher living standard for all Americans.

The business cycle is the fluctuation between expansion and recession that is a part of modern capitalist economies. The business cycle is a measurement of the real GDP. Although we have seen an overall increase in growth it has really been a series of peaks and valleys that make up the business cycle. Inflation is the rise in the general level of prices as measured by the Consumer Price Index (CPI). CPI is a statistical measure of a weighted average of a specific list of goods and services purchased by consumers. Hyperinflation is an inflation rate in excess of 200% lasting more than one year.

Stagflation is the occurrence of inflation and rising unemployment. A recession is a decline in real GDP and is evidenced by declines in investments, a decline in production, and an increase in unemployment. A trade deficit is the amount by which the value of imports exceeds the value of exports. Some view the trade imbalance as a positive by keeping prices low and thereby avoiding inflationary pressures. The trade deficit may also reflect declining production in the U.S. and eventually an increase in unemployment. Unemployment is the inability of the labor force participants to find work. The unemployment rate measures the percentage in individuals out of work who are looking for work. The unemployment rate may be the most important economic measure for politicians. Americans tend to vote their pocketbook and blame the president for downturns in the economy and rising unemployment. Full employment is achieved when unemployment drops to 3%. Fiscal policy is the use of taxing and spending to promote a nation's macroeconomic goals of full employment, price stability, and economic growth. Monetary policy is the use of the money supply to promote a nation's macroeconomic goals of full employment, price stability, and economic growth.

U.S. Economic Policy: The Tools of Fiscal and Monetary Policy

Generating Revenue

Taxation is the primary source of revenue for any government. All taxes discriminate, and the policy question is how should the government raise revenue with the desired discrimination?

Types of taxes

Tariffs are taxes on imported goods and were the most important tax of the 1800s and are still used today to generate revenue and control imports. U.S. steel producers supported a 40% tariff in 2002 on steel to protect U.S. markets. Bush imposed 8% to 30% tariffs on steel products but was met with international opposition to U.S. goods. The tariffs were subsequently dropped after the World Trade Organization found them in violation of trade agreements. The European Union threats to impose tariffs on U.S. goods were also dropped.

The value of imported goods and tariffs

Excise taxes are indirect taxes or duties on items within the United States to generate revenue and also to serve as sin taxes to control behavior/consumption. The fuel tax is an example, with the federal excise tax of 18.4¢ per gallon and the Texas excise tax of 20¢ per gallon.

Sales taxes are levied on consumers at point of sale. The sales tax in Texas is 6.25%. Most cities add a local sales tax rate of 2.0%. An example is Friendswood's local rate of 1.5%.

Value-added tax taxes every increase in value along the production line. Property taxes are levied on the value of real property. Property taxes are used primarily at the local level.

Federal Open Markets Committee (FOMC)

Members include the seven members of the Board of Governors and five of the presidents of the Federal Reserve Banks. It is responsible for adopting monetary policy that will promote economic growth, full employment, stable prices, and a sustainable level of international trade and payments. The FOMC makes key decisions regarding the sale and purchase of government securities. The FOMC also recommends changes in the Federal Funds Rate.

Federal Reserve Banks

Twelve Regional Banks and Twenty-Five Districts

1. Boston
2. New York
3. Philadelphia
4. Richmond
5. Cleveland
6. Atlanta
7. Chicago
8. St. Louis
9. Minneapolis
10. Kansas City
11. Dallas
12. San Francisco

Services of Federal Reserve Banks

Depository for payments to the federal government such as unemployment taxes, income taxes, corporate taxes, and certain excise taxes. They serve as a depository for required reserves, making loans to member banks, and a clearinghouse for checks, supply the economy with currency and coins, issue and redeem government securities, and supervise member banks and state-chartered banks.

Directors of the Federal Reserve Banks meet every two weeks to establish the discount rate, subject to approval by the Board of Governors.

Controlling the Money Supply—Tools of the Fed

The discount rate is the interest rate the Fed charges member banks to borrow money. In a recession, the Fed would lower the discount rate to encourage member banks to borrow money and make short-term loans at a lower rate thereby increasing the money supply. During periods of high inflation, the Fed will increase the discount rate to slow borrowing from the member banks resulting in fewer loans being made and thereby decreasing the money supply. The Federal Funds Rate is the interest rate on overnight loans to member banks required to meet reserve requirements, and changes are usually reflected in the prime interest rate. Buying and selling of government securities is called open market operations. The purchase of long-term bonds from the Fed by member banks reduces the money supply. The sale of long-term bonds to the Fed by member banks increases the money supply. Reserve requirements are the amount of liquid assets and ready cash that banks are required to hold to meet depositors' demands for their money. An increase in the reserve requirement decreases the money supply. Decreasing the reserve requirement increases the money supply.

Economic Theories on the Role of Government in the Economy

Classical Economics and Say's Law, 1789–1932

During the 1700s, the Physiocrats urged government to adopt a "laissez-faire" approach to the economy. It was believed that the government that governs best is the government that governs least. Physiocrats believed that the government should have a minimal role in trade. Adam Smith, who tutored in France, was heavily influenced by the principles of laissez-faire economics, resulting in his publication of *The Wealth of Nations*. This philosophy became the foundation for free-market capitalism, which holds that the government should avoid competing with the private sector for goods and services for fear of destabilizing the economy. For example, inflation may result from too many dollars chasing too few goods. Inflation is a consistent increase in the general level of prices and is a problem every administration since Washington has faced. In the early days of the Republic, the national government promoted rather than regulated the economy. A free-market economy will naturally develop inflationary and recessionary periods, but it was believed that the economy would self-correct given the guidance of Smith's "invisible hand." In fact, the economy rebounded from inflationary and recessionary periods as part of the normal business cycle from 1789 to 1929. Many believed that this was a product of Say's Law that holds that supply creates demand. However, in October 1929, the stock market crashed and the U.S. entered the Great Depression.

The Depression, the New Deal and Keynesian Economics, 1932–1980

Unlike previous recessions/depressions, the economy did not bounce back from the downturn of the late 1920s. Unemployment continued to rise as businesses failed.

Unemployment Rates during the Great Depression

- 15.9% in 1931
- 23.6% in 1932
- 24.9% in 1933
- 21.7% in 1934
- 20.1% in 1935
- 16.9% in 1936
- 14.7% in 1937
- 19.0% in 1938
- 17.2% in 1939
- 14.6% in 1940

The Great Depression had many questioning the traditional role of the government with regard to the economy as the states were unable to deal with rising unemployment and poverty. John

Maynard Keynes, in *The General Theory of Employment, Interest and Money,* argued that deficit spending could be used to stimulate the economy. Government expenditures would be used to fund programs that would create jobs thereby creating the demand needed to revitalize the business sector. Contrary to Say's Law, demand drives supply. Once the economy has rebounded, the debt incurred from deficit financing could be paid with the new revenue generated from a robust economy. President Roosevelt's New Deal programs took the role of the government to new levels in the depression as advocated by Keynes. However, it is doubtful that the New Deal led to an economic recovery. It is generally accepted that WWII led the United States out of the depression as unemployment dropped to a low of 1.2% in 1944.

- 9.9% in 1941
- 4.7% in 1942
- 1.9% in 1943
- 1.2% in 1944
- 1.9% in 1945
- 3.9% in 1946
- 3.9% in 1947

Regardless, Keynesian economic theory would be utilized for the next forty years as Congress became accustomed to deficit spending.

Stagflation and Supply-side Economics, 1980–1988

During the 1970s, the American economy experienced rising inflation and rising unemployment contrary to the Phillips Curve. The Phillips Curve suggests that stagflation, which is rising inflation and rising unemployment, is impossible in that inflation and unemployment are in an inverse relationship. Stagflation was possibly a result of a sudden rise in the price of oil that created a massive shock to the economy resulting in businesses raising prices and laying off employees to maintain profits. Nixon and Congress implemented wage and price controls that failed to stabilize the economy. Carter asked Americans to turn down their thermostats and devised the Misery Index (Inflation + Unemployment = Misery) and told the nation it was in a "state of malaise."

Ronald Reagan Returns the U.S. to Supply-Side Economics

Ronald Reagan adopted a supply-side approach to the economy when he argued that the economic problems facing the nation were caused by excessive government spending, high taxes, and government regulation. The Laffer Curve suggests that the government can tax up to a certain level before tax revenues begin to drop. Reagan and his economists believed that these factors deterred production in the private sector and reforms were needed to promote the supply-side of the economy. The Kemp-Roth Tax of 1981 was passed to stimulate the economy by reducing the tax burden on Americans with the hope of spurring investment. Reagan's attempt to cut federal spending was met with opposition by the Democrats who would not increase defense spending without increases in social spending. Deregulation was stalled by the federal agencies. Paul Volcker and the Federal Reserve Board tightened the money supply by raising interest rates. The economy was thrown into a recession, thereby reconciling an economic downturn with unemployment.

The Inflation Rate in:

- 1980 was 12.5%
- 1981 was 8.9%
- 1983 was 3.8%
- 1984 was 3.8%
- 1985 was 3.8%
- 1986 was 1.1%
- 1987 was 4.4%

The Fed slowly eased the money supply and a recovery was in place by 1984, thus allowing Reagan to win reelection carrying all the states with the exception of Minnesota.

SOCIAL WELFARE POLICY

American Political Culture and Social Policy: Liberty versus Equality

Liberty and equality are the basic values of American political culture that guide us in our policy approach to success and failure, wealth and poverty. Americans strongly support the notion of political and economic liberty that makes America the land of opportunity. Americans also believe that all Americans should be given an equal opportunity to succeed. As a society, we provide K–12 education to all Americans through our public school systems. Equal Employment Opportunity laws require employers to provide all Americans equal access to employment. Thomas Jefferson writes in the Declaration of Independence that "all men are created equal," which seems to suggest that given an opportunity everyone could and should succeed. The question is whether simply providing equality of opportunity is enough to guarantee success. We must ask ourselves, are we are truly equal with another? And if not, at what expense to liberty must we go to achieve equality?

Are We Created Equal?

In looking at why people succeed or fail we can draw two different conclusions. Conservatives/Republicans argue that economic failure is a function of individual responsibility or irresponsibility. Liberals/Democrats view economic failure as a product of societal factors. We know that individuals are not equal because of individual differences, and these differences produce different economic outcomes.

- Intelligence
- Knowledge
- Skills
- Talents
- Ambition

But there are also societal inequalities that prevent economic success.

- Inequities of class
- Inequities of educational opportunities
- Prejudice and discrimination

So we are now back to the basic question, is economic success or failure a function of individual responsibility or societal failure?

Poverty in America

Poverty was first defined using a calculation developed by Mollie Orshansky of the Social Security Administration. Orshansky used an "economy food plan" developed by the U.S. Department of Agriculture. In 1955, families spent approximately one-third of their after-tax income on food. In other words, consider the average cost of living and take thirty percent of their income for food. By multiplying the "economy food plan" by a multiplier of three for a family of three the poverty threshold was created. The poverty threshold is now adjusted annually by the Consumer Price Index (CPI).

The Census Bureau defines poverty by the poverty threshold, which is the annual cash income that falls below what is required to maintain a decent standard of living.

- A family of three (Mother and two children) is $17,568
- A family of four (Mother and three children) is $22,190

The Department of Health and Human Services poverty threshold:

- A family of three $19,090
- A family of four $23,050

How Many Americans are Considered Poor?

- The poverty rate for 2010 was 15.3%
- The total number is 46,215,956

Poverty Conditions in 2010[1]

- The official poverty rate in 2010 was 15.1%—up from 14.3% in 2009. This was the third consecutive annual increase in the poverty rate. Since 2007, the poverty rate has increased by 2.6 percentage points, from 12.5% to 15.1%.
- In 2010, 46.2 million people were in poverty, up from 43.6 million in 2009—the fourth consecutive annual increase in the number of people in poverty.
- Between 2009 and 2010, the poverty rate increased for non-Hispanic Whites (from 9.4% to 9.9%), for African Americans (from 25.8% to 27.4%), and for Hispanics (from 25.3% to 26.6%). For Asians, the 2010 poverty rate (12.1%) was not statistically different from the 2009 poverty rate.

- The poverty rate in 2010 (15.1%) was the highest poverty rate since 1993 but was 7.3 percentage points lower than the poverty rate in 1959, the first year for which poverty estimates are available.
- The number of people in poverty in 2010 (46.2 million) is the largest number in the 52 years for which poverty estimates have been published.
- Between 2009 and 2010, the poverty rate increased for children under age 18 (from 20.7% to 22.0%) and people aged 18 to 64 (from 12.9% to 13.7%), but was not statistically different for people aged 65 and older (9.0%).

WHO ARE THE POOR?

Socioeconomic Characteristics of the Poor (2003):

- 8.2% (15.9 million) non-Hispanic Whites below the poverty level
- 24.4% (8.7 million) African Americans below the poverty level
- 22.5% (9 million) Hispanics below the poverty level
- 30.0% (12.4 million) of Female Headed Households (FHH)
- 21.1% for White FHH
- 37.4% for Black FHH
- 38.4% for Hispanic FHH

Income and Employment Differences:

- Median Household Income for 2000 was $42,148
- $45,904 for Whites
- $30,449 for Blacks
- $33,447 for Hispanics

Per-Capita Income for 2000 was $22,199

- $23,415 for Whites
- $15,197 for Blacks
- $12,306 for Hispanics

Unemployment Rates for Teens

The unemployment rate for teens rose to 24.5% in June of 2011, up from 24.2% in May.

- 16.4% for Whites
- 37.0% for Blacks
- 30.4% for Hispanics

Recipients of Temporary Assistance to Needy Families

Family Size

- The average family size is 2.8
- Two out of 5 families had only 1 child
- Only 1 in 10 have more than 3 children

Education

- 43.5% had not completed high school
- 37.9% completed high school
- 18.6% completed 1 or more years of college

Age

- 28.2% were 15–24 years of age
- 47.5% were 25–34 years of age
- 24.3% were 35+ years of age

Urban versus Rural

- 81% Metropolitan
- 19% Non-metropolitan

Marital Status

- 48% never married
- 23% widowed or divorced
- 17% married husband absent
- 13% married husband present

Criticisms of the Definition of Poverty

Liberal critics of the definition claim that poverty is underestimated. The near poor are excluded from the definition of poverty. This does not take into account regional differences in cost of living and does not take into consideration what people need to live on. Conservative critics counter that poverty is overestimated. The definition does not consider the value of family assets. Many counted as poor do not consider themselves poor. Cash income is unreported.

Temporary vs. Persistent Poverty, Temporary Poverty

The poor are generally envisioned as a permanent "underclass" living most of their lives in poverty.

Median Duration of Poverty

- 51.3% of poverty spells ended within 4 months
- 80.3% of poverty spells ended within 12 months
- 88.6% of poverty spells ended within 20 months
- 11.4% of poverty spells extend more than 20 months
- 37.5% of African Americans live in poverty 3 years or more
- 5% of Hispanics live in poverty 3 years or more

Individuals Living in Poverty by Number of Years (1982–1991)

- 0 years 78.8%
- 1–2 years 11.3%
- 3–5 years 5.3%
- 6–8 years 2.8%
- 9–10 years 1.8%

Going on Welfare[2]

- 42.1% married women become FHH
- 38.8% unmarried women became FHH
- 7.1% FHH had earnings fall
- 11.0% other income factors

Getting off Welfare

- 29.4% FHH got married
- 25.0% FHH saw earnings improve
- 12.1% saw transfer payments increase
- 10.8% no longer had eligible child
- 6.7% had a family earnings increase

Persistent Poverty

Neighborhoods are considered in a state of persistent poverty if at least 20% of the population lives in poverty for three decades. Neighborhoods marked by persistent poverty experience a higher degree of social problems, such as:

- Teen pregnancy
- Family instability
- Drugs and alcohol abuse
- Crime rates
- Alienation, apathy, and irresponsibility

Poverty spells exceeding four years correlates to a 90% probability that the family will remain poor for the rest of their lives. The homeless population is estimated between 500,000 and 600,000 at any one time or 3.5 million individuals in a given year.

Profile of the homeless

Age:

- 25% of the urban homeless are children under 18
- 3% of those under 18 were unaccompanied minors
- 51% are between ages 31 and 50

Gender:

- 45% of the urban homeless are single males
- 14% of the urban homeless are single women

Families:

- 40% of the homeless are families with children
- 2% of the homeless are victims of domestic violence

Ethnicity:

- 49% are African American
- 32% White
- 12% Hispanic

Military status:

- 22–40% are veterans
- 76% of homeless vets have substantial substance abuse and/or mental health problems
- 47% of homeless vets served during Vietnam
- 17% of homeless vets served after Vietnam

Mental Illness and Drug/Alcohol Addiction

- 65% of the homeless are drug or alcohol dependent
- 20–25% suffer from persistent mental illness

Poverty, Government, and the Welfare State

Early Social Programs in the United States

Until the early 1900s, welfare programs were operated by private, non-profit charitable organizations. Programs varied from community to community. Social policy in the United States was largely modeled on Great Britain with the use of workhouses. There were 7000 children in workhouses in the U.S. in 1880. Conditions were harsh to discourage idleness. Counties provided some outdoor relief programs, and work was required for the poor who were capable of working. Programs were underfunded by property taxes. County officials decided who would go to the workhouse or orphanage and who would receive aid at home. Officials discriminated against the poor and denied benefits to those viewed as "unfit" because of race, nationality, or religion. State governments created workers' compensation programs and unemployment programs between 1900 and 1932. Maryland enacted the first workers' comp program in 1902. Texas enacted its first workers' comp in 1913. Wisconsin enacted the first unemployment program in 1932. Aid to Mothers with Dependent Children or Mothers Pensions was implemented between 1911 and 1926. Illinois was the first to create a program to aid mothers and children in 1911, and forty-six states followed by 1926. Mothers were excused from working outside the home as it was viewed as beneficial to society to have children raised by their mothers as a means of avoiding juvenile delinquency. A mother generally had to prove that she was fit and qualified (i.e., children were legitimate) to receive benefits. The program benefitted widowed white females. Women who were divorced or deserted, the unmarried, and minorities were viewed as "unfit" and denied benefits. Aid to the elderly poor existed in thirty states prior to the Great Depression, as it was believed that individuals had a responsibility to save for old age.

The Development of the American Welfare State (1935–1968)

The Great Depression

Business cycles were accepted as part of a free economy, and poverty was believed to be a product of individual irresponsibility. The Great Depression was the longest and deepest downturn in U.S. history. Significant economic misfortune was widespread with an excess of 20% of the workforce unemployed in the first years of the Great Depression. Unemployment was 25% in 1932, with millions more underemployed. Nothing seemed to turn the economy around as businesses continued layoffs to cut costs, which reduced demand and caused further cuts. The Great Depression essentially destroyed private and state social programs as the demand for relief overwhelmed funding levels. Policymakers now realized that poverty was a result of economic conditions and not necessarily a function of "mental fitness."

The New Deal, World War II, and the 1950s

The 1930s and the New Deal

The early New Deal programs attempted to boost prices and lower unemployment. The second round of New Deal programs were aimed at helping individuals. The U.S. Supreme Court held the programs as unconstitutional. Roosevelt proposed increasing the size of the Supreme Court from nine to fourteen and packing it with pro-New Deal justices. The Supreme Court, in response to the threat and public mood, began to broaden their view of government powers in upholding the second phase of the New Deal programs as constitutional. The American "Welfare State" began with the Social Security Act of 1935 and Aid to Dependent Children. Unemployment remained at 17% in 1939, despite the implementation of the New Deal programs.

World War II

WWII provided the necessary economic surge to put the country back to work. War production maximized employment and production. Unemployment reached a low of 1.2% during the war.

The post-war period: 1946–1959.

The U.S. began to experience economic growth in the post-war period. The GI Bill provided an opportunity for many returning GI's to attend college and increase their earning capacity. The U.S. also experienced a "baby boom" from 1946 to 1964. Families moved to suburban communities, bought cars, televisions, and washers and dryers. Post-war prosperity throughout the 1950s hid poverty evident in the country's darker corners.

The New Frontier and the Great Society

President Kennedy was elected in 1960 on an idealistic platform of social improvement that he referred to as the New Frontier. However, the election was close and Kennedy and his staff were aware of the nature of politics and limits of economy. Accordingly, the Kennedy Administration was restrained in taking broad steps to promote equality. Kennedy's assassination on November 22, 1963, cut short Kennedy's New Frontier but gave momentum to social reform for his successor Lyndon B. Johnson. Johnson was a social reformer and his Great Society programs were designed to promote equality and eliminate poverty. They included:

- Civil Rights Legislation
- Civil Rights Act of 1964
- Voting Rights Act of 1965

Johnson's War on Poverty

The war on poverty was to eradicate poverty in ten years by providing "a hand up not a hand out." The Economic Opportunity Act (1964) included *Head Start* and *Jobs Corp.* The Social Security Act of 1965 created Medicare and Medicaid. The War on Poverty sputtered as funding was diverted to America's other war—Vietnam. Stagflation of the 1970s prevented Nixon, Ford, or Carter from addressing the need so America's poor had high inflation rates, and unemployment contributed to the "misery" of all Americans.

Ronald Reagan and the War on Welfare

Ronald Reagan challenged welfare as we know it. Reagan, building on the myth of the "welfare queen," was elected on a platform of conservative change and the public was ready. Nothing really changed as he was met with opposition from Democrats. Reagan did set the stage for welfare reform in the 1990s.

The Contract with America

In 1994, Republicans pushed for welfare reform. The Contract with America promised to change the welfare system. With majority control of the House and Senate, Republicans proposed significant cuts in social programs. Clinton refused to go along with the cuts, which forced a showdown with congressional Republicans. Democrats possessed the high ground, and the public opposed the Republican cuts. Clinton also ran under the promise of changing the welfare system. The Contract with America put pressure on Clinton to live up to his promise. Clinton vetoed the first two proposals, but signed the third thereby abolishing Aid to Families with Dependent Children (AFDC) and creating Temporary Assistance to Needy Families (TANF).

The 1996 Welfare Reform Act: TANF

- Provides block grants to the states to run their own programs
- Recipients must work within two years of receiving assistance

- Recipients have a five-year limit on benefits
- $1 billion for performance bonuses to state agencies for moving recipients to jobs and reducing out-of-wedlock births and abortions

A Look at Social Programs

The Federal Government, Redistribution of Income, and the Federal Budget

Tax revenues are used to redistribute income from one sector of society to another through transfer payments or goods and services. Direct payments to individuals (i.e., Social Security, TANF, and VA pensions) make up 45% of all federal government outlays. Between 50% and 60% of the federal budget is spent on social programs when non-cash benefits are included (Medicaid, Medicare, Food Stamps). That would be $1.1 trillion out of a $2.2 trillion budget.

Definitions

Contributory programs are financed by a direct tax to fund future payments to the taxpayer Social Security (1935)

- Unemployment Compensation (1935)
- Medicare (1965)

Non-contributory programs do not require beneficiaries to make contributions to receive benefits (funded through federal budget)

- AFDC (1935) was replaced with TANF (1996)
- Housing Assistance (1937)
- School Lunch Programs (1946)
- Food Stamps (1964)
- Medicaid (1965)
- SSI (1974)

Means-tested programs require proof of financial eligibility. *COLA* is a cost of living adjustment tied to the inflation rate.

Overview of the Programs

Programs for the Elderly

Social Security (1935)

Social Security is the largest spending program in federal budget. It is funded by 15.30% payroll tax on employees and employers with 96% of the paid work force covered. Benefits are indexed to rise with inflation (COLA). Social Security is a "pay as you go" system, which means that current employees are paying the benefits for current recipients.

The Boomer Problem

The Baby Boom (1946–1964) produced 76 million Boomers that are now moving through the political and economic system. This represents 25% of the total population. Boomers began to retire in 2011. Between 2011 and 2029, the over-65 population of the U.S. will double. The Gen X (46 million born 1964–1976) population that follows is 35% smaller and whose peak earning period will not generate sufficient income to support the Boomers. Gen Y (60 million born 1977–1993) is a product of the Boomers and is closer in size to the Boomers, but will not reach peak earning years until after 2029.

Ratio of workers to recipients is declining:

- 1950—16 to 1
- 2003—3 to 1
- 2011—2 to 1

Life expectancy has risen:

- 61.7 in 1935
- 69.7 in 1960
- 73.7 in 1980
- 77.0 in 2000
- 78.7 in 2010

Early payments were low compared to paid benefits. Contributions were capped at $60/year at the inception of the program. The tax rate was under 5% as late as 1977. In 1977, the average annual salary was $10,000 and in 2000 the average annual salary was $32,000. The average benefit level in 2001 was $894. It is estimated that current recipients exhaust their own contributions within four years of entering Social Security.

The result is that there will not be enough funds generated to cover the benefits paid to retirees.

- In 2017, the deficit will near $80 billion
- In 2030, the deficit will reach $275 billion
- In 2040, the deficit will be $429 billion.

A number of possible reforms have been suggested:

- Increase the tax rate
- Raise the retirement age
- Apply means-testing

Medicare

Medicare provides healthcare for the elderly and those with disabilities. The AMA opposed governmental attempts for a national healthcare plan fearing socialized medicine. Medicare was a compromise reached in 1965. Medicare consists of four parts:

- Part A provides for hospital care and is paid for through a direct tax on wages
- Part B provides for physician care and is paid in part by a premium
- Part C is a private Medicare HMO plan
- Part D is a prescription drug plan (2006)

Medicare costs are rising at 10.5% per year, but the tax contribution is 2.9% on employer and employee. About 1% of recipients have two or more chronic conditions. About 10% of recipients account for 69% of expenditures. Congress is considering a number of reforms to Medicare. Raising the tax to 6.42%, would greatly reduce disposable income and result in a recession. As far as implementing private sector approaches to Medicare, there is managed healthcare (HMOs), medical savings accounts, and flexible spending and cafeteria plans.

Supplemental Security Income (SSI, 1974)

SSI is an income assistance program that provides monthly cash payments to the needy elderly, blind, or disabled. It is funded through federal income tax and is means tested (resources below $2000). The benefits are indexed to rise with inflation (COLA).

Programs for Workers

Unemployment Compensation (1935)

Unemployment compensation is a Department of Labor program to temporarily replace part of the wages of workers who lose their jobs involuntarily. States administer their own programs subject to federal guidelines. Benefits are funded by federal and state unemployment taxes on employers based on their unemployment history. The Federal rate is .8% on the first $7000 paid by an employer to each employee. The Texas rate for new employers is 2.7% on the first $9000 to each employee. The Texas average rate is 1.74% on the first $9000 to each employee. Recipients must meet certain requirements:

- Employed for a specified amount of time and meet earnings requirements
- Unemployed due to a reduction in force or layoffs
- Eligible and looking for work

There are certain disqualifications:

- If unable to work
- If left work voluntarily without good cause
- If the employee is terminated for cause

Texas benefit levels:

- $330 per week for 26 weeks maximum benefit
- $261 per week for 17 weeks average benefit
- $4,249 average annual benefit

Social Security Disability Insurance (1956)

This program provides monthly cash benefits to disabled workers and their dependents. A twenty-year-old worker has a 3 in 10 chance of becoming disabled during his or her lifetime. Employees must meet eligibility requirements, such as having worked on a job covered by Social Security and having a medical condition that meets the Social Security definition of a disability.

A thirty-five-year-old employee earning $30,000 a year would receive a monthly disability benefit of $1000 with a maximum family benefit of $1800 per month and also be eligible for Medicare.

Programs for the Poor

Aid to Families with Dependent Children (AFDC, 1935) was created by the Social Security Act of 1935. It was designed to assist needy children with cash payments. It is a means-tested program operated by states that define need and set their own benefit levels and establish income and resource limits (within federal guidelines).

Temporary Assistance to Needy Families (TANF, 1996)

The goal of TANF is to reduce the number of individuals on welfare. The number of recipients dropped 20% within the first year of the law. In Texas, the number of recipients dropped 28%. In Louisiana, the number of recipients dropped 44%. Families moving from AFDC to TANF declined. The Texas caseload dropped 55% from 1993 to 1998. The national caseload dropped 42% from 1993 to 1998.

TANF in Texas (Family of Three):

- Means-tested
- Earnings limit of $4,812
- Asset limit of $2,000
- Must be in work/education program within two years
- $208 maximum monthly benefit and $2,496 year
- Sixty-month maximum duration
- New spouse income disregarded for first six months
- Texas spent an average of $1,560 per family (2002)

Food Stamps (1964)

Food stamps provide low-income households with coupons (in Texas, they receive the Lone Star Card) with which they can purchase enough food to provide a minimal, nutritious diet. States operate under federal guidelines based on U.S. Dept of Agriculture's Thrifty Food Plan. It is means-tested at the 130% of poverty line level. They generally exclude purchase of alcohol, tobacco, prepared foods, drugs or other controlled substances.

Food Stamps in Texas (Family of Three) Means Test:

- Liquid assets of less than $5000
- Monthly income less than $1,698
- Maximum monthly benefits for family of three is $393
- Maximum annual benefits for family of three is $4,716
- Average monthly benefit of $222.40 (2004)

Medicaid (1965) and CHIPs (1997)

Medicaid is a joint federal-state program under the Social Security Act that provides healthcare to low-income Americans. Feds pay about 60% while the states pay 40%.

Medicaid in Texas

- Average annual cost per recipient in Texas is $3,767 (2002)
- Income limit of $20,841 with children 1 to 5

About 59% of recipients are non-disabled children, and they account for 25% of the cost ($1,604 per capita). About 9% of recipients are over 65, but they account for 25% of the cost ($10,887 per capita). Then 11% of recipients are disabled and blind and they account for 36% of the cost ($12,344 per capita).

Children's Health Insurance Program (CHIP)

CHIP is a national plan that provides low-cost insurance to families that do not qualify for Medicaid, but cannot afford health insurance. The income limit is $2,682 for a family of three.

Women, Infants, and Children (WIC, 1974)

WIC provides food assistance and nutritional screening to low-income and postpartum women and their infants and children to age five. WIC provides food items and vouchers for milk, eggs, cheese, infant formula, cereal, and juices. The cutoff is at 185% of poverty level. WIC serves 47% of all infants born in the U.S. WIC serves 93% of all those eligible for benefits.

> WIC in Texas:
> Income limit of $2,416 per month
> Average monthly benefit of $37.54 per participant
> Federal Earned Income Tax Credit
> Reduces the taxes that low- to moderate-income working families are required to pay
> Where income tax is not owed provides a rebate

National School Lunch Program (1946)

The National School Lunch Act of 1946 provides nutritionally balanced, low-cost or free meals to children in public and private schools. Participating school districts receive cash subsidies and donated commodities from the U.S. Department of Agriculture for each meal they serve.

Eligibility requirements:

- Free lunch at 130% of poverty level
- Reduced lunch (<40 cents) at 185% of poverty level

Housing Programs

The public housing and the development of the "projects"

The Techwood Homes in Atlanta was the first housing project in the U.S. It was built in 1936 to eliminate slums. It was once the most violent neighborhood in Georgia. It was demolished for the 1996 Olympics. Queensbridge is the largest housing project in the U.S. with 3,142 units and is owned by the New York Housing Authority. Section 8 vouchers are replacing public housing. A family pays up to 30% of rent and utilities and the voucher covers the remainder. Most applicants are put on a waiting list. The landlord must be willing to accept the voucher.

Head Start

Head Start was created in 1965 to provide comprehensive early childhood development to low-income children with the goal of improving school readiness. The purpose of Head Start is to teach children and their parents habits that will permit them to be successful throughout their lives. Head Start coordinates activities with WIC and Medicaid to promote the physical and mental health of preschoolers.

Job Training

Most of the programs are administered by the Department of Labor, Department of Education, or Department of Health and Human Services.

- Jobs Corp (DOL)
- Dislocated Workers Program (DOL)
- Community-Based Job Training Grants (DOL)
- Workforce Investment Act (DOL)
- Carl Perkins Vocational Training (DOEd)
- Job Opportunities and Basic Skills (HHS)
- College Education Assistance
- Pell Grants
- Guaranteed student loans
- Work-study programs

FOREIGN POLICY

Who Makes Foreign Policy?

Inside the Government

The president has significant foreign policy power. He serves as head of state, has diplomatic powers, and is the Commander in Chief. He negotiates treaties and executive agreements.

The Bureaucracy
Department of State
Department of Defense
Department of Homeland Security
Department of Commerce
Director of National Intelligence
National Security Council

Joint Chiefs of Staff
Congress

The Senate has the power of advice and consent on treaties. Congress also has the "power of the purse" and thereby controls the budget of the executive branch departments. Congressional standing and select committees monitor execution of foreign policy. Congress has the power to declare war, although a war has not been declared since 1941, and the War Powers Act.

Outside the Government

Interest groups provide support as well as opposition to foreign policies adopted by the president. Amnesty International monitors human rights violations. Jewish-American groups support Israel. Business groups promote U.S. economic interests. Greenpeace challenges world environmental policies.

The media shapes public policy through news coverage of events, visual images, and news angles. Public opinion drives policymakers to adopt or alter policies. American public opinion went from isolationism to war after the attack at Pearl Harbor on December 7, 1941. A change in public opinion after 1968 brought about the end of the Vietnam War. The impact of public opinion on the War on Terrorism and the War in Iraq has yet to be determined.

What Shapes Foreign Policy? The Two Policy Paradigms

The Munich Paradigm

The Munich Paradigm attempts to avoid mistakes made prior to WWII that allowed Hitler to control Europe early. Hitler invaded Sudetenland in 1938. Chamberlain and Hitler signed Munich Pact September 1938. Hitler followed with the occupation of Czechoslovakia and Poland in September 1939. Britain declared war September 1939. Over 52 million deaths occurred during WWII. The Soviet expansion was viewed as similar to German expansion. The Soviet's ceded control of Eastern Europe at Yalta in 1945. Churchill gave his "Iron Curtain" speech in March 1946. The Communists expanded into Greece and Turkey in 1947. The Truman Doctrine called for U.S. economic and military aid to countries fighting against communist revolutions. George F. Kennan introduced "containment" with the goal of promoting order by containing communist expansion through strong military establishment. The Berlin Blockade occurred in 1948. The Soviet Union exploded the first A-bomb July 14, 1949. The Communists expanded into Korea in 1950 and expanded into Vietnam in 1956.

The Vietnam Paradigm

This paradigm seeks to avoid mistakes made in entering the Vietnam quagmire. It was founded on the belief that turmoil in underdeveloped countries is not caused by communist expansion, but by internal poverty, nationalism, and anti-colonialism. It rejects military solutions and prefers diplomacy, detente, disarmament and arms control, and developmental aid.

Roles Nations Plays

The Napoleonic Role promotes the expansion of democracy to ensure national security even if force is required.

The Holy Alliance Role attempts to ensure the stability of existing political regimes against any uprising.

The Balance of Power Role is an effort to play the major powers against each other.

The Economic Expansionist Role attempts to promote capitalism to benefit the success of domestic corporations.

The Values in American Foreign Policy

The Goal of National Security

International politics is a struggle for power. Struggle involves all the nations and peoples of the world. Foreign policy goal is to protect and preserve national interests, including but not limited to national security.

ISOLATIONISM VERSUS GLOBALISM

George Washington warned of involvement in European affairs in his Farewell Address of 1796 suggesting a policy of isolationism. Isolationism is a national policy of avoiding participation in foreign affairs. Unilateralism is a national policy of acting without consulting others. The U.S. continued to engage in international economic trade because the U.S. needed foreign trade. There was undeclared war with France in the 1790s following seizure of U.S. ships trading with France's enemies. Barbary Wars in the 1790s followed seizure of U.S. ships and seaman by North African Barbary states. The War of 1812 with Britain had its origin in the impressments of merchant sailors and the Embargo Act of 1807. In 1823, President Monroe staked out U.S. interests with the Monroe Doctrine that declared the Americas off-limits to European involvement. Manifest Destiny defined foreign policy over the next 100 years as the U.S. expanded its sphere of influence throughout the Americas, the Caribbean, and the Pacific.

- Louisiana Purchase in 1803
- Indian Wars from 1776–1890
- Mexican War from 1846–1848
- Spanish American War in 1898
- Cuba
- Puerto Rico
- Guam
- Philippines
- Hawaii in 1893

Teddy Roosevelt's Roosevelt Corollary argued that it was the responsibility of the U.S. to insure the stability of Latin America. This included:

- Panama Canal Zone
- Cuba
- Dominican Republic
- Haiti
- Nicaragua

By 1914, U.S. influence extended from the Caribbean to the Pacific Rim.

THE BALANCE OF POWER SYSTEM AND WORLD WAR I

The balance of power model creates a system of alliances among nations so that the relative strength of each alliance balances that of the others. The model worked from the end of the Napoleonic War (1815) until the outbreak of World War I (1914).

World War I

- June 28, 1914—Archduke Franz Ferdinand, heir to the throne of the Austro-Hungarian Empire, is assassinated in Sarajevo
- July 28—Austria-Hungary declares war on Russia
- August 1—Germany declares war on Russia
- August 3—Germany declares war on France
- August 4—Germany invades neutral Belgium
- August 4—Great Britain declares war on Germany

The U.S. initially maintained a policy of "isolationism" or "neutrality." German subs torpedoed U.S. ships bringing the U.S. into the war in 1917. World War I grew out of this system of alliances as a small regional conflict drew in the great powers on opposite sides with 10 million casualties on the battlefield and 66 million total deaths. Allies included England, France, Russia, and the United States. Central Powers included Germany, Austria-Hungary, and Turkey.

THE END OF WORLD WAR I AND COLLECTIVE SECURITY

The failure of the Balance of Power System led to the creation of a new arrangement—collective security. Under collective security, all nations would join together to guarantee territorial integrity and existing political independence against external aggression by any nation.

LEAGUE OF NATIONS FORMED IN 1919

The United States' opposition to international involvement after WWI was so great that the Senate refused to enroll the United States in the League. The U.S. returned to its policy of isolationism/unilateralism.

THE FAILURE OF COLLECTIVE SECURITY AND WORLD WAR II

Difficult economic conditions in Europe led to the rise of Adolph Hitler and Benito Mussolini. Fascism grew out of a fear of Bolshevism following the Russian Revolution and the failure of laissez-faire economics in the 1920s. Italians and Germans both felt the economic effects of treatment by the Allies following World War I. The rise of Mussolini and Hitler led to aggressive acts. Italy invaded Ethiopia in 1935. Germany invaded Czechoslovakia and Poland in 1939. The League of Nations failed to deal with these acts of aggression. The result was WWII with more than 66 million casualties. The war ended with the U.S. dropping atomic bombs on Nagasaki and Hiroshima, beginning a new era in warfare and new fears for humanity.

THE UNITED NATIONS: COLLECTIVE SECURITY PART DEUX

Even after WWII, the idea of collective security remained the model for the victorious Allied powers. The United Nations (1945) was the new collective security arrangement. The General Assembly is composed of all the member nations, each with a single vote. The U.N. has grown from 51 to 191 member states. No nation has a veto power over the General Assembly. The Secretariat is headed by a Secretary General with a staff at UN headquarters in New York. There are special bodies to handle specialized affairs; for example, the Economic and Social Council, the Trusteeship Council, and the International Court of Justice is at The Hague in the Netherlands. The Security Council has fifteen member nations and five of which are permanent members (United States, Russia, Britain, France, and China). The Security Council has the primary responsibility of maintaining international peace and security. The five permanent members have the power to veto any action by the Security Council. From 1946 to 1989, a significant number of the member nations were headed by authoritarian regimes supported by the Soviet Union. The U.S. was repeatedly outnumbered in the General Assembly, and the USSR used its veto power to prevent action in the Security Council. This occurred despite the fact that the U.S. is the biggest contributor to the UN. The U.S. provided 40% of the U.N. budget in 1946.

The U.S. is the largest contributor to the U.N. Each nation's contribution is based on "ability to pay." This has led some to call for the U.S. to leave the U.N. or to withhold funding, which has been done repeatedly over the years. Recent scandals involving the Oil for Food Scandal and nepotism have only added to the perception that the U.N. is a corrupt and ineffective organization.

Regional Security:

The Balance of Power Part Deux

The ineffectiveness of the UN to protect the interests of the U.S. and the Western democracies led to the formation of regional security agreements. The North Atlantic Treaty Organization was formed in 1949. Founders include the U.S., Canada, Belgium, Denmark, France, Iceland, Italy, Luxembourg, the Netherlands, Norway, Portugal, and the UK. It was agreed that an armed attack against one or more NATO nations shall be considered an attack against them all. The United States made a specific commitment to defend Western Europe in the event of a Soviet attack. New members have been added over the years with recent additions coming from the former Warsaw Pact nations.

- West Germany in 1955
- Spain in 1982
- Turkey in 1952
- Greece in 1952
- Poland in 1999
- Hungary in 1999
- Czech Republic in 1999
- Bulgaria in 2004
- Estonia in 2004
- Latvia in 2004
- Lithuania in 2004
- Romania in 2004
- Slovakia in 2004
- Slovenia in 2004

The Australian, New Zealand, U.S. Security Treaty (ANZUS) in 1951 was originally a defense agreement between the three member countries. A dispute between the U.S. and New Zealand over U.S. use of New Zealand ports for nuclear armed or powered vessels led to the dropping of New Zealand from the pact. The Southeast Asia Treaty Organization (SEATO) was formed in 1954. Members include the U.S., the U.K., France, Australia, New Zealand, Pakistan, Thailand, and the Philippines. It was abandoned in 1977 as a result of a lack of consensus on issues such as intervention in Laos and Vietnam.

The Central Treaty Organization (CENTO) was formed in 1958, and the member nations include Iraq, Turkey, Iran, Pakistan, the U.K., and the U.S. Tensions over the years led to the eventual demise of the pact. The Warsaw Pact was formed by the USSR in 1955. Members included Albania, Bulgaria, Czechoslovakia, East Germany, Hungary, Poland, Romania, and the USSR. The Warsaw Pact disintegrated following the collapse of the communist governments of Eastern Europe in 1989. Former Warsaw Pact nations (Poland, Hungary, Romania, Bulgaria, and East Germany) threw out their communist regimes and demanded the withdrawal of Soviet troops.

The Berlin Wall fell in 1989, and Germany was reunified in 1990. The pact was formally dissolved July 1, 1991. The USSR collapsed and ceased to exist as of December 31, 1991.

ECONOMIC DEVELOPMENT IN THE POST-WAR ERA

The Marshall Plan (Economic Assistance Act of 1948) was created to provide for the relief, reconstruction, and economic recovery of Western Europe. It provided $6 billion in its year 1948–1949. That is approximately $13 billion which was spent to rebuild Europe. The Marshall Plan is considered a success especially when compared to the approach taken towards Germany following World War I.

THE INTERNATIONAL MONETARY FUND (IMF)

The IMF was established in 1944 at Bretton Woods, New Hampshire. The IMF is entrusted with overseeing the global financial system by monitoring foreign exchange rates and balance of payments. The principal architects were John Maynard Keynes and the U.S. Secretary of Treasury, Harry White. Current criticism of the World Bank centers on conspiracies of elites trying to control the world.

THE WORLD BANK

The World Bank was established in 1944 at Bretton Woods, New Hampshire. The original mission was to finance reconstruction projects in countries ravaged by World War II. The World Bank's stated purpose is to reduce poverty and improve living standards through sustainable growth and investment in people. The World Bank provides long-term loans, grants, technical assistance, and economic development advice to developing countries. The World Bank is often criticized for its approach to social and environmental issues.

THE COLD WAR HEATS UP

Origins of the Cold War

The Cold War was a state of tension between the U.S. and the Soviet Union following World War II. George Orwell (1984, *Animal Farm*) coined the phrase "cold war" in his 1945 essay titled "You and the Atomic Bomb." The phrase was later popularized by Bernard Baruch, an advisor to President Truman, in several speeches in 1947. During WWII, the U.S. and the Soviet Union joined forces to eliminate the Nazi threat to the world. However, a rivalry between the USSR and U.S. began towards the end of WWII as the two armies raced toward Berlin. The U.S. "allowed" the Soviets to take Berlin, and Europe was divided into occupation zones at Yalta. Stalin used the revitalized Soviet forces to install communist governments in the nations of Eastern Europe to "protect" the Soviet Union from future acts of aggression. On June 24, 1948, Stalin attempted to oust the U.S., Britain, and France from a jointly occupied Berlin by blockading Western access to Berlin forcing the Berlin airlift, which lasted 324 days. General Lucius Clay recommended a convoy down the autobahn. President Truman feared this might lead to war opted for the airlift. Soviet Union exploded their first A-bomb on July 14, 1949. The world was now in an atomic age and the potential for nuclear war was ever present and any one incident could trigger a nuclear holocaust. The Berlin Wall (1961) symbolized the split between the two sides. The wall would lead to numerous conflicts that would bring the world to the brink of nuclear war. On October 27, 1961, U.S. and Soviet tanks squared off against one another for twenty-four hours over disputed crossings at Checkpoint Charlie (DEFCON 3). On August 17, 1962, Peter Fechter (an eighteen-year-old East German) was shot in the hip and bled to death on the barbed-wire fence at Checkpoint Charlie as he attempted to escape from East Germany.

CHINA, KOREA, AND THE DOCTRINE OF CONTAINMENT APPLIED

The fall of China to Communists (Mao Tse Tung) occurred in 1949 with aid of Soviets. In June 1950, communist North Korean armies invaded South Korea, with the assistance of Soviets and the Chinese. Korea had been divided into Soviet and U.S. spheres of influence after its liberation from Japan at the end of World War II. The dividing line was the 38th Parallel. Korea was to be unified, but the Soviets refused to allow participation, instead handing control over to the Korean communists under the leadership of Kim Il-Sung. The U.S. brought the matter to the UN Security Council and passed a resolution calling on member nations to send troops to Korea to repel the invasion (Soviets boycotted the meeting). The Korean War was really the first of the proxy wars in which countries were used as pawns in the Cold War conflict between the U.S. and the Soviet Union. The conflict in Korea ended July 1953, with a truce that is still in effect and Korea divided (communism in the North and democracy in the South) near the 38th Parallel. Eisenhower had become president in 1953 and emphasized deterrence. There was a policy of mutual assured destruction.

THE CUBAN CRISIS

Castro overthrew Batista in 1959 with U.S. approval, but he allied his government with the Soviet Union angering the U.S. by planting communism ninety miles off the Florida coast. Eisenhower was presented with plans for a counterrevolution, but his term ended before the plan could be executed. Kennedy inherited the plan and initially gave his "full" support to the Bay of Pigs invasion on April 15, 1961. The plans were poorly developed. The U.S. failed to provide full air/military support. The invasion failed, and 1189 of the 1500 invaders were captured and paraded in front of the world media embarrassing the United States. Review of the plan's failure gives us the concept of "groupthink."

CUBAN MISSILE CRISIS IN OCTOBER OF 1962

U.S. intelligence photographed missile sites being constructed on Cuba. Kennedy warned Khrushchev that the U.S. would not allow deployment of missiles on Cuban soil. Kennedy then imposed a blockade on Cuba, and the Soviet Navy began to bear down on the U.S. Navy (DEF-CON 2). War was averted when the Soviets agreed to stop deployment and the U.S. agreed to remove missiles from Turkey with a promise not to invade or support an invasion of Cuba. Robert McNamara began to develop the doctrine of Mutual Assured Destruction premised on the notion that Soviets and the U.S. had the capability to destroy one another in the event of nuclear war.

CONTAINMENT AND INDOCHINA

France began colonization of Vietnam in the mid-1800s. Japan seized Vietnam during World War II, and Japan ceded control to Ho Chi Minh's at the conclusion of the war. Ho Chi Minh sought to free Vietnam from French influence and initially sought assistance from the U.S. The U.S. declined because of loyalty to France. The Soviets and Chinese provide the necessary support. Ho Chi Minh defeated the French forces at Dien Ben Phou in 1954. Eisenhower was concerned about the fall of other nations to the communists if Vietnam were to fall—giving rise to the Domino Theory. The U.S. now intervenes and assists in the resulting Treaty of Paris. North Vietnam was controlled by the communists, and South Vietnam was controlled by French/U.S. puppet governments. Eisenhower provided training for South Vietnamese army. The South Vietnamese communists (Viet Cong) threatened the South Vietnamese government in the early 1960s. President Kennedy sent in 12,000 "advisors." By 1964, Viet Cong, with assistance of North Vietnam, controlled most of S. Vietnam. An incident in the Gulf of Tonkin led to the passage of Gulf of Tonkin Resolution of 1964. North Vietnamese PT boats attacked a U.S. destroyer August 2, 1964. Congress granted Johnson broad powers with regard to military. Johnson ordered bombings pursuant to Operation Rolling Thunder. Johnson began deployment of ground troops in 1965 reaching a maximum ground force of 500,000 men. On January 30, 1968, the Tet offensive began and inflicted massive political losses on the United States.

Opposition to War in the U.S. Grew
On March 31, 1968, Johnson, opposed by McCarthy (antiwar-student support), ended bombing and withdrew from the race. Nixon defeated Humphrey in the 1968 election and escalated the bombings. Nixon defeated McCarthy in 1972, and eventually began withdrawal of troops in 1973 after negotiating "peace with honor" in early 1973. In April 1975, the communists took control of Vietnam.

Soviet Expansion

The USSR expanded political and military presence in Asia, Africa, the Middle East, Central America, and the Caribbean in the late 1970s. As late as 1989, Soviet troops were stationed in Vietnam, Cambodia, Laos, Mongolia, Angola, Congo, Ethiopia, Mali, Mozambique, Libya, Algeria, Iraq, Syria, South Yemen, Cuba, Grenada, Nicaragua, and Peru.

Nixon: Detente, China, and the Soviet Union

Nixon began his political career as a staunch anti-communist in Congress and later as vice president under Eisenhower. Nixon campaigned against communist sympathizers and served on the House Un-American Activities Committee. He brought down Alger Hiss, a state department employee who was suspected of being a communist but denied the allegations. Nixon relied on detente (the relaxation of tensions through the use of diplomacy) to open relations with China.

Exchange of U.S. and Chinese Ping Pong Teams in 1971–1972
Nixon's Trip to China in 1972
Nixon's overtures towards China had the effect of pitting the Soviet Union and China against one another resulting in a number of border clashes. The Soviets, in turn, attempted to soften its position towards the U.S., and agreements were sought to achieve "strategic parity" on nuclear weapons.

The Nixon Doctrine was adopted towards the end of the Vietnam War and held that the U.S. would provide military equipment and arms, but no troops. The groundwork carried out by Nixon led to a number of agreements between the two superpowers in the span of 1972 through 1975.

- SALT I in 1972
- ABM Treaty in 1972
- Helsinki Accords in 1975

Carter's Search for a New Foreign Policy

Carter dismissed the Soviets as a cause for international upheaval. He believed the Iranian and Nicaraguan Revolutions were the result of internal problems and not Communist expansion. Carter emphasized human rights and achieved peace between Egypt and Israel with the Camp David Accords on September 17, 1978. Carter's presidency was damaged by events in Iran and Afghanistan. There was a hostage crisis in Iran from November 1979 to January 1981, and a Soviet invasion of Afghanistan in December 1979. Carter authorized increased defense spending and covert action against the Soviets in Afghanistan.

The Carter Doctrine provided that the Persian Gulf was vital to U.S. interests and the U.S. would fight to maintain access. Carter was weakened by the domestic economy, Iran, and Afghanistan and would lose the 1980 presidential election to Ronald Reagan.

Reagan, Communism, and the Munich Paradigm

Reagan revived the Munich Paradigm as he blamed Soviets for world instability and believed the only thing the Soviet leaders respected was military strength and a willingness to use it. Reagan increased defense spending through 1985. Military force was used in Libya and Grenada.

The Reagan Doctrine provided military assistance to anti-communist groups fighting against pro-Soviet governments.

- Afghanistan
- Angola

- Mozambique
- Nicaragua

The Cold War intensified until the Soviets began drowning in internal problems and the expense of maintaining communist satellite states. Three leaders died between 1982 and 1985. Internal economic issues developed as the government spent money on defense rather than domestic goods. Gorbachev ascended to power and was committed to perestroika ("restructuring") by seeking a more open economic and political system. He achieved many agreements with the U.S. with promises of an open system. In 1988, Gorbachev announced that the Soviet Union would no longer use its military forces to support communist governments in Eastern Europe.

George H. W. Bush and the New World Order

Bush inherited a collapsing Soviet Union in 1989, and Gorbachev's decision not to use Soviet troops to prop up communist regimes resulted in democratic uprisings in Poland, Czechoslovakia, Hungary, Bulgaria, Romania, and East Germany. Soviet troops remained in their barracks, and the communist regimes fell. In 1990, Saddam Hussein invaded Kuwait. Bush organized a response by the U.N., and Congress issued a resolution authorizing military force. Operation Desert Storm was a quick and decisive victory as Iraq was expelled from Kuwait in a matter of weeks. However, a decision to follow Saddam's army into Baghdad was rejected given that the objective of expulsion from Kuwait had been achieved. Gorbachev now faced opposition inside the USSR.

A Failed Coup in 1991

The economy was in shambles, and there was internal dissent and nationalistic movements. The Soviet Union was replaced by the Russian Federation in 1991. Nuclear deployment is still an issue for the four "nuclear republics" of Russia, Ukraine, Byelorussia, and Kazakhstan. The U.S. must balance interest in promoting democratic reforms with fear of being seen as meddling in Russia's domestic affairs, which is opposed by many of the old hardliners in Russia. The U.S. is also concerned about the sale of nuclear weapons to other countries by Russia and the other nuclear republics. The absence of a strong Soviet regime to control the new breakaway republics has led to conflicts throughout Africa and Eastern Europe. The collapse of the Soviet Union eliminated financial support for communist regimes in Asia, Africa, the Middle East, and the Americas. These countries must turn to the democratic nations of the west for financial support and turn toward market-oriented economies as has been achieved in Vietnam. Alternatively, these former Soviet states exploded in bloodshed.

- Angola
- Somalia
- Bosnia
- Kosovo

Clinton and the Complexities of a World with the Soviets

Clinton adopted the policies of engagement and enlargement. Engagement meant the U.S. would remain actively involved in foreign affairs. Enlargement meant the U.S. would promote the expansion of democracy and free markets throughout the world. Clinton exerted U.S. influence throughout his presidency. Here are some examples.

- Somalia in 1993
- Iraq in 1993
- Haiti in 1994
- Bosnia in 1995
- Iraq in 1996
- Iraq in 1998
- Kosovo in 1998–1999
- World Trade Center Bombing in 1993
- Khobar Towers in 1996
- U.S. Embassy bombings in Kenya and Tanzania in 1998
- U.S.S. Cole while docked in Yemen in 2000

George W. Bush and the Post-9/11 World

On September 11, 2001, terrorists struck the twin World Trade Center towers and the Pentagon killing 2,986. Bush responded with the War on Terrorism, the War in Afghanistan, and the War in Iraq.

Iran

Iran has been rebuilding its army, navy, and air force. China and Russia have supplied surface-to-surface missiles to Iran, and Iran is believed to be developing nuclear weapons. Iran is also believed to sponsor terrorism.

North Korea

North Korea is one of the most authoritarian and militaristic regimes in the world. It has a one-million member army with 4000 tanks, a large air force, and a large submarine force and an advanced nuclear weapons program. Kim Il-Sung never renounced his intention to reunify Korea by force. Current economic problems have magnified tensions.

China

China has the largest military in the world in terms of active duty personnel with at least 2.5 million soldiers (600,000 reserve). There has been a longstanding conflict over Taiwan. Hong Kong was turned over to Beijing in 1997, and China is becoming more capitalistic, which may lessen tensions unless those in political power fear the loss of that power.

India versus Pakistan

Conflicts between the countries have brought the world to the brink of nuclear war. India has approximately 60 nuclear weapons compared to Pakistan's 30 to 48 nuclear weapons. The U.S. has intervened on numerous occasions to reduce the risk of a nuclear war.

Israel versus the Palestinians

Despite attempts by numerous presidents, the "Roadmap to Peace" remains uncharted. The core problem seems to be unwillingness on either side to recognize the other side's right to exist or if there is a right to exist on what land.

ENDNOTES

1. The data presented here are from the Current Population Survey (CPS), 2011 Annual Social and Economic Supplement (ASEC), the source of official poverty estimates. The CPS ASEC is a sample survey of approximately 100,000 households nationwide. These data reflect conditions in calendar year 2010.
2. *See* Bane and Ellwood *Welfare Realities* 1994.

Chapter 9

THE ORIGIN AND DEVELOPMENT OF THE TEXAS CONSTITUTION

THE TEXAS CONSTITUTION

Texas History and the Texas Constitution

The Early Constitutions

The Constitution of Coahuila y Tejas, 1827

This constitution was drafted upon Mexico gaining its independence from Spain and the creation of the State of Coahuila y Tejas. It borrows from the U.S. Constitution with three branches and closely resembles the Spanish Constitution of 1812. Catholicism was adopted as the established state religion. It attempted to curtail the spread of slavery and established the principle of community property, and it exempted homesteads from bankruptcy. The legislature was unicameral with twelve deputies elected by popular vote. Texas was one of three districts called Bexar with two of the twelve deputies.

THE CONSTITUTION OF THE REPUBLIC OF TEXAS, 1836

Colonists from the United States objected to the tyrannical rule of Mexican government and, relying on American experiences, declared their independence from Mexico in 1836. They imposed a strict separation of church and state. There were term limits for elected officials. However, it maintained important provisions from Spanish-Mexican law, such as community property, homestead exemptions, and debtor relief. More importantly, it protected the institution of slavery. Slave owners could not free their slaves without permission. It allowed Texans to maintain their property and allowed new settlers to bring their slaves with them. The slave population grew from 1836 to 1860. In 1836, Texas had a slave population of 5000 and by 1850, the slave population had risen to 58,161 (25% of the state's population). By 1860, the number of slaves in the state exceeded 182,000 (30% of the state's population). Otherwise, it was modeled after the U.S. Constitution and the constitutions of the Southern states.

STATEHOOD, SECESSION, AND STATEHOOD REDUX

The Constitution of the State of Texas—1845: Texas Joins the Union

Texas remained an independent republic for nine years in part due to conflict over the admission of another slave state. In 1845, the United States Congress adopted a resolution that would bring Texas into the Union as a state. Texas ceded all military armaments, bases, and facilities pertaining to public defense to the United States. It retained a right to all its vacant and unappropriated lands. Moreover, Texas had permission to break up into four additional states. The Constitution of 1845 borrowed from the Constitution of 1836, the U.S. Constitution, and the constitutions of the Southern states. It retained the debtor protections and property laws of Spanish-Mexican legal system.

The Constitution of 1861: Texas Joins the Confederacy

Texas was divided over the issue of secession, and Sam Houston was a staunch Unionist and refused to call a special session of the legislature to discuss secession until others in the state mobilized a convention to call for secession. It prohibited the emancipation of slaves and raised the debt ceiling. Basically, it replaced the United States with the Confederate States of America throughout the Constitution of 1845.

The Constitution of 1866: Texas Rejoins the Union

The defeat of the Confederacy in the Civil War led to the adoption of a constitution in 1866 for the purposes of rejoining the Union. Texas, as well as the other Southern states, had to renounce the right of secession, repudiate the war debt incurred by the state, and accept the abolition of slavery. The Constitution of 1866 did not state that secession was unconstitutional, ratify the Thirteenth Amendment, or guarantee the civil rights of the newly freed slaves.

Reconstruction and its Aftermath

The Reconstruction Constitution of 1869

The Congressional Reconstruction Act of 1867 forced the adoption of yet another constitution in 1869. Texas was under the control of General Winfield Scott Hancock, the commander of the Texas and Louisiana Military District. He had called a constitutional convention, which was dominated by Radical Republicans and newly enfranchised African Americans. Under the Reconstruction Constitution of 1869, the U.S. Constitution was declared supreme law of the land. Political power was centralized in the office of governor and provided for annual legislative sessions. The Thirteenth Amendment was ratified in 1870, and Edmund J. Davis governed under this constitution until 1872. Democrats regained control of the state government with the election of Richard Coke as governor in 1874.

The Constitution of 1876

The Democrats attempted to prevent a return to Republican control by adopting a new constitution. The Constitutional Convention was dominated by farmers and members of the Grange, a militant farming organization. These framers created a very weak state government in which control was guaranteed to the people of Texas. It cut salaries for government officials, placed strict limits on property taxes, stripped the governor of powers, and established elected plural executive. The legislature would meet every other year, and most legislation would be adopted by constitutional action.

Understanding the Current Constitution

Comparison to the United States Constitution

Length and Detail

The U.S. Constitution is brief and flexible having been amended a total of twenty-seven times in more than 200 years. The Texas Constitution is the second longest constitution in the nation having been amended over 450 times and counting. The Texas Constitution goes to great lengths to limit the political powers of officeholders, whereas the U.S. Constitution attempts to give the national government more power than it possessed under the Articles of Confederation.

Similarities between the U.S. and Texas Constitutions

The Texas and the U.S. Constitutions are similar in that power originates from the people and is delegated to government with specific limitations. The Texas and the U.S. Constitutions both create three branches of government—legislative, executive, and judicial. The Texas and the U.S. Constitutions provide for a system of checks and balances. The Texas and U.S. Constitutions stress the importance of individual rights. Both constitutions also recognize the existence of a federal system.

Differences between the U.S. and Texas Constitutions

Texas is limited by Article VI of the U.S. Constitution, which provides that the U.S. Constitution and laws of the United States are the supreme law of the land. Texas judges, as well as judges in other states, are bound by the U.S. Constitution. The Texas Constitution does not grant implied powers to the state government as the necessary and proper clause of Article I, Section 8 of the U.S. Constitution provides.

The Texas Constitution
The Preamble

The preamble is very short, which is surprising considering the length of the overall document. Humbly invoking the blessings of Almighty God, the people of the State of Texas do ordain and establish this Constitution.

Article I: The Bill of Rights

Texas places its Bill of Rights first, in contrast to the Bill of Rights in the U.S. Constitution. Texas guarantees many of the rights embodied in the U.S. Constitution and Bill of Rights: equality, freedom of speech, freedom of press, right to a jury trial. Texas also provides additional protections: the right to a republican government, and monopolies that are contrary to the public interest are forbidden.

Article II: The Powers of Government

The doctrine of separation of powers is guaranteed by this article. It also prohibits anyone from serving in two or more branches at the same time.

Article III: Legislative Department

It creates a bicameral legislature with a House containing 150 State Representatives serving two-year terms and Senate with 31 State Senators serving four-year terms. Every two years, one-half of the Senators are up for election, 15 in one cycle and 16 in the next cycle. Salaries are set by the

Texas Constitution, currently $7200 year. The Constitution requires residency in the state and the district. The legislature meets once every odd year for 140 days, and only the governor may call special session. Special session can last no more than 30 days, which is limited to topics specified by the governor. There is a balanced budget mandated by the Texas Constitution.

Article IV: Executive Department

The governor is elected by the voters as are other members of the plural executive, which restricts the governor's ability to control the executive branch. In addition to the governor, there is a Lieutenant (Lt.) Governor who presides over the Senate. The Lt. Governor is elected for a four-year term. There is an attorney general that represents the state in legal matters involving the state and is elected to a four-year term. There is a land commissioner that administers Texas land and is elected to a four-year term. The agriculture commissioner is responsible for promoting agriculture products in Texas and is elected to a four-year term.

The governor has rather limited powers in comparison to the governors of other states, but note that the governor can call special sessions, which last no more than 30 days. The governor also has the power of the line-item veto; however, he does not have the pocket veto power.

Article V: Judicial Department

The Texas court system is bifurcated and has elected judges except for municipalities. The system has a variety of levels with two high courts: the Supreme Court for civil matters and the Court of Criminal Appeals for criminal matters. Both of these high courts are appellate courts. Just below these high courts is a Court of Appeals. Trial courts consist of district courts, county courts, and justice of the peace courts. Appellate judges serve six-year terms, and trial judges serve four-year terms except for justice of the peace courts, which serve two-year terms.

Article VI: Suffrage

Suffrage is the right to vote. This article says that persons less than 18 years of age, those who have been determined mentally incompetent by a court, and those convicted of any felony, shall not be allowed to vote. In addition, the legislature shall enact laws to exclude from the right of suffrage persons who have been convicted of bribery, perjury, forgery, or other high crimes.

Article VII: Education

This article says that there will be support and maintenance of a system of public free schools. Moreover, it says a general diffusion of knowledge being essential to the preservation of the liberties and rights of the people, it shall be the duty of the legislature of the state to establish and make suitable provision for the support and maintenance of an efficient system of public free schools.

There will also be the creation of a perpetual school fund. All funds, lands, and other property heretofore set apart and appropriated for the support of public schools; all the alternate sections of land reserved by the state out of grants heretofore made or that may hereafter be made to railroads or other corporations of any nature whatsoever; one half of the public domain of the state; and all sums of money that may come to the state from the sale of any portion of the same, shall constitute a perpetual public school fund.

Independent school districts and junior college districts will also be created. The governing body of any such district, without the necessity of an additional election, shall have the power to assess, levy, and collect ad valorem taxes on all taxable property within the boundaries of the district and such governing body also shall have the power, without the necessity of an additional election, to sell and deliver any unissued bonds voted in the district.

The Legislature shall provide by law for a State Board of Education, whose members shall be appointed or elected in such manner and by such authority and shall serve for such terms as the Legislature shall prescribe not to exceed six years. The said board shall perform such duties as may be prescribed by law.

Article VIII: Taxation and Revenue

No state ad valorem taxes shall be levied upon any property within this state. A general law enacted by the legislature that imposes a tax on the net incomes of natural persons, including a person's share of partnership and unincorporated association income, must provide that the portion of the law imposing the tax not take effect until approved by a majority of the registered voters voting in a statewide referendum held on the question of imposing the tax. This is highly unlikely in Texas. The referendum must specify the rate of the tax that will apply to taxable income as defined by law.

Article IX and XI: Local Government and Municipal Corporations

Cities and towns with a population of 5,000 or less will be chartered as general law cities. Cities of more than 5,000 inhabitants may, by a majority vote of the qualified voters of said city, at an election held for that purpose, adopt or amend their charters. This is referred to as a Home Rule city. The adoption or amendment of charters is subject to such limitations as may be prescribed by the legislature, and no charter or any ordinance passed under said charter shall contain any provision inconsistent with the Constitution of the State or of the general laws enacted by the legislature of this state. This essentially makes Texas a form of unitary government.

Article X: Railroads

Railroads constructed in Texas are declared public highways, railroad companies, and common carriers. The legislature shall pass laws to regulate railroad, freight, and passenger tariffs; to correct abuses and prevent unjust discrimination and extortion in the rates of freight and passenger tariffs on the different railroads in this state and enforce the same by adequate penalties; and to the further accomplishment of these objects and purposes, may provide and establish all requisite means and agencies invested with such powers as may be deemed adequate and advisable.

Article XII: Private Corporations

No private corporation shall be created except by general laws. General laws shall be enacted providing for the creation of private corporations, and shall therein provide fully for the adequate protection of the public and of the individual stockholders.

Article XIII: Spanish and Mexican Land Grants (Repealed Aug. 5, 1969)

Article XIV: Public Lands and Land Office

There shall be one General Land Office in the state, which shall be at the seat of government, where all land titles that have emanated or may hereafter emanate from the state shall be registered, except those titles the registration of which may be prohibited by the constitution. It shall be the duty of the Legislature at the earliest practicable time to make the land office self-sustaining and, from time to time, the legislature may establish such subordinate offices as may be deemed necessary.

Article XV: Impeachment

The power of impeachment shall be vested in the House of Representatives. Impeachment of the governor, lieutenant governor, attorney general, and commissioner of the general land office, comptroller and the judges of the supreme court, court of appeals, and district court shall be tried by the Senate.

When the Senate is sitting as a court of impeachment, the senators shall be on oath, or affirmation impartially to try the party impeached, and no person shall be convicted without the concurrence of two-thirds of the senators present.

Judgment in cases of impeachment shall extend only to removal from office, and disqualification from holding any office of honor, trust, or profit under this state. A party convicted on impeachment shall also be subject to indictment, trial, and punishment according to law.

Texas has impeached a sitting governor even though the Constitution does not specify the grounds for impeachment. Jim, Pa, Ferguson was impeached and convicted for tampering with UT money. Texans turned around and elected Miriam, Ma, Ferguson—thereby getting two governors for the price of one.

Article XVI: General Provisions

This is one of the lengthiest in the document with seventy-three sections. I have often called this the "kitchen sink" article because it seems as if anything that would not fit into another category wound up here. One of the provisions worth noting is that all elected and appointed officers, before they enter upon the duties of their offices, shall take the following oath or affirmation:

"I, _____, do solemnly swear (or affirm), that I will faithfully execute the duties of the office of _____ of the State of Texas, and will to the best of my ability preserve, protect, and defend the Constitution and laws of the United States and of this State, so help me God." And, "I, _____, do solemnly swear (or affirm) that I have not directly or indirectly paid, offered, promised to pay, contributed, or promised to contribute any money or thing of value, or promised any public office or employment for the giving or withholding of a vote at the election at which I was elected or as a reward to secure my appointment or confirmation, whichever the case may be, so help me God." No member of Congress, nor person holding or exercising any office of profit or trust, under the United States, or either of them, or under any foreign power, shall be eligible as a member of the legislature, or hold or exercise any office of profit or trust under this state. All officers within this state shall continue to perform the duties of their offices until their successors shall be duly qualified.

Article XVII: Amending the Constitution

Constitutional amendments must be proposed by two-thirds of the Texas Legislature and approved by a simple majority of the voters of the State of Texas. Over 450 amendments have been ratified. Attempts to rewrite the Texas Constitution have been soundly defeated. A brief explanatory statement of the nature of a proposed amendment, together with the date of the election and the wording of the proposition as it is to appear on the ballot, shall be published twice in each newspaper in the state which meets requirements set by the legislature for the publication of official notices of offices and departments of the state government. The explanatory statement shall be prepared by the secretary of state and shall be approved by the attorney general. The secretary of state shall send a full and complete copy of the proposed amendment or amendments to each county clerk who shall post the same in a public place in the courthouse at least thirty days prior to the election on said amendment. The first notice shall be published not more than sixty days or less than fifty days before the date of the election, and the second notice shall be published on the same day in the succeeding week. The legislature shall fix the standards for the rate of charge for the publication, which may not be higher than the newspaper's published national rate for advertising per column inch.

If it appears from the returns that a majority of the votes cast have been cast in favor of an amendment, it shall become a part of this constitution and proclamation thereof shall be made by the governor.

Chapter 10

LOCAL GOVERNMENT IN TEXAS

© 2012 Brandon Seidel. Used under license with Shutterstock, Inc.

The origins of local government come from the foundation of American democracy. Alexis de Tocqueville recognized the importance Americans placed in local government when he wrote his monumental work *Democracy in America*. The strength of free peoples resides in the local community. Local institutions are to liberty what primary schools are to science; they put it within the people's reach; they teach the people to appreciate its peaceful enjoyment and accustom them to make use of it. Without local institutions a nation may give itself a free government, but it has not got the spirit of liberty. There are essentially three forms of local government in Texas: counties, cities, and special districts. Ultimately, any level of government can perform a function; however, some levels of government are better suited to perform certain tasks. For example, counties could provide education, but Texans believe a government closer to the community is best. It is easier to control and hold accountable. That is the essence of local government—responding to the needs of the community. The principle authority in the state is the state legislature, and all local government answers to the state. This provides a unitary structure.

There are approximately 4700 local governments in Texas.

- 1431 general purpose governments
  - ▷ 254 county governments
  - ▷ 1177 municipal governments
- 3269 special purpose governments
  - ▷ 1087 school districts
  - ▷ 2182 special districts

Local governments provide water, electricity, and sewer services, as well as police protection and public education.

County governments in Texas are granted authority under the constitution. Texas has 254 counties, more than any other state, but the Texas Constitution places strict limits on their operation (i.e., generally they lack the power to legislate). They are basically the administrative arms of the state. The structure of the county is called the Commissioners Court. Besides the Commissioners Court, the county is run by a multitude of elected officials, which continues the state preference for a decentralized and publicly controlled government. The leader of the Commissioners Court is the county judge who is elected in a countywide/at-large election to a four-year term. The county judge presides over the Commissioners Court (criminal and civil cases such as probate matters) and is responsible for the administration of the county.

There are four commissioners elected from equal-sized precincts—numbers one through four. These are not to be confused with election precincts or constable precincts. The main duty of the commissioners is the construction and maintenance of roads and bridges in their respective precincts. They also set the county tax rate and the county budget, build and maintain county jail facilities, and provide indigent healthcare services.

OTHER COUNTY AND PRECINCT-LEVEL ELECTED OFFICIALS

- County Court at Law Judges: Judge the county courts
- County and District Attorney: Represents the county in legal matters and prosecutes criminal cases in the county

- County and District Clerk: Issues marriage certificates and other government documents, and the record keeper of the district court
- County Tax Assessor-Collector: Collects taxes for the county
- County Treasurer: Manages the county funds
- Justices of the Peace: Judges the justice of the peace courts
- Constables: Provide law enforcement in the county

CITY GOVERNMENT IN TEXAS

Texas municipalities have constitutional authority. There are 1177 municipal governments incorporated in Texas ranging in size from 24 residents to over 1.7 million. Municipal governments are creations of the state of Texas. Cities with populations in excess of 5000 may adopt home-rule charters. Home-rule charters provide operational rules for the municipality. Also, they provide for the type of local government: Mayor–council; Council–manager; or Commission. They are authorized to borrow money, annex land adjacent to the municipality, and set property taxes up to $2.50 per $100 valuation. There are approximately 310 home-rule cities in Texas. Cities smaller than 5000 are chartered by general statute, which means they are limited to operation pursuant to statutes passed by the state legislature. The limit on property tax is $1.50 per $100 valuation.

FORMS OF GOVERNMENT IN TEXAS CITIES

The mayor–council form is the oldest form of government in Texas. It consists of an elected mayor and city council. The mayor is elected at-large, and the council members are elected from single member districts, combined districts, and at-large elections. They can operate under either a strong-mayor or weak-mayor model.

Council–Manager

The Council and a Mayor are elected, but the administrative arm of local government is controlled by a city manager that is hired by council. This form of government was an attempt by progressives to control the dangers associated with machine politics. By the 1990s, 251 of the home-rule cities operated under a council manager form of government. City managers are trained professionals and serve as chief executive and administrative officer for the municipality.

Local Council–Manager Municipalities

Commissioner

The city is run by a small commission composed of between five and seven members generally elected on an at-large basis. As a group, commissioners pass laws for the city. As individuals, commissioners are in charge of one of a variety of departments. They were popular in Texas around the turn of the century but fell out of favor following World War I. Currently, no city in

Texas operates under a pure commission form and those that claim to be operating under a quasi-commission form are really operating as council forms of government.

Special Districts in Texas

Types of Special Districts

A special district is a unit of local government that performs a single service in a limited geographical area. These governments cross borders of existing units of local governments or perform services that other local governments are unwilling or unable to perform.

- Hospital districts
- Mosquito control
- Navigation
- Flood control
- Sanitation
- Drainage
- Law enforcement

There are two types of special districts in Texas: school and non-school.

School districts offer public education from pre-kindergarten through twelfth grade. The school district boundaries may not match municipal boundaries. They are governed by an elected board of trustees. The board employs a superintendent. They establish policy for the district; the tax rate for the district; adopt textbooks; hire principals, faculty, and support staff; set the school calendar; and determine salaries and benefits for employees.

Non-school Special Districts

- Municipal Utility Districts
- Flood Control Districts
- Community College Districts
- San Jacinto Community College District
- Houston Community College District
- Mosquito Control Districts
- Harris County Mosquito Control District

Creating a Special District

Special districts are created by voters of the area to be served. Creating a special district requires a petition signed by the residents requesting that the legislature to authorize provides for a special election to create the district. A simple majority of those voting in the special election are required.

Governing a Special District

Most special districts are governed by elected boards. The board of trustees, board of regents, or board of directors sets policy for the district.

Revenues

Property taxes are the primary source of revenue for special districts. User fees also contribute to the operational revenues of the district.

Councils of Government

The overlapping nature of local governments and the multitude of demands on these local governments have led to calls for a coordinated effort. The Regional Planning Act of 1965 authorized the creation of regional councils of government (COG). There are twenty-four regional councils in Texas today.

Responsibilities of the COGs

The basic responsibilities of the COG include planning for the economic development of an area, helping local governments carry out regional projects, and reviewing applications for state and federal financial assistance. Originally, COGs focused on federal mandates for water and sewer provision, open space, and housing planning. Currently, COGs have become more involved in a broad range of policy areas: aging, employment and training, criminal justice, economic development, environmental quality, and transportation.

Chapter 11

SEPARATION OF POWERS AND CHECKS AND BALANCES IN BOTH THEORY AND PRACTICE IN TEXAS

THE TEXAS CONSTITUTION

Unlike the U.S. Constitution, the Texas Constitution in Article 2 specifies that there will be a division of powers with three separate departments. Section 1 says: "The powers of the Government of the State of Texas shall be divided into three distinct departments, each of which shall be confided to a separate body of magistracy, to wit: Those which are Legislative to one; those which are Executive to another, and those which are Judicial to another; and no person, or collection of persons, being of one of these departments, shall exercise any power properly attached to either of the others, except in the instances herein expressly permitted." It is thought that the inclusion of this article was to emphasize the need for separation of powers and not leave it to interpretation.

The model for this could have come from the United States Constitution; however, it is more likely to have been conceived as a result of the Governorship of Edmund J. Davis. Davis was a Union Army officer and Republican Reconstruction governor of Texas. Davis won the election of 1869 against Andrew J. Hamilton, Republican, in a closely disputed race. He was a member of the 1866 Texas Constitutional Convention prior to election, and he supported the rights of the freed slaves and urged the division of Texas into several Republican-controlled states. His administration was controversial. His programs called for law and order backed by a state police and restoration of the militia, public schools, and internal improvements, bureaus of immigration and geology, and protection of the frontier. The Davis administration was marked by a commitment to the civil rights of African Americans. These measures encountered strong attacks from both Democratic and Republican opponents and added to the controversy of Reconstruction. Davis ran for reelection in December 1873 and was defeated by Richard Coke by a vote of two to one. Davis believed that the Republican national administration was partly responsible for his defeat, and relations between the governor and Washington were tense. Davis contested the results and refused to leave his office until he was removed by Democrats the following January in what is known as the Coke-Davis controversy.

The separation of powers in Texas operates in a similar way as the federal government; however, there are a couple of considerations. One consideration is that the executive branch is significantly different in Texas. The executive is referred to as a plural executive because there are multiple, seven, elected officials, all of which execute the laws of the state and are independently elected. Each member is elected to four-year terms and held accountable by the people. The focal point of the plural executive is the governor, although, the lieutenant governor has considerable authority over the legislature which puts the Lt. governor in the legislative branch. In other words, the Lt. governor is the presiding officer of the Senate and as such controls one house of the legislature. It is also worth noting that the governor has the power of the line-item veto, which means that appropriations bills can be altered before signed into law. The president does not have this power. The governor also has the traditional veto power although it can be overridden by two-thirds of both chambers and it is difficult to override the governor's veto because most vetoes occur after the legislature has adjourned and a two-thirds vote of each chamber is difficult to come by. However, Republicans currently have two-thirds of the House and a simple majority of the Senate with the Republican Lieutenant Governor as the presiding officer. Moreover, the governor can call a thirty-day special session in which he alone sets the agenda. Essentially, this gives the governor power over the legislature.

The governor is commander in chief of the Texas Rangers and National Guard. Although the governor is the chief law enforcement officer in the state, most law enforcement exists at the local level. The governor also has limited powers of clemency, which gives the governor the capacity to grant relief from criminal punishment. Unlike governors in many states, the Texas Governor cannot independently issue a pardon or sentence commutation. In death penalty cases, the governor can issue one thirty-day reprieve. The governor can also make recommendations to the

Board of Pardons and Paroles and can either approve or reject the board's recommendations on pardons or sentence reductions.

A second consideration is the nature of the judicial branch. Unlike the federal court system, the judges in the judicial branch in Texas are elected rather than appointed. Therefore, the control of the judiciary is in the hands of the people. However, appointments may be filled by the governor with the consent of the legislature. Therefore, this gives the governor considerable power to shape the judiciary. Often, these appointments translate into electoral victories because the public favors incumbents.

In addition to the judiciary, the governor has other appointments that can influence the bureaucracy. Up until 1972, the governor could not fire appointees but now can and is still subject to two-thirds Senate vote; however, the governor cannot remove the appointees of his predecessor. Appointees must pass political inspection by the home-area senator. This is called Senatorial Courtesy, which allows a senator to block the confirmation of a gubernatorial appointee who lives in the senator's district.

SEPARATED BUDGETARY POWERS

The governor may submit budget proposals to the state legislature, but the Legislative Budget Board's (LBB) proposals carry more weight and it is headed by the Lt. governor. The governor has also been granted limited budget execution authority, which allows the governor to transfer money between state agencies when the legislature is not in session. An agency's appropriation cut cannot be more than 10% or increased more than 5%. The LBB must accept or reject this fund transfer proposal before the governor can transfer the fund.

Although the legislature is ultimately responsible for the budget, the comptroller estimates state revenues for the upcoming two-year budget cycle to certify that the appropriation bill falls within revenue estimates to prevent deficit spending. Moreover, the finances for the state are heavily influenced by the federal government and the economy. Local governments are largely responsible for their own finances.

The legislature is the more powerful branch because the executive branch is fragmented and the judiciary is elected. The legislature has great influence over the bureaucracy through the sunset review process, but this takes place infrequently and is not very effective. The legislature is also limited by biennial 140-day sessions.

$$Chapter\ 12$$

THE LEGISLATIVE, EXECUTIVE, AND JUDICIAL BRANCHES OF TEXAS GOVERNMENT

© 2012 Chad Zuber. Used under license with Shutterstock, Inc.

THE STRUCTURE OF THE TEXAS LEGISLATURE

Composition

The Texas legislature has a bicameral structure. Nebraska is the only state with a unicameral legislature. One chamber is referred to as the House of Representatives, and the other is called the Senate. The two chambers are divided into single-member districts with 150 members in the House and 31 members in the Senate.

ELECTIONS AND TERMS OF OFFICE

Elections are held in even-numbered years with members serving in the House of Representatives for two-year terms, and Senators serving staggered four-year terms except after redistricting, which occurs in first odd year of the decade. Senators draw lots to determine who will serve the initial two-year term and the others serve four-year terms. Vacancies are filled by special election. Expulsion requires a two-thirds vote in the legislator's chamber.

SESSIONS

The regular session is 140 days, which begins on the second Tuesday in January of odd-numbered years. This is considered a part-time legislature. Special sessions of thirty days may be called by the governor in which legislative work is restricted to matters stated by the governor. The legislature can also perform housekeeping functions. Special sessions are unpopular due to a half-million-dollar price tag.

CONSTITUTIONAL MANDATES AND REDISTRICTING

State and U.S. congressional districts are redrawn by the legislature of the states. If the legislature fails to redistrict, the task falls to the Legislative Redistricting Board, which is comprised of the following individuals.

- Lt. Governor
- Speaker of the House
- Attorney General Comptroller
- Commissioner of the General Land Office

COMPENSATION

Comparative legislative salaries in the U.S.

- Texas $7200 last updated in 1975
- Rhode Island pays $300 per year
- New Hampshire pays $100 per year
- Florida pays $27,900 per year (60 calendar days extended by 3/5 vote)
- New York pays $79,500 per year
- California pays $99,000 per year (285-day session)

Lawmakers receive a per diem expense allowance of $125 and contingency expense allowances. Representatives receive $7500 for office expenses and $2650 per month for staff salaries. Senators receive $22,000 per month for secretary and office staff and no limit for salary of legislative staff. Moreover, they receive a retirement pension which requires 12 years of ser-vice and 50 years of age and ranges from $20,000 to $65,000.

MEMBERSHIP

The formal qualifications of the Senate are that you must be a U.S. citizen, qualified voter, 26 years of age or older, and lived in state 5 years and in district 1 year. The formal qualifications of the House are that you must be a U.S. citizen, qualified voter, 21 years of age or older, and lived in Texas 2 years and 1 year in district.

SNAPSHOT OF THE 82ND LEGISLATURE (2011)

Overview of Characteristics

Members of the Texas legislature tend to be White, Anglo-Saxon, Protestant, Males, generally in their forties or fifties (Avg. 51 House and 57.5 Senate). Nearly all of the members, 80–85% have college, graduate, or professional degrees (i.e., law). Most are businessmen or lawyers. In the Senate, 52% of the members are from business and 33% of the House. In the Senate, 23% of the members are lawyers and 31% of the House. In terms of gender and race the Senate has 25 males and 6 females, and the House has 118 males and 32 females. The Senate has 22 Anglos, 7 Hispanic-Americans, and 2 African Americans. The House has 101 Anglos, 30 Hispanic-Americans, 17 African Americans, and 2 Asians.

Party Identification

In 1960, there were no Republicans in the Texas Legislature. By 1992, there were 13 Republicans in the Senate and 58 in the House. In 2011, the House had 49 Democrats and 151 Republicans. The Senate had 12 Democrats and 19 Republicans. The Democratic Party once dominated Texas politics. They gained power following Reconstruction and gained strength during Roosevelt's New Deal. The resurgence of the Republican Party occurred particularly in West Texas, the Panhandle, and urban areas. This transformation was partially a result of presidential elections. When popular Republicans were on the national ticket, it helped lift the Republican candidates lower on the ballot. Now, the Texas legislature is dominated by Conservative Democrats and Conservative Republicans.

Religious Affiliation

Catholics have a plurality with 35%, followed by Baptists with 22%, Methodists with 15%, and Episcopalians at 6%.

Money to Run Campaigns

It costs more than $75,000 for House election campaign and more than $250,000 for a Senate election. However, in competitive urban districts expenditures can exceed $500,000. Business-oriented PACS are very influential.

FUNCTIONS OF LEGISLATIVE BODIES: POWERS AND IMMUNITIES

Formal Functions

Lawmaking is the most fundamental purpose of any legislature. The purpose of making law is that it is the primary source of public policy. Therefore, the basic prerogative for writing, amending, and passing legislation belongs to members of the legislature. Another responsibility is reapportionment and redistricting. This is performed every ten years following the census. Realignment of both state and federal legislative districts is required. The next function concerns constitutional amendments. The legislature is empowered to prepare constitutional amendments and ratify amendments to the United States Constitution. There is also a judicial function with the power to impeach and convict judicial or executive branch officials. One example is Governor Pa Ferguson who was impeached and convicted. The legislature has an electoral function in that it settles election disputes, and it has an administrative function in that it provides oversight of the bureaucracy. For example, the Sunset Act of 1977 provides for review of administrative agencies. Therefore, the legislature is allowed to review rules and regulations of administrative agencies. In addition, the legislature has the ability to audit state expenditures. The legislature has an investigatory function to determine if there is wrongdoing within the bureaucracy.

Informal Functions

Informal functions of the legislature include casework, providing education, and information.

LEGISLATIVE POWERS

Legislative powers include considering simple resolutions (H.R. or S.R.) which involve action by one house and is not sent to the governor. A majority vote is required. This is used for rule of the House or Senate, procedures, and invitations to non-members to address legislature. Concurrent resolutions (H.C.R. and S.C.R.) require a simple majority in both houses, which is then sent to the governor who may sign the resolution, veto it, or allow it to pass without his signature. It is used to request action by the United States Congress, request information from state agencies, or to establish joint study committees. Joint resolutions (H.J.R. or S.J.R.) require approval of both houses and do not need the governor's approval. These are used to propose amendments to the Texas Constitution (2/3 vote of both houses) and to ratify amendments to the United States Constitution (simple majority). Bills are referred to as H.B. or S.B. along with the number of the bill. Special bills grant exception to general laws to an individual, class, or corporation. General bills apply to all citizens and require a simple majority vote. They go into effect ninety days after adjournment unless an emergency (2/3 vote), which goes into effect upon governor's signature. Local bills affect a single unit of local government. Members of the legislature enjoy certain immunity, which means that they may not be sued for statements made in a speech or during debate during legislative session. And, they may not be arrested while attending or traveling to and from legislative session unless charged with treason, felony, or breach of the peace.

Presiding Officers

Lieutenant Governor

David Dewhurst is the Lt. governor and was elected in a statewide election to serve as Lt. governor. As the Lt. governor, he serves as president of the Senate and serves a four-year term. The Lt. governor succeeds the governor in case of death or resignation and when the governor is out of the state. For example, Rick Perry served as acting governor when Bush was out of state campaigning for president. He became governor following the November 2000 election.

Other Powers of the Lt. Governor

He appoints all committee chairs and appoints committee members; however, there is a limitation based on seniority. He recognizes the speaker on the floor of the Senate. He can cast a tie-breaking vote. He also serves on the Legislative Council, Legislative Audit Committee, Chairs the Legislative Budget Board, and Co-Chairs Legislative Criminal Justice Board. He also assigns bills to committee.

Speaker of the House

Joe Straus is the Speaker of the House and was selected by his fellow House members in 2009. The Speaker of the House presides over the House of Representatives and is elected by House membership for a two-year term. The Speaker of the House appoints committee chairs and vice-chairs, all committee members for the House procedural committees, committee members to substantive committees subject to seniority, recognizes speakers on the floor, assigns bills to committee, serves on the Legislative Council, is vice-chair of the Legislative Budget Board, and co-chairs Legislative Criminal Justice Board.

Committee System

Standing committees and subcommittees are permanent and consider bills and exercise oversight of administrative agencies. Subcommittees are a division of standing committees and consider bills within an area of specialization. Ad hoc committees are temporary committees that consider special issues or problems. The Conference Committee reaches compromise between the House and Senate versions of a bill. Interim committees meet when the legislature is not in session to consider proposed legislation for the next session or to consider a problem that arose since last session.

House Committee Assignments

The House has provided for a limited seniority system for all substantive committees since 1973, but not for procedural committees. A maximum of half of the membership is based on seniority. The representative designates three preferences for committee assignment and is given top available position. The remaining positions are assigned by the Speaker. They are limited to two substantive committee assignments.

Senate Committee Assignments

Senators are limited to three committee assignments and one chairmanship. The Lt. governor makes all appointments for all committee members.

Calendar

The presiding officers control the flow of legislation. In the House, a calendar committee is appointed by the Speaker. In the Senate, the Lt. governor is influential in getting bills to floor or blocking consideration (need 2/3 vote to take out of order).

Floor Action

The presiding officers control debate on the floor. A filibuster is limited to one Senator.

INFLUENCES ON THE LEGISLATIVE PROCESS

Internal influences derive from caucuses. Party caucuses exist in the House. The Democratic Caucus was formed in 1981, and the Republican Caucus formed in 1989. There are also racial caucuses. For example, there is a Legislative Black Caucus and a Mexican American Legislative Caucus. There are Ideological Caucuses such as the Texas Conservative Coalition formed by conservative Democrats and Republicans in 1985 and the Legislative Study Group formed by liberal Democrats in 1993. Influence also comes from the legislative research organizations, the Legislative Council, the House Research Organization, and the Senate Research Center.

External influences include the governor, judges of the federal and state government, the attorney general, the comptroller, lobbyists, and the media.

THE TEXAS EXECUTIVE BRANCH

The Governor

Qualifications

There are only three formal requirements to serve as governor: be at least thirty years of age, a U.S. citizen, and live in Texas five years prior to the election. Generally, Texas governors have been white, Anglo-Saxon, protestant males, and Democrats but politically moderate or conservative, wealthy, and with prior considerable political experience. Texas has elected two women to serve as governor: Miriam "Ma" Ferguson (1925–1927, 1933–1935) and Ann Richards (1991–1995). No minorities have served as governor or been nominated by the Democratic or Republican parties. William Clements (1978–1982) was the first Republican to be elected since Reconstruction. George W. Bush (1994–2000) was the first Republican to win back-to-back terms as governor. Rick Perry (2000–) was elected three times and is the longest serving governor in the country. A campaign for the governor can cost between $25–60 million per candidate.

Election and Term of Office

Prior to 1974, Texas governors served two-year terms, with most serving a maximum of two consecutive two-year terms. Coke Stevens, Price Daniel, and John Connally served for six years. Allan Shivers served for eight years. A 1972 constitutional amendment provided a four-year term. Dolph Briscoe (1974–1978) was the first governor to serve a four-year term. George W. Bush was the first to be elected to consecutive four-year terms. Gubernatorial elections are held in off years to prevent undue influence from the presidential election, either a popular Republican candidate or an unpopular Democratic candidate.

Campaigns

The campaign for governor lasts for ten months, the primary from January to March and the general election from March to November. The media costs for a campaign can run close to $15 million. There are twenty-seven media markets in the state, and no single media source can hope to reach the majority of the states' registered voters. However, considerable attention is directed towards the Houston and Dallas-Fort Worth areas.

Removal of a Governor

The governor may be removed by impeachment and conviction. Impeachment means to accuse or to indict the governor alleging grounds sufficient to warrant removal from office. The Texas Constitution is silent with regards to the grounds for impeachment. However, the impeachment and conviction of James "Pa" Ferguson (1915–1917) has since given the legislature some guidance. The University of Texas refused to remove faculty members that Governor Ferguson found objectionable. Governor Ferguson then vetoed UT's appropriations. On July 21, 1917, a Travis County grand jury indicted Governor Ferguson on nine charges of misapplication of public funds, embezzlement, and diversion of funds. The House Speaker called the legislature into special session and issued twenty-one Articles of Impeachment. Ferguson was found guilty on ten counts of the Articles of Impeachment, but resigned as governor before the final vote was taken, thereby arguing that he could not be convicted under the Articles of Impeachment and removed from office. The Texas Supreme Court ruled that the conviction stood and that Ferguson was prohibited from holding office. Ferguson later ran his wife's (Miriam "Ma" Ferguson) successful campaign to become the first woman to be elected to serve as governor. There has been some who compare the Fergusons to Bill and Hillary Clinton.

Succession

The Texas Constitution provides for the lieutenant governor to become governor if the office becomes vacant through impeachment and conviction, death, resignation, or the governor's absence from the state. When George W. Bush became president-elect of the United States, he resigned as governor and was replaced by his lieutenant governor, Rick Perry. The Lt. governor receives the governor's salary for each day the governor is out of the state.

Compensation

The governor's salary is set by the legislature. For fiscal year 2008 the salary was $115,345, which is seventh highest in the nation. The governor also enjoys living in the governor's mansion, use of a state car, state-owned aircraft, and a personal staff.

Staff

The governor's staff consists of more than 200 individuals. The staff includes a chief of staff, deputy chief of staff, general counsel, press secretary, and a scheduler. The staff keeps the governor informed about issues and problems, assists the governor in making appointments, deal with the staffs of state representatives, and track legislation.

Executive Powers of the Governor

Appointment Power

Texas has a board or agency form of government with approximately 200 state boards, commissions, and agencies. The governor's power of appointment is his most significant executive power by allowing the governor to exercise patronage. Governor Bush made 334 appointments in 1997 and 483 in 1998. The governor's power of appointment is checked by the Senate's power to confirm the appointments. An appointee that was confirmed by the Senate cannot be removed by the governor unless cause is shown and two-thirds of the Senate approves. The governor's appointment power is also limited in that many of the major agencies, boards, and commissions are headed by elected officials rather than a gubernatorial appointment.

Budgetary Power

Officially, the governor is the state's chief budget officer, but in reality the Texas legislature is really in control primarily through the Legislative Budget Board. William Clements realized the futility of preparing a budget and simply endorsed the LBB's proposal. Ann Richards followed Clements precedent, but George W. Bush tried to take a more active role in budget preparation. The governor does have the power of a line-item veto, but he cannot impound funds or transfer funds from one agency to another. In the mid-1990s, a decline in oil revenues resulted in a budget crisis in the nature of a $1 billion shortfall in revenues. All Governor Mark White could do was request that the state agencies reduce expenditures, as he lacked any legal power to back the request.

Military Power

The governor is commander-in-chief of the state's national guard units when they are not under presidential orders. These units are headed by the adjutant general, who is appointed by the governor. The governor can declare martial law to protect lives and property during riots or natural disasters.

Police Power

Law enforcement is generally considered a local responsibility (i.e., municipal police departments and county law enforcement agencies). The governor appoints with Senate approval a three-member Public Safety Commission that directs the Department of Public Safety. The DPS is responsible for highway traffic enforcement, driver's licensing, motor vehicle inspection, truck weighing stations, and the Texas Rangers.

Legislative Powers of the Governor

The governor will provide a state of the state message. The governor has the power to veto legislation, including the line-item veto. The governor does not have the power of a pocket veto. The 140-day legislative session allows the governor to execute a post-adjournment veto, which cannot be overridden. Of the 148 bills vetoed during one four-year period, 145 were post-adjournment vetoes. The line-item veto was used seven times in 1999, and like the post-adjournment veto, the line-item veto cannot be overridden.

The Governor May Call a Special Session

Special sessions are limited to thirty days and are not very popular because the cost of a single session will approach $1 million. Special sessions are also limited to the subject matter designated by the governor.

Judicial Power of the Governor

The governor will appoint state court judges if a vacancy occurs between elections; otherwise all Texas state court judges are elected. More than 95% of state judicial incumbents are reelected.

The Plural Executive

The framers of the Texas Constitution of 1876 attempted to limit executive power by dispersing the power to a multitude of elected executive officials. This plural executive dramatically restricts the power of the governor by giving the voters in the state more control over state government.

Secretary of State

The secretary of state is one of the few state executives appointed by the governor. Once considered the official keeper of state records, this official is now is primarily responsible for administering elections, managing corporate entities operating in the State of Texas, and maintaining debt and UCC filings.

Lieutenant Governor

The Lt. governor is elected in a statewide election and serves as presiding officer (President) of the Texas Senate and as acting-governor when the governor is out of the state.

Attorney General

The attorney general is elected in a statewide election to a four-year term. The AG serves as the attorney for the state in civil matters, provides advisory opinions to state agencies, and manages the state child support collection efforts. Criminal matters are handled by local district attorneys at the county level.

Commissioner of the General Land Office

The commissioner is elected in a statewide election to a four-year term and manages state-owned land. Texas owns 20.3 million acres of land. The mineral interests such as oil and gas as well as grazing rights contribute significantly to state revenues most of which goes to the Permanent School Fund and Permanent University Fund. Texas also has rights to all submerged lands up to 10 miles into the Gulf of Mexico. All of Texas's Gulf Coast beaches are publicly owned and under the jurisdiction of the general land office. The commissioner is responsible for 18,000 producing wells.

Commissioner of Agriculture

The commissioner is elected in a statewide election to a four-year term and is primarily responsible for enforcing agricultural laws, animal quarantine laws, food inspection, and the enforcement of disease and pest control programs. The commissioner is also responsible for weights and measures, meat markets, produce scales, and gasoline pumps.

Comptroller of Public Accounts

The comptroller is elected in a statewide election to a four-year term and is responsible for certifying state revenues in compliance with the balanced budget requirement. In addition, the comptroller is responsible for collecting state tax and non-tax revenues. The comptroller is also responsible for returning abandoned or lost money or property by publishing a list of individuals with unclaimed property or assets. Unclaimed money is forfeited to the state.

State Treasurer

Texas had a state treasurer until 1996. The treasurer at that time (Martha Whitehead) had campaigned that if elected she would eliminate the office. She won and she carried out her campaign promise by eliminating the state treasurer's office. The responsibilities of the treasurer were transferred to the comptroller.

Boards, Commissions, and Regulatory Agencies
Appointed Officials

Most boards and commissions in Texas are headed by members appointed by the governor, confirmed by the Senate, and serve staggered six-year terms.

Public Utilities Commission (PUC)

The PUC was established in 1975 to protect consumers and curb the rate at which utility costs were increasing. The commission is responsible for local telephone rates and some electric rates. Local telephone rates vary from one part of the state to the next, but all rates in a service area are the same. The PUC determines the maximum charge for pay telephones. The PUC also approves additional services such as Caller ID, call waiting, and call forwarding. A 1999 law gives the PUC the authority to lower intrastate long distance rates and prohibiting local service from being disconnected for failure to pay long distance bills. The commission sets electric rates for private companies offering service to those residing outside city limits. Cities may continue to set rates or allow the PUC to set rates. Electric companies may appeal to the PUC those rates set by a city.

Texas Alcoholic Beverage Commission (TABC)

The Twenty-First Amendment to the U.S. Constitution gives the states the responsibility for enforcing regulations concerning the alcoholic beverage commission. The TABC regulates the industry in the state of Texas with a $124 billion budget and 500 employees. Regulate all aspects of the manufacture, importation, transportation, and sale of alcoholic beverages. The TABC establishes the alcoholic content of beer. The TABC prohibits the outdoor advertising or the manufacture of alcoholic beverages in areas that prohibit the sale of alcoholic beverages; transporting beer, wine, or liquor through a dry area; assisting in the enforcement of the minimum drinking age; checking hours of operation; issuing permits and licenses; and leveling fines that raise approximately $170 million a year.

Texas Lottery Commission

The commission is responsible for administering the state lottery and is made of three members appointed by the governor. Pursuant to statute, one member of the Lottery Commission must be a bingo expert (Texas Government Code, § 467.021).

Elected Officials

The State Board of Education is a fifteen-member board elected to four-year terms from single-member districts. Policy for public education (pre-K to grade 12) is set by the State Board of Education. The Texas Education Agency is the bureaucratic arm of the State Board of Education and is responsible for enforcing rules and regulations affecting Texas public schools. Together the SBOE and TEA determine license requirements for teachers, set minimum graduation requirements, establish accreditation guidelines, and adopt public school textbooks.

Railroad Commission

The RRC has three members who are elected to staggered six-year terms. One member is elected every two years. At one time, the RRC was one of the most powerful state agencies in the nation because it regulated intrastate railroads, trucks, and bus transportation and supervised the oil and gas industry. Court decisions, deregulation of the transportation industry, and other state and federal legislation has significantly weakened the RRC.

Sunset: Maintaining Accountability

The Sunset Advisory Commission (1975) is responsible for reviewed the effectiveness of state agencies. The review process is conducted once every twelve years. The ten-member Sunset Advisory Commission has four members from the Texas Senate, one public member appointed by the lieutenant governor, four members from the House, and one public member appointed by the Speaker of the House. Forty-two agencies have been eliminated through Sunset and more than a dozen agencies have been merged with existing bodies.

STATE COURTS: TEXAS JUDICIAL SYSTEM

Trial Courts

Trial courts are courts of original jurisdiction and finders of fact. There are five distinct trial courts in Texas: municipal courts, justice of the peace courts, constitutional county courts, county courts at law, and district courts.

Municipal (882 municipal courts) courts deal with criminal misdemeanors with fines only and no jail and municipal ordinance violations. The justice of the peace courts (835 JP courts) deal with civil actions not exceeding $5000, small claims, and criminal misdemeanors with fines only and no jail. Constitutional county courts (254 courts) deal with civil actions between $200 and $5000, probate cases (17 specialized probate courts), appeals from lower courts, de novo from JP courts, and on record from municipal courts. County courts at law (209 county courts at law) deal with limited civil actions under $100,000, limited criminal misdemeanors, and appeals from lower courts. District courts (420 district courts) deal with original jurisdiction in civil actions over $200/$500, divorce cases, land titles, elections, original jurisdiction in felony criminal matters, and juvenile matters. Some district courts specialize in criminal, civil, or family law cases.

Courts of Appeal (14 Courts of Appeal)

There are fourteen courts of appeal in Texas and each court has a chief justice and between two and twelve justices who are elected in partisan elections. Cases are usually heard by three justices and may be heard by the entire court (*en banc*). Courts of appeal review the record of the trial court. Generally, the attorneys for the parties will raise legal challenges in their motions for appeal and legal briefs that the trial judge erred in a ruling of law or evidence.

Texas Supreme Court and the Texas Court of Criminal Appeals

The Texas Supreme Court hears appeals on civil matters and juvenile cases. There is a chief justice and eight associate justices elected by the voters of the state in partisan elections. The Texas Court of Criminal Appeals hears appeals on criminal matters, such as death penalty cases that are appealed directly to the court of criminal appeals. There is a presiding judge and eight justices elected by the voters of the state in partisan elections. These courts review the record of the trial court to determine if an error in law has been made by either the trial court or a court of appeals in ruling on the law or the admission of evidence. Both courts are considered courts of last resort, but a case may be appealed to the U.S. Supreme Court if a federal question (i.e., constitutional issue) is raised. This court system is referred to as bifurcated. Texas and Oklahoma are the only two states with this system.

Participants in the Trial Process

Participants in the trial process include judges, attorneys, the jury, parties to the case, and witnesses to the case. All judges are elected in partisan elections with the exception of municipal court judges. Justices of the peace judges do not have to be lawyers, only "well informed in the law." In criminal cases the district attorney would be required.

Applicable law

State criminal statutes vary by state because each state maintains its own penal code. These statutes are generally similar but there are differences. The Texas Penal Code is derived from the common law. The Louisiana Penal Law is based on the Napoleonic Code and is the only civil-law state in the country. Each state has a body of common law. Common law will vary from state to state as each jurisdiction has defined the common law over the years. Many states have adopted uniform codes that codify the common law. The uniform commercial code was adopted to reduce interstate differences in commercial transactions. However, many differences still exist as the courts interpret the codes. Rules of evidence and rules of procedure govern the operation of the courts and use of evidence at trial.

Chapter 13

THE ROLE OF PUBLIC OPINION, INTEREST GROUPS, AND POLITICAL PARTIES IN TEXAS

© 2012 Lawrence Roberg. Used under license with Shutterstock, Inc.

THE ROLE OF PUBLIC OPINION

Public opinion is essential to a democratic society for the simple reason that it is an effective means of communicating the desires of the public to elected and non-elected officials. It may or may not be the case that these officials listen or respect the wishes of the public. Texas is similar to the United States when it comes to the role of public opinion. There are government officials at all levels with different responsibilities. For example, at the national level we have the president with his role as chief executive and commander in chief. There is Congress, of course, and they are responsible for making laws that are national in scope. As for the state, the governor is responsible for executing state law and to that extent may be influenced by public opinion. However, there is very little media attention given to the governor. It may not be the case that the public knows very much about what the governor is doing or how his position influences the lives of Texans. The Texas legislature is one institution at the state level that does receive considerable attention particularly during the regular session in odd-numbered years. The reason so much attention is placed on the legislature is due to the laws that are passed and the budget. In recent years, great controversies emerged over such issues as the funding of public schools. Naturally, polling organizations are going to focus their questions on those issues that are discussed in the media. Again, it may or may not be the case that these lawmakers listen to the public. The ultimate public opinion poll is an election. We see a growing number of Republicans elected to the statehouse each election cycle, which suggests that Republicans are in favor with the public. At the local level, we see the same dynamic. Mayors, council members, and county officials sense the desires of the public by virtue of polling although local issues are not often discussed as much as you may think. The national news appears to dominate.

REASONS FOR POLITICAL CONFLICT

Politics is a process of conflict originating from a variety of differences that exist among the members of society. Marxists argue that conflict is caused by differences in economic class. Others include ethnic, cultural, geographic, gender, religious, value, and historical differences as causal factors of our many differences. The result is a variety of factions that, on occasion, become organized. An interest group is an organization with members who share common views and objectives and seek to influence government to achieve group objectives. One in three Americans joins an interest group. The government is protected from interest group control through decentralization (federalism and separation of powers).

REASONS FOR POLITICAL CONFLICT

The differences among interest groups causes conflict. This is generally related to economic costs or rewards. Many of the interest groups in Texas seek tangible economic gain from the political system.

Values

Some values are based on religious beliefs, ethical commitments, or cultural backgrounds. These values can create bitter and violent conflicts because it is difficult to reach a compromise. Gender and racial equality may include both values and economic interests. The Christian Life Commission and the Baptist General Convention oppose issues such as liquor by the drink, state lottery, gambling. The NAACP and NOW seek equal treatment for African Americans and women.

Ideology

Ideology can be a complex system of values relating to the nature and purpose of the political system. Examples include the John Birch Society on the right, the Socialists Workers Party on the left, Americans for Conservative Action (conservatives), and the Texas Civil Liberties Union (liberal).

Interests in Texas

Business

One of the dominant interests in Texas is the business community. Legislators are drawn from business, and there is a respect for the business spirit in Texas. Business interests favor policies that protect their economic interests, and they are effective in controlling labor laws. Texas is one of twenty-one right-to-work states with weak employee protection laws. Texas was the last to adopt minimum wage and a no maximum hour law. There are low unemployment and workers compensation benefits. Business taxes are low. A couple groups are the Texas Association of Business (formerly Texas Manufacturers Assoc.) and the Texas Research League.

There are professional groups such as the Texas Medical Association and the Texas State Teachers Associations, which are considered two of the most effective groups in Texas.

Agricultural Groups

The Farm Bureau Federation represents large commercial farmers, and the Farmers Union represents small farmers.

Labor

Labor groups are small, scattered and weak, and they have few members because of a pro-business atmosphere, limited to Houston and Beaumont areas.

Ethnic Groups

The NAACP represents African Americans, and LULAC and MALDEF represent Mexican-Americans.

The State Party System

The State Political Party exists in the form of committees. Texas has been a one-party state in that at one time or another it has been controlled by just one party. For most of Texas history it has been controlled by the Democrats, and since 2000 it has been controlled by Republicans. The party exists at the state, county, and precinct level. The county political party is also a committee. The precinct is the building block of the process and is designated by a number on the voter registration card. Of course, there are Republicans and Democrats in the state legislature. However, they are not organized for control as they are at the national level. The lack of strong party organization in the statehouse is the product of a strong conservative ideology that runs through both parties. The most significant role of parties in the state is the organization of elections for the national, state, and local levels. Even so, the national party apparatus seems to wield great influence. For example, the state primaries this year were held on May 29. This is long after the Republican nominee will have been determined by other states. Basically, this reduces the role of the state.

Chapter 14

POLITICAL PARTICIPATION AND ELECTIONS IN TEXAS

© 2012 Vepar5. Used under license with Shutterstock, Inc.

THE POLITICS OF ELECTIONS

The qualifications to vote in Texas are that you must be a citizen of U.S., at least 18 years of age, and a resident of the state and county. You must not be mentally incompetent or a felon without a pardon or two years from completion of sentence. You may register by mail or in person anytime during year. Residence is determined by voters' intent. You can vote after thirty days processing time. Ballots are printed in English and Spanish in counties where the population is 5% or more Mexican-American. Ballots in Harris County are also printed in Vietnamese.

VOTERS

The following is a list of Amendments designed to remove legal barriers to voting:

- Fifteenth Amendment
- Nineteenth Amendment
- Twenty-sixth Amendment

The Voting Rights Act of 1965 abolished literacy tests and waiting periods longer than thirty days. For most Texans, voting is their principal or only political activity. There has been a decline in voter turnout nationally and in Texas. The young are less likely to vote, but there was a slight reversal in 2008. The same general trend exists in Texas (forty-eighth in voter turnout). Since 1960, about 45% of eligible voters participated in presidential elections. Turnout in local elections is approximately 25%. Particular political factors influenced turnout, such as corruption (Watergate) and assassinations (JFK, MLK, RFK).

REASONS FOR LOW TURNOUT IN TEXAS

The political culture in Texas is a mixture of individualistic and traditionalistic culture, which places less importance on political participation. Socioeconomic factors contribute to low voter turnout. Texas has a high rate of poverty, is a minority state, and has low levels of educational achievement. In terms of the political structure, Texas has a long ballot in which in an urban county can have 150–200 positions being voted on at any one time increasing burden of voting. Also, there are numerous elections each year. Federal and state elections are every even year and municipal elections are in odd years.

Legal Factors

The Poll Tax was adopted in 1902 ($1.75) but held unconstitutional (1966). White primaries were used until 1944 but ruled unconstitutional in *Smith v. Allwright.* One year, 1972, residency requirements were abolished. There was early registration by January 31 until 1971 and annual registration. Texas did not use a literacy test and the grandfather clause. There was also property ownership for bond and tax elections.

Elections in Texas

There are a variety of elections in Texas. The first primary was used in 1906. Primaries are used by a political party to nominate a candidate for the general election. Caucuses do pretty much the same thing; however, it is done in a different manner. Texas has a dual primary in that if no candidate wins 51% of the vote a runoff is held between the top two candidates. This is used in the South. A plurality is required elsewhere. A closed primary is limited to party members. Texas and forty other states use this method. A voter can only vote in one primary on election day and cannot vote in another party runoff race or convention. If a voter did not vote in the primary, the voter is free to choose either party in the runoff race. Crossover voting and raiding is the practice of voting in another party's primary with the intention of electing the least favorable candidate so that they will be easily defeated in the general election. Crossover voting was used by Republicans in Texas as part of Limbaugh's Operation Chaos. He urged listeners to vote in the Democratic Primary for Hillary Clinton. This method is easier to accomplish when there is an incumbent. In other words, if Obama is the incumbent, Democrats know he will receive the nomination and can freely crossover and raid the Republican primary.

The primary is usually scheduled for the second Tuesday in March; however, in 2012, the election was delayed due to redistricting lawsuits. The runoff election is one month later, usually in April. An early primary can help a party heal the wounds of the primary battle before the general election.

The Texas Election Code requires a primary for parties receiving 20% of gubernatorial vote. Others can use a convention system but must file a list of supporters equal to 1% of total vote for governor in last election.

Primaries are funded by the state treasury. A candidate must pay a filing fee to get on primary ballot or file a petition with 5000 voters for statewide office (less for local offices).

General Elections

Voters elect the actual representative in the general election. It is decided by plurality vote rather than majority vote. They are held biannually on the first Tuesday after the first Monday in November. State candidates usually tie the election with a popular president. This is not the trend in Texas because of the conservative nature of Texas Democrats. Texas historically voted Republican for president and Democrat for lower seats. Since 1980, the Republican Party gained political power and is now dominant.

Special Elections

Special elections are for emergency needs, such as ratification of constitutional amendments or filling vacant offices to legislative bodies (U.S. House/Senate, Texas House/Senate, City Councils). Judgeships and the county commissioner vacancies are filled by appointment until the next election. The majority of votes are required rather than a plurality as previously required.

Conduct and Administration of Elections

County-Level Administration

Since 1973, the Secretary of State disperses money for elections. The general elections are conducted by county officials. Texas uses a party column type of ballot with the party listed at the top of each column. The office runs down the left side. A voter can vote straight ticket with one vote. A split ticket requires more effort. Straight-ticket voting enhances the coattail effect. The winner of governor's office gets preferred first column.

To get your name on the ballot, you must be the nominee of a major party. Minor parties have a difficult time getting on the ballot. Independent presidential candidates must have a petition with a number equal to 1% of the vote in the last presidential election. The minor party candidate needs only 1% of vote for governor (also applicable for all other offices). Write-in candidates are possible but not successful. It requires early registration with the secretary of state, and the person must register prior to absentee voting and forty-five days before primary.

Voting is by secret ballot in that a private voting area is essential. Most voting now is done with computer in most places and the voter is not required to sign the ballot as in past.

Absentee Voting

Traditionally only members of the armed services and those who would be out of town or who were ill could vote absentee. Now anyone can vote absentee between four and twenty days before election or first primary (4 to 10 days before runoff). The voter does not have to swear to be out of town. Voting takes place in some sub-courthouses across county and by mail if you are ill or confined.

DEVELOPMENT OF THE TEXAS PARTY SYSTEM

Democrats and the One-Party Tradition in Texas, 1865–1960

There was very little party activity in the Republic during this period. Politics were usually pro- or anti-Sam Houston. After the Civil War, the Democratic Party dominated Texas politics. In early 1900, challenges did not come from Republicans, but liberal third parties Progressives and Populists. The Democratic primary became the chief election. The Great Depression further locked Democrats in power because Republicans were linked to the Great Depression Factions in the Democratic Party. Conservatives benefitted from no Republican party because Republicans voted in the Democratic primary and general elections. Liberals now controlled the Democratic Party in Texas as the Republican Party gained strength and traditional conservatives switched parties.

Rise of the Republican Party, 1952–2011

The state voted Republican in seven of eleven presidential elections after 1952. It began with the election of Republican John Tower in 1961 to the U.S. Senate, and in 1978, Texans elected Bill Clements the first Republican governor since Reconstruction. Ronald Reagan transformed Southern politics. Evidence is found in the election of Phil Gramm to the U.S. Senate in 1984 and Kay Bailey Hutchinson in 1993, which gave Texas two Republican U.S. Senators. This was followed by George W. Bush who was elected governor in 1998. Republicans captured the Texas Legislature in 2000, and all statewide elected officials are held by Republicans. Moreover, Rick Perry was elected to a third term in 2010. Presently, two-thirds of the House is controlled by Republicans.

Chapter 15

THE RIGHTS AND RESPONSIBILITIES OF CITIZENS

© 2012 Mastering_Microstock. Used under license with Shutterstock, Inc.

There are three methods of becoming an American citizen, birth in the country—birth to a U.S. citizen, and naturalization. Citizenship by birth is the most common way people become citizens. Any person born on American soil, either in the U.S. or in one of its territories, automatically becomes a citizen. This is true even if the child's parents are not American citizens. However, there is an exception to this that affects children of foreign diplomats working in the U.S. While here, the diplomats are representatives of other countries, and their children would not become citizens. Any person born outside the U.S. to parents who are American citizens automatically becomes a citizen at birth. The only requirement is that one of the parents once lived in the U.S. If only one of the child's parents is an American citizen, this condition still applies. Finally, citizenship can be obtained by naturalization. Those people who come to the United States as citizens of other countries and who desire to stay here permanently are called immigrants.

RIGHTS OF AMERICAN CITIZENS

As Thomas Jefferson said in the Declaration of Independence, our rights come from God and/or nature. They are natural rights, which means that rights cannot be given or taken away by man. The government's purpose is to protect these rights. Such rights include the right to life, liberty, and the pursuit of happiness. Some people believe the rights we have fall into one of three categories: security, equality, and liberty. Security means protection from unfair and unreasonable actions by the government and others. The government, for example, cannot arrest, imprison, or punish people or search or seize their property without good reason and without following certain rules. Other people do not have a right to take your property. The concept of property rights is an essential element to a free society. The principle of "due process of law" protects these rights for all Americans, which is found in the Fifth and Fourteenth Amendments, which states that no person shall be deprived of "life, liberty, or property, without due process of law." Due process means that the laws and the process of executing and enforcing laws must be fair and reasonable, must be in accordance with the Constitution, and must apply to everyone equally. Due process also applies to property rights. If a state takes property to build a highway, it must pay the owner or owners of the property a just compensation for their losses. The right of equality means that everyone is entitled to the equal protection of all the laws in the U.S. That is, all people have a right to be treated the same, regardless of race, religion, or political beliefs. This right is found in the Fourteenth Amendment. However, it does not mean you have a right to other people's property. It means equality of opportunity and treatment, not equality of outcomes. Our fundamental freedoms are spelled out in the Bill of Rights and the so-called "Civil War Amendments"—Thirteen, Fourteen, and Fifteen.

DUTIES AND RESPONSIBILITIES OF AMERICAN CITIZENS

We have an obligation to carry out certain duties and responsibilities. Duties are things we are required to do; if we fail to perform them, we are subject to legal penalties, such as fines or imprisonment. Responsibilities are things we should do. We fulfill these obligations voluntarily. Fulfilling both our duties and our responsibilities helps ensure that we have good government and that we continue to enjoy our rights.

Duties include:

- Obeying the law. We may not agree with a law; however, we must obey it.
- Paying taxes. We may not agree with the taxes we pay; however, we must pay them.
- Defending the country. We may be called to serve our country in time of war.
- Serving as a juror. We may be called to jury duty. We must do it.
- Attending school. The path to success requires education.
- Voting. A system that is not used will not work. Democracy requires participation.

With these new rights, citizenship also brings with it some important responsibilities. As a U.S. citizen, it is your duty to give back to your adopted nation by fulfilling these responsibilities. Some of these responsibilities are legally required of every citizen, but all are important to ensuring that America remains a free and prosperous nation.

ADDITIONAL RESPONSIBILITIES OF U.S. CITIZENS

- Support and defend the Constitution
- Respect and obey federal, state, and local laws
- Participate in your local community
- Being informed about the government and knowing your rights in order to preserve them
- Participating in government. This could include writing a letter, donating money, or voting.
- Respecting the rights of others. Do unto others as you would have them do unto you.
- Respecting diversity. Civil society requires that individuals respect the differences among them.

VOTING AND ELECTIONS IN THE UNITED STATES

Before you can vote, you must register. However, registering is only one part of getting ready to vote. People should exercise their right to vote for several reasons. Voting gives citizens a chance to choose their government leaders. It also gives them an opportunity to voice their opinion on the past performance of public officials. If the voters are dissatisfied, they can elect new leaders. Voting also allows citizens to express their opinions on public issues. Upon entering the polling places, the locations where votes are cast, voters give their names to an election worker, who checks the names against a master list. The voters are then given a ballot and directed to a voting booth. Voters cast their ballots in one of three ways; by computerized machine, by mechanical machine, or by paper ballot. With a computerized voting machine, votes are cast by touching certain spots on the screen, by pushing certain buttons, or by marking a ballot. With a mechanical voting machine, votes are cast by pulling small levers next to the names of the candidates chosen. With a paper ballot, a square is marked or a hole punched next to the names of the candidates chosen.

Becoming an American citizen with all the freedoms and opportunities this nation has to offer is the dream of many immigrants. Those who are fortunate enough to be in a position to pursue naturalization gain the same rights and privileges of citizenship as natural-born American citizens save one: naturalized U.S. citizens are not eligible for the Office of the President.

RIGHTS OF U.S. CITIZENS

- Serve on a jury
- Bring family members to the United States
- Obtain citizenship for children born abroad
- Travel with a U.S. passport
- Become eligible for federal grants and scholarships
- Freedom to express yourself
- Freedom to worship as you wish

- Right to a prompt, fair trial by jury
- Right to vote in elections for public officials
- Right to apply for federal employment
- Right to run for elected office

To become a U.S. citizen, you must take the Oath of Allegiance. When you take the oath, you must promise to:

- Renounce foreign allegiances
- Support and defend the Constitution and laws of the United States
- Fight in the U.S. Armed Forces, perform noncombatant service in the Armed Forces, and perform civilian service in the U.S.

If you are against serving in the military because of your religious beliefs, you may be exempted from the Armed Forces requirements.

The Oath of Allegiance

I hereby declare, on oath, that I absolutely and entirely renounce and abjure all allegiance and fidelity to any foreign prince, potentate, state, or sovereignty of whom or which I have heretofore been a subject or citizen; that I will support and defend the Constitution and laws of the United States of America against all enemies, foreign and domestic; that I will bear true faith and allegiance to the same; that I will bear arms on behalf of the United States when required by the law; that I will perform noncombatant service in the Armed Forces of the United States when required by the law; that I will perform work of national importance under civilian direction when required by the law; and that I take this obligation freely without any mental reservation or purpose of evasion; so help me God.

In some cases, *U.S. Citizenship and Immigration Services* allows the oath to be taken without the clauses: "*. . . that I will bear arms on behalf of the United States when required by law; that I will perform noncombatant service in the Armed Forces of the United States when required by law. . .*"

Citizenship is the common thread that connects all Americans. We are a nation bound not by race or religion, but by the shared values of freedom, liberty, and equality. Throughout our history, the United States has welcomed newcomers from all over the world. The contributions of immigrants have helped shape and define the country we know today. More than 200 years after our founding, naturalized citizens are still an important part of our democracy. By becoming a U.S. citizen, you too will have a voice in how our nation is governed. The decision to apply is a significant one. Citizenship offers many benefits and equally important responsibilities. By applying, you are demonstrating your commitment to this country and our form of government.

Chapter 16

PUBLIC POLICY IN TEXAS

THE ECONOMY AND TEXAS

Constraints on Policy

The Texas Constitution of 1876 mandates a balanced budget, which is generally achieved by low tax rates and low to moderate levels of government spending. Federal spending declined in the 1980s, creating strains on state and local budgets. The Texas state government was forced to cope with a growing population, rising poverty rates, increased education, and medical and prison costs. The apparent unending mandates from the courts and federal government led to revenue shortfalls during recessionary periods. The Texas economy is always in transition. One reason for this is that it is generally driven by the price of oil. A one dollar per barrel increase means an additional $50 million in oil severance taxes for the state and the creation of new jobs but may bring about inflationary pressures. It may also reduce economic activity because people will drive less. It will also add to the cost of transportation for individuals, businesses, and governments. A drop in the price per barrel has a negative impact on the economy because it brings less revenue. Of course, the Texas economy is not isolated. There are imports and exports to other states and other nations. The environment also plays a major role. Texas recently experienced wild fires and a major draught. This impacts agriculture, livestock, property values, and the price and availability of water.

Texas Has Been Striving to Diversify Its Economy

There are budget demands and public school pressures. By 1990, financing public education had become a persistent policy issue and will always be one. In 1983, the Select Committee on Public Education (headed by Ross Perot) and a 1989 Texas Supreme Court decision mandating reform of financing system pushed education to forefront. Between 1991 and 1993, the Texas Supreme Court twice invalidated the state's system for raising public school revenue. The legislature proposed a constitutional amendment in which wealthy school districts would share $400 million in revenues with poorer districts. Voters rejected this proposal in a special election held on May 1, 1993.

Highway Demands

Much of the Texas highway system was built during the 1960s and 70s. The average age of Texas Highways was 18 in 1984 (designed to last 18–20 years). The projected maintenance and construction costs were $60 billion over 20 years. It was estimated that $25.5 billion would be needed just for the decade of the 90s, but that gasoline tax revenues would generate only about $11 billion during that same 10 years.

Prison Stresses

A federal court decision in 1980 condemned the overcrowded, substandard conditions of the Texas prison system. The state was ordered to improve the conditions of the prisons, which required additional funding.

Welfare Strains

Changes in inflation, federal spending, and an increase in recipients made the $80 million per year ceiling on welfare spending for AFDC inadequate by 1982. The ceiling was raised to $160 million for the 1982–1983 biennium by constitutional amendment in 1982. Texas, however, remains at the bottom for welfare spending.

TRADITIONAL FISCAL POLICIES

Budget Policy

Texas fiscal policy is shaped by hostility to state indebtedness, opposition to taxes, and limited spending for public services. Opposition to debt is demonstrated in constitutional and statutory provisions designed to force the state to operate on a pay-as-you-go balanced budget. The Texas Constitution prohibits borrowing except to supply casual deficiencies of revenue, repel invasion, suppress insurrection, and to defend the state in war. The comptroller must submit to the legislature prior to each session a sworn accounting of cash on hand and revenue anticipated for the next two years. Appropriation bills are limited to not more than the amount certified unless passed by four-fifths majority in each house or unless new revenue sources are provided.

Taxing Policy

Texans favor regressive taxes that have greater impact on the poor. The Texas tax system is the second most regressive in the nation. State tax revenue is based on a 6.25% general sales tax and other selective sales taxes. Texas does not have a personal income tax, which could only be enacted by popular referendum. A consumption tax of this nature makes the state vulnerable when there are fluctuations in the national economy. Tax revenues go down when there is a recession and go up when there is growth.

Spending Policy

Public expenditures in Texas are relatively low in comparison to other states. Texas has $1,301 in spending per capita. California has $2,237 in spending per capita. New York has $2,554 in spending per capita. Texas spends most of its money on highways, roads, and other public improvements rather than welfare programs, recreational facilities, and similar social services. Local governments such as school districts and universities receive money from the state; however, when the state cuts back on spending the local governments have to make up the difference by raising taxes and fees or reduce their spending.

POLITICS OF REVENUE AND DEBT MANAGEMENT

The Politics of Taxation

A tax is a compulsory contribution for a public purpose. Another way to look at it is that it is simply a transfer of money from you, the taxpayer, to the government. It is designed to pay for the operation of the government.

Theoretically taxes should be just and equitable

Current Trends in Texas Taxation

Taxation based on petroleum, petroleum revenues, sales tax, consumption taxes on motor fuels, alcoholic beverages and tobacco, and finally taxes on business gross receipts (franchise tax, insurance company tax, and public utilities) make up 50% of state revenue. The sales tax is most important single source of tax revenue. It accounts for three-fifths of all state tax revenue and is regressive, which places the burden on those that make less. This is a product of the Texas independent political culture which says that an individual should keep what he earns. A communitarian culture would redistribute earnings for the good of the community. The general sales tax was first used in 1961 and is applicable to all tangible personal property (exempted items include water, telephone, food not used for immediate consumption, and prescriptions). Selective sales taxes have been used since 1931 when the legislature imposed a tax on cigarettes and now include highway user taxes (motor fuels, motor vehicle sales and rentals, registration), sin taxes (cigarettes, chewing tobacco, snuff, pipe or smoking tobacco, cigars, liquor, wine, malt liquor, beer and mixed drinks), and miscellaneous sales taxes (hotel and motel room rates). Business taxes account for 35% of state revenue. Businesses pay general and selective business taxes. General business taxes include: sales tax, franchise tax, unemployment compensation, and payroll tax. Selective business taxes are levied on oil and gas production, insurance company's gross premiums, public utilities' gross receipts, other taxes, and the death tax on estates. A drug tax enacted in 1989 requires drug dealers to purchase tax stamps. They must then affix them to packages of illegal drugs. Failure to pay the tax authorizes the government to seize assets to collect the taxes owed to the state. These are constitutionally questionable. The income tax is not politically popular.

Revenue from Gambling

Parimutuel wagering legalized on horse and dog races in 1988 raised over $15 million dollars for the state in four years. The state receives 1% of the first $100 million wagered on horse races and 2% of the first $100 million at greyhound tracks (states take increases by 1% for each additional $100 million). The lottery was approved by voters in 1991. Revenues are allocated as follows:

- 45% for prizes awarded winners
- 45% profit for the state
- 10% to private management for running the lottery
- 5% commissions to ticket sellers

From May 29, 1992 to August 31, 1994, more than $5 billion in lottery tickets had been sold. The state's share was $1.7 billion by the end of 1994 fiscal year ($2.7 billion in prizes). The money is deposited in General Revenue Fund. Bingo was authorized in 1981 to benefit charities with a 5% tax on prizes imposed in 1993.

Non-tax Revenues

The state receives a substantial amount of money from federal grants, land revenues, fees, permits and investments, motor vehicle inspection fees, college tuition, patient fees at state hospitals, liquor, wine, beer, and cigarette permits. There are also Texas sales of bonds to finance debt. It might be worth remembering that money that comes from the federal government originated in the states and was collected by the federal income tax. Therefore, the federal government is redistributing money that it took from the states. Also, fees are essentially a tax. Whenever money is collected from the taxpayer and distributed to the government, it becomes a tax. Employers collect income taxes for the federal government. Businesses collect taxes for the state through purchases. Local governments collect taxes based on property values. Businesses pass taxes on to the consumer. Therefore, citizens and non-citizens bear the burden of taxation.

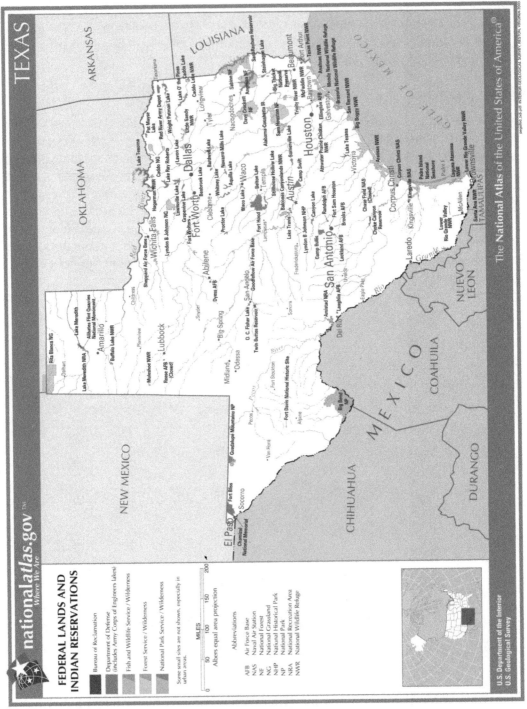